地方矿冶文化的传译

——以湖北省黄石市为例

赵小红　编译

Interpretation of Local Mining and Metallurgical Culture

Taking Huangshi of Hubei as an Example

WUHAN UNIVERSITY PRESS
武汉大学出版社

图书在版编目(CIP)数据

地方矿冶文化的传译:以湖北省黄石市为例=Interpretation of Local Mining and Metallurgical Culture——Taking Huangshi of Hubei as an Example:汉文、英文/赵小红编译.—武汉:武汉大学出版社,2021.11
ISBN 978-7-307-22502-2

Ⅰ.地… Ⅱ.赵… Ⅲ.①矿业—工业产业—地方文化—介绍—黄石—汉、英 ②冶金工业—工业产业—地方文化—介绍—黄石—汉、英 Ⅳ.F426.32

中国版本图书馆 CIP 数据核字(2021)第 154664 号

责任编辑:李晶晶　　责任校对:李孟潇　　版式设计:马　佳

出版发行:**武汉大学出版社**　(430072　武昌　珞珈山)
(电子邮箱:cbs22@whu.edu.cn　网址:www.wdp.whu.edu.cn)
印刷:武汉邮科印务有限公司
开本:720×1000　1/16　印张:21.25　字数:303 千字　插页:1
版次:2021 年 11 月第 1 版　2021 年 11 月第 1 次印刷
ISBN 978-7-307-22502-2　定价:59.00 元

前　言

根据笔者掌握的文献，国外学者自20世纪就已开始对矿冶文化进行研究。赫伯特·胡佛的《采矿和冶金收藏》（Rae，1980）为学者提供了技术史的基础资料，是有关人类社会和工业组织的丰富信息宝库。Long（1991）探索了矿冶作家的实践，发现他们主张知识开放，将工艺知识转化为公开的文字形式。而国内学者是于21世纪初涉足矿冶文化领域的。李蕾蕾（2002）以德国鲁尔工业区为例，介绍了工业遗产旅游的新观念，提出了一些值得我国学界进一步研究和探讨的议题。

进入21世纪以来，国外矿冶文化领域的研究主要集中在矿冶语言（Bigelow，2020）、矿冶知识传承（Habashi，2003）、矿冶文化建设（Liu，2010，2017；Ou，2013）等方面。国内矿冶文化作为一个文化概念被提出始于湖北省黄石市（石璋铭、项锐，2008）。此后，该领域的研究成果逐渐增多。专家学者从矿冶文学（李社教、周进珍，2008；周进珍等，2009；陈继林等，2009；李社教，2010；方红等，2012）、矿冶文化建设（王载册，2009、2013；曹庆波，2010；肖步云，2011、2016；刘梦恒、吴堪，2012；王勇刚，2014；赵青，2018；曹宇，2019）、矿冶文化旅游（舒韶雄、张红英，2011a、b；孙少山、孙发友，2012；张大鹏，2015；刘金林，2016；张亚微，2018；张大鹏等，2019）、矿冶文化翻译（邵春美，2011；方晓梅、邵春美，2014；曹芸，2015；郭淑英，2016；李睿，2020）等方面开展了卓有成效的研究。

根据前期矿冶文化研究成果的梳理可以看出，国内外学者围绕矿冶文化传承、矿冶文化建设、矿冶文化旅游、矿冶文化翻译、矿冶语言、矿冶文学等内容对人类矿冶文明展开了多角度的探索与研究。但是还有许多尚待深入探讨的地方，如矿冶文化发展脉络的研究以及纵向发展研究、矿冶文化的翻译与传播研究以及横向比较研究等。总的来说，现有研究对矿冶文化的翻译与传播问题关注不够，关涉地方矿冶文化“走出去”的研究更是少见。本书对黄石博物馆矿冶文化展、铜绿山古铜矿遗址、大冶铁矿博物馆和黄石国家矿山公园四个矿冶文化场馆的解说词进行了编辑和翻译，从翻译学和语言学角度对矿冶文化和矿冶文学展开研究，着眼于传播当地矿冶文化，构建文化新形象，提升黄石市在国内外的文化知名度，为地方经济文化建设创造机遇。

本书收录的四个矿冶文化场馆在黄石极具代表性，基本上可以借此了解黄石市的矿冶文化现状。我们对解说词中涉及的矿冶文化术语进行了梳理，并精选了部分矿冶文化器物和遗址图片及介绍作为附录，同时附上相应的英文，帮助读者理解书中的专业术语和专业知识。翻译过程中，我们参考了大量网络及相关资源，借鉴了许多黄石地方外宣资料的翻译经验，同时依据英文需要进行适当的变通，力图保持解说词的原貌及其功用。

本书兼具理论性与实践性，既可为矿冶文化的翻译学和语言学研究贡献新的理论，也可为矿冶文化领域的理论建构提供支撑。同时，本书还可作为英语专业学生与教师的教学用书和汉英翻译学习者与从业者的参考用书。另外，本书还可作为翻译学或语言学研究的素材。本书收录的四个矿冶文化场馆也可以此书为外宣资料，其他矿冶文化场馆对外宣传时亦可借鉴。基于上述几点，本书具有一定的理论意义和重要的现实意义。

本书的读者对象为高等院校英语专业和翻译专业的本科生和研究生，从事翻译学或语言学研究的专业人员，以及其他对翻译学或语言学研究感兴趣的读者。本书在编写过程中参考了许多国内外出版的专著、报纸杂志，以及网络资源，在此对相关作者及出版单位表示诚恳的感谢。

作　者

2021年1月

Preface

According to the present literature, foreign scholars have been studying the culture of mining and metallurgy since the 20th century. *The Herbert Hoover Collection of Mining and Metallurgy* is available to scholars as a basic source of technology history, which is itself a rich information treasure of human society and industrial organization (Rae, 1980). Based on a study of the authorship practice, Long (1991) concluded that mining and metallurgical writers consistently urged that knowledge be open, and they parlayed craft knowledge into openly written form. However, domestic scholars' research in the field of mining and metallurgical culture began in the early 21st century. Taking the Ruhr area of Germany as an example, Li Leilei (2002) introduced some new concepts and ideas of industrial heritage tourism and put forward some issues and points for further discussion.

Since the beginning of the 21st century, overseas research in the field of mining and metallurgical culture has mainly focused on mining and metallurgical language (Bigelow, 2020), the inheritance of mining and metallurgical knowledge (Habashi, 2003), the construction of mining and metallurgical culture (Liu, 2010, 2017; Ou, 2013), etc. As a cultural concept, domestic mining and metallurgical culture was first proposed in Huangshi City, Hubei Province (Shi Zhangming & Xiang Rui, 2008). Since then, the research achievements in the field have gradually increased. Experts and scholars have carried out fruitful research on the following aspects: mining and metallurgical literature (Li Shejiao & Zhou Jinzhen, 2008; Zhou Jinzhen et al., 2009; Chen Jilin et al., 2009; Li Shejiao, 2010; Fang Hong et al., 2012), construction of mining and metallurgical culture (Wang Zaice, 2009, 2013; Cao Qingbo, 2010; Xiao Buyun, 2011, 2016; Liu Mengheng & Wu Kan, 2012; Wang Yonggang, 2014; Zhao Qing, 2018; Cao Yu, 2019), tourism of mining and metallurgical culture (Shu Shaoxiong & Zhang Hongying, 2011a, b; Sun Shaoshan & Sun Fayou, 2012; Zhang Dapeng, 2015; Liu Jinlin, 2016; Zhang Yawei, 2018; Zhang Dapeng et al., 2019), translation of mining and metallurgical culture (Shao Chunmei, 2011; Fang Xiaomei & Shao Chunmei, 2014; Cao Yun, 2015; Guo Shuying, 2016; Li Rui, 2020), etc..

Through the combing of the previous research of mining and metallurgical culture, it is clear that scholars at home and abroad have launched a multi-angle exploration of mining and metallurgical civilization, centering on mining and metallurgical culture heritage, mining and metallurgical culture construction, mining and metallurgical culture tourism, mining and metallurgical culture translation, mining and metallurgical language, mining and metallurgical literature, etc.. However, there are many fields left to be further discussed, such as the study of the development context of mining and metallurgical culture, the study of vertical development, the study of translation and dissemination of mining and metallurgical culture, and the study of horizontal comparison, etc.. At present, attention paid to the translation and dissemination of mining and metallurgical culture is insufficient, and the research concerning the "going out" of local mining and metallurgical culture is even rarer. Therefore, the tour guide manuals of the four mining and metallurgical culture venues are edited and translated, including Huangshi Museum's Mining and Metallurgical Culture Exhibition, Tonglushan Ancient Copper Mine Site, Daye Iron Mine Museum and Huangshi National Mine Park. In addition to the translation studies and linguistic studies of mining and metallurgical culture and literature, this book aims at the dissemination of Huangshi mining and metallurgical culture, which may help to increase the popularity of Huangshi City, and create opportunities for local economic and cultural construction.

The four mining and metallurgical culture venues included in this book are most representative in Huangshi, based on which we can see the status quo of the city's mining and metallurgical culture. As appendices, we sorted out the terminology of mining and metallurgical culture in the tour guide manuals, along with the pictures and introduction of the artifacts and sites of mining and metallurgical culture. At the same time, the corresponding English version is attached to help readers understand the technical terms and professional knowledge in the book. In the process of translation, we consulted a large number of Internet and paper resources, learnt from the translation experiences of many local publicity materials, and made appropriate adaptations according to the English usage. As a result, the originality and function of the tour guide manuals is preserved.

This book is both theoretical and practical. It can not only contribute new theories to translation studies and linguistic studies of mining and metallurgical culture, but also provide support for the theoretical construction of the field. It can be used as a textbook for English majors and teachers, as a reference book for Chinese-English translation learners and practitioners, and as a material for translation studies or linguistic studies. It can also be used as international publicity materials by the four mining and metallurgical culture venues and as a reference by other similar venues for their international publicity. Therefore, this book is of both theoretical and practical significance.

The readership is for undergraduates and postgraduates majoring in English and translation in colleges and universities, professionals engaged in translation or linguistic studies, and other readers interested in translation or linguistic studies. In the process of compiling, many domestic and foreign published monographs, periodicals, newspapers, as well as network resources and electronic resources, etc. , have been consulted. I hereby express my respect and gratitude to their authors and publishers.

Author

January, 2021

目　　录
CONTENTS

第一章
黄石矿冶文化场馆中英文解说词

Chinese and English Tour Guide Manuals of Huangshi Mining and Metallurgical Culture Venues

第一节　黄石博物馆矿冶文化展中英文解说词

Chinese and English Tour Guide Manual of Huangshi Museum's Mining and Metallurgical Culture Exhibition

中庭《天地一洪炉——黄石矿冶文化展》展标前

At the Entrance Hall, in front of the Exhibition Poster

《天地一洪炉——黄石矿冶文化展》是黄石博物馆主办的主题展，也是目前国内首次以矿冶文化为专题的展览，同时也是国内关于矿冶遗址发掘和研究成果最集中的展示。希望您参观完展览后，能对黄石悠久的矿冶历史以及中国的矿冶文化有更多的了解。

Huangshi Mining and Metallurgical Culture Exhibition is the theme exhibition of Huangshi Museum. In China, it is the first time to take mining and metallurgical culture as the special subject of an exhibition, including a large collection of ancient relics and scientific studies about mining and metallurgy. After our visit, we will have a good knowledge of Huangshi mining history and China's mining and metallurgical culture.

序厅前言

The Preface of the Introductory Hall

现在，我们一起共同追溯黄石历史的源头，早在二三十万年前的旧石器时代，我们的祖先就在这里繁衍生息，创造了考古学上的“石龙头文化”，并由此拉开了黄石历史的帷幕。黄石的矿冶文化也在这时开始孕育。

Now let's trace the origin of Huangshi history. Our ancestors thrived here in the Paleolithic Age of 200 or 300 thousand years ago. They created the "Shilongtou Culture" according to archaeology, opening the curtain of Huangshi history. Then mining and metallurgical culture came into being at that time.

在距今一万年至四千年的新石器时代，考古工作者还在这里发现了数十处新石器时代遗址。新石器时代晚期，黄石的矿冶文化已经初现端倪。

In the period between ten and four thousand years ago, archaeologists have discovered dozens of mining and smelting sites of the Neolithic Age. In the late period of Neolithic Age, Huangshi mining and metallurgical culture began to emerge.

夏、商、周三代王朝所处的青铜时代是黄石矿冶文化的兴盛时期。黄石的先民在这里凿岩开矿，筑炉炼铜，为中国社会的发展做出了卓越贡献。

The Bronze Age is the boom time of Huangshi mining and metallurgical culture, which covers three dynasties: Xia, Shang, and Zhou. At that time, ancestors of Huangshi started to drill rocks, explore mines, build furnaces, and smelt ores into copper. They made great contributions to the development of Chinese society.

汉唐至明清，黄石的矿冶业仍持续不断发展。清末汉冶萍煤铁厂矿公司的创办，确立了黄石在中国近代工业发展中的先驱地位。

From the Han and Tang Dynasties to the Ming and Qing Dynasties, Huangshi Mining and Metallurgy industry continued to develop. In the Late Qing Dynasty, Han-Ye-Ping Coal and Iron Factory and Mine Co. Ltd. was founded, which established Huangshi's pioneer position in China's modern industrial development.

黄石地区矿区分布图

The Map of Mine Distribution in Huangshi

我们首先参观的展厅是《黄石矿冶文化展》的序厅。在这个展厅里请大家留意以下几个看点。

Let's first visit the introductory hall of Huangshi Mining and Metallurgical Culture Exhibition. Here please pay attention to the following aspects.

一是黄石丰富的矿产资源。矿产资源是黄石矿冶文化赖以产生、发展的物质基础。正因为黄石有着丰富的矿产资源，黄石的矿冶文化才得以在数千年的历史长河中不断延续。

The first one is the richness and variety of the mineral resources in Huangshi which are the material basis of the formation and development of Huangshi mining and metallurgical culture. It is because Huangshi is rich in mineral resources that its mining and metallurgical culture runs through several thousand years.

地台下是黄石、大冶、阳新的矿产分布图。根据地质资料显示，目前黄石地区已探明的矿产有：金、银、铜、铁、铅、锌、钴、钨、磷、锰、硫、硅质石、方解石、大理石、石膏、石棉、煤炭等50余种。尤其是铜、铁的藏量最为丰富。以著名的大冶铁矿、铜绿山铜铁矿为代表的数十座矿山，至今仍在大规模地开采。

Now please turn to the glass floor to see the Map of Mineral

Distribution in Huangshi, Daye, and Yangxin. According to the geological data, there are more than 50 kinds of minerals in Huangshi, such as gold, silver, copper, iron, lead, zinc, cobalt, tungsten, phosphorous, manganese, sulfur, limestone, calcite, marble, gypsum, asbestos, coal, etc. But the richest reserves are copper and iron. Dozens of mines are still under massive extraction, among which Daye Iron Mine and Tonglushan Copper and Iron Mine are the representatives.

黄石地区矿冶遗址分布图

The Map of Ancient Mining and Smelting Sites in Huangshi

请大家留意的第二个看点是丰富的矿冶文化遗产。

Now let's turn to the second aspect of the exhibition: the rich relics of mining and metallurgical culture.

右侧地台下陈列的是黄石、大冶、阳新采矿、冶炼遗址分布图。经过考古工作者多年的努力，在黄石地区目前已经发现古代采矿遗址 10 处，冶炼遗址 57 处。与矿冶文化有关的文化遗存还有旧石器时代遗址 1 处、新石器时代遗址 64 处、古城址 3 处。这些遗址的发现和发掘，为认识和研究黄石的矿冶文化提供了丰富的实物资料。

Beneath the floor, we can see the Map of Ancient Mining and Smelting Sites in Huangshi, Daye and Yangxin. After years of exploration and excavation, archaeologists have discovered 10 ancient mining sites and 57 smelting sites in Huangshi area. Other cultural remains related to mining and metallurgical culture include one site of the Paleolithic Age, 64 sites of the Neolithic Age, and 3 sites of ancient cities. These findings and excavations provide authentic data to understand and explore Huangshi mining and metallurgical culture.

请大家留意的第三个看点是序厅左右两侧的仿铜雕壁画。这两幅浮雕壁画再现了青铜时代黄石矿冶工匠从事采矿和冶炼生产的劳动场景。从浮雕壁画上我们可以对古代的矿冶生产有一个形象的了解。同时，我们在参观中也可以得到一种艺术的享受。

Now let's come to the third aspect. Please look at the bronze imitation murals on the walls. These two relief murals revive the scenes of mining and smelting at the Bronze Age, which offers us a vivid knowledge of the ancient mining. At the same time, we can also enjoy the remarkable art during the visit.

序厅中央井巷剖面

The Cross-section of the Shaft and Tunnel in the Center of the Introductory Hall

第四个看点是序厅中央的古代采矿井巷剖面。

The fourth aspect is the cross-section of the ancient mining shaft and tunnel in the center of the introductory hall.

这个井巷剖面是依据战国时期采矿井巷缩小一定比例制作而成的。在井巷剖面中，我们利用幻影成像技术，再现古代矿工在井下采掘、运输、提升等劳作的情景。

This cross-section is a reduced representation of ancient mining shaft and tunnel in the Warring States Period, where the working scenes of ancient miners' digging, hauling, and hoisting are reproduced through phantom imaging technology.

中央地台下陈列的是黄石地区的部分矿物标本，其中有色彩斑斓的孔雀石、蓝铜矿、赤铜矿；有光彩夺目的黄铁矿晶体；有晶莹剔透的水晶、方解石；还有褐铁矿、磁铁矿等。这些矿物巧夺天工，令人叹为观止。有些矿物品种还是制作珠宝的原料。

Under the central platform, some mineral specimens of Huangshi are displayed, among which are colorful malachite, azurite and cuprite, dazzling pyrite crystal, sparkling crystal and calcite, and limonite, magnetite, etc.. All these minerals are intricate and amazing. Some of them are the raw materials for jewelries.

下面请大家跟随我一起，穿过时空隧道进入地下的采矿平巷，身临其境体会古代采矿工匠的生产环境。

Now let's go through the Time Tunnel to the underground mining tunnel, where we can experience the working conditions of the ancient miners.

这是一处复原的古代井巷，依据战国时期铜绿山古铜矿遗址中最大的一条平巷复原而成。目的是为了安全，也便于参观浏览。而早于战国时期的井巷，比现在我们见到的井巷要窄小得多，平巷断面只有 1 米左右。可见当时的生产环境十分艰苦。然而，勤劳智慧的黄石先民就是在这样艰苦的环境中，开采出一筐又一筐，一吨又一吨矿石，并将矿石百炼成铜，以满足当时社会发展的需要。

This is the restoration of the ancient shaft and tunnel which is built according to the largest tunnel in Tonglushan Ancient Copper Mine Site in the Warring States Period. Both safety and convenience of the visit are considered in the reconstruction. Before the Warring States Period, shafts and tunnels were much smaller than what we see now. The cross-section of the tunnel was only one meter. Thus we can imagine the hard working conditions at that time. However, those diligent and intelligent ancestors of Huangshi extracted tons of ores and smelted them into copper in order to meet the needs of social development.

值得大家注意的是：这些经过木材支护的矿井，虽然历经两千多年，至今仍保存完好，说明当时支护技术已经相当成熟，基本上能够保证采矿生产的安全。古代地下开采技术除了进行井巷的开拓和支护以外，还要解决矿井排水、矿井提升、矿井通信、井下照明等一系列技术问题。古代采矿工匠是怎样解决这些问题的，我们将通过参观下面的几个展厅，为大家解答。

One point is worth special attention. After more than 2000 years, those mines are still well-reserved with timber support, which proves that the supporting techniques of that time are mature enough to guarantee the safety of the mine production. The underground mining techniques not only include the extension and support of shaft and tunnel, but also include mine draining, mine hoisting, mine communication, and underground lighting etc.. How do the ancient miners solve all these problems? We will find the answer after we visit the next few exhibition halls.

请大家跟随我一起穿越地下巷道，真实体验古代采矿情景。

Now let's go through the underground tunnel to experience the ancient mining scenes.

春秋时期古矿井现场复原

Restoration of the Ancient Mine during the Spring and Autumn Period

我们现在看到的是铜绿山古铜矿遗址，其向我们展示的是春秋时期古矿井发掘出土的情景。墙上的照片是全景照。地台下是按 1∶1 的比例复原的局部。

Here is Tonglushan Ancient Copper Mine Site which displays the scene of ancient mine excavation during the Spring and Autumn Period. On the wall is the panoramic picture. Under the platform is the restoration of part of a mine according to 1∶1 ratio.

这处采矿遗址是 1979 年至 1980 年由中国社会科学院考古研究所考古发掘的，共清理出竖井、盲井 65 个，平巷、斜巷 19 条，排水巷道 1 条。这处遗址的上部原是一座小山，在矿山生产中已剥离了近 20 米。经过考古勘探，在遗址下部15米处还发现了古矿井的支护木，说明当时古矿井的开采深度最少已达到地下35米。

The site was excavated by the Archaeological Institute of Chinese Academy of Social Sciences from 1979 to 1980. About 65 vertical and blind shafts, 19 level and inclined tunnels, and a draining tunnel were sorted out. There was once a hill on the top of the site which was stripped nearly 20 meters in the process of mine production. After archeological survey, supporting timbers were discovered 15 meters beneath the site, which proves that the mining depth of the ancient mine is at least 35 meters underground.

2号主展厅入口

Entrance to the No. 2 Main Exhibition Hall

下面我们将要参观的是《黄石矿冶文化展》的2号主展厅。在这个展厅里请大家留意以下三个看点：一是黄石矿冶文化的源头在哪里？二是古代采矿工匠是怎样寻找地下矿床的？三是商周时是怎样进行地下开采的？

Next we go to No. 2 main exhibition hall of Huangshi Mining and Metallurgical Culture Exhibition, where there are three points of interest. The first one is the origin of Huangshi mining and metallurgical culture. The second one is how ancient miners search for the underground ore deposits. The third one is how the underground mining is carried out in the Shang Dynasty and Zhou Dynasty.

石龙头遗址展柜前

In Front of the Showcase of Shilongtou Site

现在让我和大家一起回到二三十万年前的旧石器时代。1973年，考古工作者在黄石市西塞山区河口镇一个名叫石龙头的小山上发现了一处洞穴遗址。经考古发掘，出土了 88 件打制石器，其中有石核、石片、砍砸器、刮削器等。在这处洞穴中还发现了大量哺乳动物化石，其中有大熊猫、豪猪、鬣狗、东方剑齿象、犀牛、鹿等。

Now let's go back to the Paleolithic Age of 200, 000 or 300, 000 years ago. In 1973, a cave site was discovered at Shilongtou Hill, Hekou Town, Xisaishan District, Huangshi City. After archeological excavation, 88 chipped stone tools were unearthed, among which were stone cores, stone flakes, choppers, scrapers, etc.. A large number of mammals' fossils were discovered in the cave, such as panda, porcupine, hyena, oriental stegodon, rhino, deer, etc.

这处遗址的发现，不仅翻开了黄石历史的第一页，同时也翻开了黄石矿冶文化的第一页，成为黄石矿冶文化的源头。

The discovery of the site not only turns on a new leaf of Huangshi history, but also turns on a new leaf of Huangshi mining and metallurgical culture, which becomes the origin of Huangshi mining and metallurgical culture.

从出土的石器上我们可以看出，这些石器所用的石料不是一般的石料，而是经过挑选的、硬度较高的石英岩、磁石等火成岩。而石龙头附近随处可得的硬度较低的石灰岩却没有被选用。这说明远古人类制作的石器是经过选择的。正是对石料的选择，使他们对矿物和岩石的性质有了逐步的认识，黄石的矿冶文化也正是在这一认识过程中开始孕育。

It is disclosed by the excavated stone tools that they are not made of ordinary stones, but rather igneous stones of high hardness, such as quartzite, magnetite, etc.. Limestone is available everywhere around Shilongtou, but it is not selected because of its low hardness. This manifests that ancient people select appropriate materials to make stone tools. Gradually, the choice of stone materials helps them understand the nature of minerals and stones. This knowledge begins to breed Huangshi mining and metallurgical culture since then.

石龙头遗址场景前

In Front of the Scenes of Shilongtou Site

这是我们根据石龙头遗址的发掘资料，用幻影成像技术制作的场景。从这里我们可以看到原始人类打制石器，并进行采集、狩猎活动的情形。

These scenes are created by phantom imaging technology based on the excavated materials of Shilongtou Site, by which we can see the primitive people chipping stone tools, gathering and hunting.

新石器时代遗址展柜

Showcases of the Sites of Neolithic Age

距今约一万年至四千年，人类社会由原始群落进入氏族公社时期，即考古学上的新石器时代。目前，黄石地区已发现新石器时代遗址 64 处。

Neolithic Age in archaeology refers to the period from 10,000 to 4,000 years ago. At that time, the primitive tribes developed into the clan commune. Up to now, 64 sites of Neolithic Age have been discovered in Huangshi area.

展柜中陈列的都是本地区新石器时代遗址出土的陶器，这些陶器具有明显的地域特点，由此说明这些陶器是在本地区烧制的。新石器时代与旧石器时代的区别在于：在新石器时代，石器已由打制演进为磨制并出现原始农业、家畜驯养以及陶器烧制。

Potteries in the showcase are unearthed in the local sites of Neolithic Age. They have obvious regional features, which indicate that they are made in the local area. The differences between Neolithic Age and

Paleolithic Age lie in the following aspects: stone tools develop from chipping to grinding; primitive agriculture, livestock taming and feeding and pottery burning appears.

制作陶器的原料是黏土。用黏土制成不同器型的陶坯，陶坯制成后放入陶窑，在1000℃左右的高温下烧制。烧成的陶器用于社会生活的方方面面，促进了人类社会的发展。制陶业出现的意义还在于为后来的金属冶炼奠定了技术基础。这是因为冶炼金属的炼炉是在陶窑的基础上发展起来的。烧制陶器的高温获得方法也用于金属冶炼之中。

The raw material for potteries is clay which is produced into different shapes of billet. Then they are put into pottery kilns and burned at the temperature of 1000℃. The potteries are used in all aspects of social life and promote social development. The pottery industry also lays a technical foundation for later metal smelting. As we know, the metal smelting furnaces develop from pottery kilns. The technique of obtaining high temperature in pottery burning is also applied in metal smelting.

《蚩尤作兵》油画

Oil Painting of *Chiyou in the Battlefield*

新石器时代晚期，也就是中国历史上的炎帝、黄帝时期，黄石的矿冶文化已开始萌芽。

The late period of Neolithic Age is also the period of Yan Emperor and Huang Emperor in Chinese history. At that time, Huangshi mining and metallurgical culture began to sprout.

我们看到的这幅名为《蚩尤作兵》的油画是根据文献资料“蚩尤受庐山之金而作五兵”绘制的。蚩尤和炎帝、黄帝生活在同一时代，分别是三大部落的首领。

This oil painting is named *Chiyou in the Battlefield*, which is painted according to the story about Chiyou. It is said that he forged five different weapons with metals of Lushan. Chiyou, Yan Emperor and Huang Emperor are the leaders of three powerful tribes who lived in the same period in Chinese history.

在古代，部落与部落之间为争夺生存空间常常发生战争。而蚩尤所领导的九黎族，因为掌握了冶金技术，制造的兵器精良而威震天下。所以古文献中记载："黄帝攻蚩尤，三年城不下""黄帝与蚩尤九战九不胜"。据考证，蚩尤"受庐山之金而作五兵"的地点应在湖北、江西、安徽等长江中游地区的铜矿上。

In ancient times, tribes usually fought for their living space. Then wars often took place between them. At that time, Jiuli tribe was led by Chiyou. Because the tribe mastered smelting technology, they were famous for their polished weapons. Their stories were recorded in the ancient documents as follows. "Huang Emperor had wars against Chiyou, but he couldn't get the upper hand after three years' fight." "After nine wars, Huang Emperor still couldn't defeat Chiyou." According to the historical survey, Chiyou forged weapons in the middle reaches of Yangtze River, which may include Hubei, Jiangxi and Anhui provinces where copper ores are abundant.

最终，蚩尤与黄帝大战于涿鹿，蚩尤兵败被擒杀。由此，黄河流域、长江流域进入了华夏民族的大融合时期。经过长期发展，形成日后的华夏族。

Finally, Chiyou and Huang Emperor fought fiercely in Zhuolu where Chiyou was defeated and killed. Then the Yellow River basin and Yangtze River basin entered into a period of great fusion of Chinese nations. After a long-term development, Huaxia clan came into being.

第二单元说明

Introduction to the Second Unit

公元前二十一世纪，以夏王朝的建立为开端，经商、西周和春秋，历时一千六百余年，是我国青铜文化逐步形成并进入鼎盛的时期，而青铜器的制造则依赖于矿业。在这一背景下，黄石古代的矿冶文化得以迅速发展，勤劳智慧的黄石先民在矿冶业上取得的技术成就为人类社会的发展做出了重要贡献。

It is more than 1600 years since the 21st century BC when China underwent the Xia Dynasty, Shang Dynasty, Western Zhou Dynasty, and the Spring and Autumn Period. During this time, Chinese bronze culture gradually came into being and entered into its heyday. As bronze manufacture is dependent on mining, the ancient mining and metallurgical culture in Huangshi develops rapidly. The wise and diligent ancient people in Huangshi made great achievements in mining and metallurgy, which contributes a lot to the development of human society.

利用矿物的共生关系找矿

Prospecting with the Help of Mineral Symbiotic Relationship

在展示黄石矿冶业的技术成就之前，我们应当首先了解，先民是怎样寻找矿石、矿床的？又用什么方法指导古代井巷开拓方向的？我们可以从文献资料和考古发掘资料中找到一些答案。

Before we talk about the achievements of Huangshi mining and metallurgy, we need to know the methods of the ancient people in the following areas. How do they prospect ores and deposits? How do they know the direction of shaft and tunnel excavation? Some answers can be found in the documents and archeological materials.

一种方法是利用矿物的共生关系找矿。我国的金属矿产资源经常是多种金属共生在一起的。这一特征早在战国时期以前人们就有所认识，并总结出一些规律。

One method to prospect is to make use of mineral symbiotic relationship. In China, there are many symbiotic metals in mineral deposits. Before the Warring States Period, this characteristic of minerals is recognized and some rules are summed up on the basis of experiences.

例如《管子》一书在《地数篇》中记载："出铜之山，四百六十七山；出铁之山，三千六百九十山。""上有丹砂者，下有黄金；上有兹（磁）石者，下有铜金；上有陵石者，下有铅、锡、赤铜；上有赭者，下有铁，此山之见荣者也。"除《管子》以外，古籍《山海经》中也有类似的记载。

It is recorded in *Land and Amount* of *Guanzi* that "There are 467 mountains with copper ores and 3,690 mountains with iron ores. If there is cinnabar above, there is gold below; magnetite above, copper and gold below; ling stone above, lead, tin and red copper below; ochre above, iron below. This is the appearance of prosperity of the mountain." Apart from *Guantzi*, similar records have been found in the classics *Mountains and Rivers*.

古文献中关于矿物共生关系的记载表明：一个垂直的矿体或一条矿脉，山上出现某种矿物分布，对地下赋存的另一种矿物起到指示作用。

There are many records in the ancient literature about mineral symbiotic relationship. Such as, in a vertical ore body or vein, distribution of a mineral on the surface indicates another mineral underground.

这里展示的是大冶铜绿山矿区矿体垂直分布图。从这张图上也可以看出不同矿物之间存在共生关系。这种矿物的共生关系是古代采矿工匠寻找铜矿资源的方法之一。

Here is the vertical distribution map of ore fields and bodies of Daye Tonglushan Mine, where we can see the symbiotic relationships of different minerals. This kind of symbiotic relationship is one of the methods for the ancient miners to prospect copper.

根据指示植物找矿

Prospecting with the Help of Indicator Plant

在长江中下游地区的铜矿带上生长着一种名为海州香薷的植物，俗称铜草花。花形如牙刷，紫红色。铜草只生长在含有铜元素的土壤中，其根部的灰分中含铜量高达百分之三。每当深秋，铜草花盛开时，遍布矿区的山野，极易辨认。从古代起，乃至现在，铜草都是寻找铜矿的指示植物。

There is a sort of plant named Haizhou Elsholtzia which is commonly known as copper flower. It grows on the copper belt along the middle and lower reaches of Yangtze River whose purple-red flower looks like a toothbrush. It only grows in the soil containing copper element. In the ash of its root, the copper content is about 3% . In the late autumn, copper flowers blossom everywhere in the mining area. It is very easy to identify them. Since ancient times, the copper flower has been the indicator plant to prospect copper. Until now, this method is still effective.

“重砂分析法”鉴别矿石品位

Identification of the Grade of Ores by the Method of Heavy Minerals Analysis

在开采过程中，为了鉴别矿石品位的高低，使井巷开拓在富矿带内，古代工匠采用“重砂分析法”，在井下进行鉴别。

During the mining process, ancient miners apply “the Method of Heavy Minerals Analysis” to identify the grade of ores which helps them build the shafts and tunnels on rich ore belt. The identification is often conducted underground.

考古发掘中，考古工作者在古矿井中发现了木杵、木臼、木斗等器物。经专家分析后认为，这是一组用于鉴别矿石品位的工具。采矿工匠将井巷中采集的矿土样品放入木臼内，再用木杵捣碎。捣碎后的矿土样品放入木斗，用水淘洗。由于矿物的比重大，当泥土冲走后，矿物则保留在木斗内。木斗内沉淀的矿物愈多，说明矿石的品位愈高。这种方法现代称之为“重砂分析法”。

During the process of excavation, archaeologists find wooden pestles, wooden mortars, and wooden dippers in ancient mines. According to the experts, they are tools to identify the grade of ores. Miners collect the soil samples from the shafts and tunnels, put them in the wooden mortar, smash them with the wooden pestle, and then wash them in the wooden dipper. Because the minerals are heavier than the soil, they are left in the wooden dipper while the soil is washed away. The more minerals are left in the dipper, the higher is the ores' grade. This is called the Method of Heavy Minerals Analysis in modern times.

考古发掘证实，铜绿山遗址古代井巷绝大多数分布在富矿带内，由此说明这种方法是行之有效的。

The archaeological excavations confirm that in Tonglushan site, the ancient shafts and tunnels are mostly distributed on the rich ore belt, which proves that the method is effective.

采矿井巷的开拓与支护

Extension and Supporting of Mining Shafts and Tunnels

下面，我将要向大家介绍的是商周时期的采矿方法。时间跨度大约从公元前十二世纪的晚商时期到公元前四世纪的春秋晚期。

Now we are talking about the mining methods in the Shang and Zhou Dynasties which last probably from the late Shang Dynasty to the late Spring and Autumn Period. That is from the 12th century BC to the 4th century BC.

商周时期黄石地区的采矿方法分为露天开采和地下开采。今天我们主要介绍地下开采方法，而地下开采是通过开凿地下井巷来实现的。由于黄石地区的矿体大多属于接触变质的铜铁矿床，因而井巷周围的岩石比较松软，开拓的井巷一般都需要支护才能保证生产安全。

During the Shang and Zhou Dynasties, both surface mining and underground mining are applied in Huangshi. Today we will mainly introduce underground mining which is realized by digging shafts and tunnels underground. Most ore bodies in Huangshi area are contact-metamorphic copper and iron deposits. So the rocks around shafts and tunnels are quite loose. In order to guarantee the safety of production, support is necessary.

研究古代采矿技术，一是要研究当时的井巷开拓与支护技术；二是要研究当时的生产工具；三是要研究矿井的提升、排水、通风、照明方法等。只有这些技术问题都得到了较合理的解决，矿山生产才能顺利进行。

In order to research the ancient mining technology, the following problems should be studied: first the extension and supporting techniques of shafts and tunnels; second the production tools; third the methods the hoisting, draining, ventilation, and lighting of mines. Only when these problems are well solved can mine production go on smoothly.

首先，我们看看商代的井巷开拓与支护。

First of all, let's look at the extension and supporting of shafts and tunnels in the Shang Dynasty.

黄石地区商代古矿井发现于大冶铜绿山矿区 7 号矿体。经碳 14 测定，距今约 3260 年。商代矿井井巷开拓一般采用竖井和盲井。所谓盲井就是井口不直接通往地表的竖井。竖井与竖井、竖井与盲井之间用短平巷连接，开采深度 15 米左右。井巷断面较小，一般为 50 厘米见方。井巷用木质榫接方框支护，方框外用木板护壁。

In Huangshi area, the shafts of the Shang Dynasty are discovered at No. 7 ore body in Daye Tonglushan Mine, dating back about 3260 years measured by carbon 14. At that time, vertical and blind shafts were usually adopted in extension of shafts and tunnels. The blind shaft refered to the vertical one whose wellhead doesn't lead to the surface. Short tunnels were used to connect vertical shafts and vertical shafts, vertical shafts and blind shafts. The mining depth was about 15 meters. The cross section of shafts and tunnels was as narrow as 50 cm^2. These shafts and tunnels were supported by wood mortised frames, around which wood boards were used to protect the walls.

西周时期的井巷开拓与支护

Extension and Supporting of Shafts and Tunnels in the Western Zhou Dynasty

西周时期采矿井巷的开拓与支护与商代矿井有明显的继承关系。除采用竖井、平巷外，还出现了斜井。开采深度 30 米左右。井巷断面较商代有所加大。竖井仍然采用间隔式方框支护，但方框构件一端或两端砍成矛状，这样可以嵌入井壁，以防井框滑落。平巷已经出现倒叉式棚架。井巷四周一般用木棍和竹席护壁。

Obviously, the extension and supporting of shafts and tunnels in the Western Zhou Dynasty inherited that of the Shang Dynasty. Apart from vertical shafts and tunnels, there were also inclined shafts. The mining depth was about 30 meters. The cross section of the shafts and tunnels was wider than that of the Shang Dynasty. The segmented frame supporting was still adopted in vertical shafts. But one end or both ends of the components were sharpened like spear, so they can be embedded into the wall to prevent the frames from sliding. Inverted fork scaffolds appeared in tunnels. Wooden sticks and bamboo mats were used to support the walls around the shafts and tunnels.

这里陈列的陶器是在考古发掘清理中出土的。这是陶甗，那是陶鬲。在考古发掘中还发现了兽骨和菱角，这些应该是当时的生活遗物。此外还发现了草棚的遗迹，说明当时井口应搭盖有草棚。

The displayed potteries are unearthed during an archaeological excavation. This is pottery yan-steamer, and that is pottery li-pot. Animal bones and water chestnuts which are living relics of that time are also found in the archeological excavation. The remains of straw sheds are also found nearby, which proves that the wellheads may be covered by straw sheds.

春秋时期的井巷开拓与支护

Extension and Supporting of Shafts and Tunnels in the Spring and Autumn Period

春秋时期的井巷开拓与支护仍沿袭前代发展，采用竖井、盲井、平巷、斜井联合开拓法。开采深度一般在 40 米左右，竖井净断面一般为 60~

70厘米见方。平巷净断面一般高100厘米，宽80厘米。井巷四周用木棍或者用木棍夹竹席护壁。

The extension and supporting of shafts and tunnels in the Spring and Autumn Period inherited that of early ages. Vertical shafts, blind shafts, tunnels and inclined shafts were adopted together. The mining depth was about 40 meters. The net cross section of vertical shafts was about $60cm^2$ or $70cm^2$. The net cross section of tunnels was 100cm high and 80cm wide. Wooden sticks and bamboo mats were used to support the walls around the shafts and tunnels.

这里陈列的是一组竖井支护方框和一组平巷支护棚架。为了使大家对古代矿井有一个全景式的了解，我们按1：1的比例，用剖面和平面相结合的表现手法制作了春秋时期的井巷复原景观，供大家观赏。

Here is a set of supporting square frames for vertical shaft and a set of supporting scaffold for tunnel. In order to achieve a panoramic view of the ancient mine, the sectional and planar perspectives are combined to restore the landscape of shafts and tunnels of the Spring and Autumn Period which is finished in a 1 : 1 ratio. So we can enjoy an immersive experience.

3号展厅：商周时期的采矿工具
Mining Tools of the Shang and Zhou Dynasties in No. 3 Exhibition Hall

商周时期采矿生产所使用的工具按质地可分为铜、木、竹、藤、石质等几类，按用途可分为采掘、装载、运输、提升、排水等几类。而用青铜制作的采掘工具决定着矿山的生产能力，也是青铜时代生产力发展水平的见证。

According to the material, the mining tools of the Shang and Zhou

Dynasties are classified into bronze, wood, bamboo, rattan, stone, etc.. According to the usage, they are classified into digging, loading, transporting, hoisting, draining, etc.. Mining tools made by bronze determine the production capacity of the mine, which is also the proof of productivity development level of the Bronze Age.

这里陈列的是木质工具和竹质工具。木质工具有木铲、木锹、木梯、木扁担等。竹制工具有竹篓、竹筐等。这些木制工具全部都是用整木雕凿的。井下工作需要不同大小、不同长短的工具，因而形成了工具系列。

Here are wooden and bamboo tools. Wooden tools include wooden shovel, wooden spade, wooden ladder, wooden shoulder pole, etc.. Bamboo tools include bamboo basket, bamboo crate, etc.. All the wooden tools are made of entire pieces of wood. Tools of different size and different length are needed in underground work which form into different series.

很多出土的工具，使用痕迹明显，有的刃部磨损严重。从这里也可以看出当时采矿工匠的艰辛。大量出土的竹制工具，虽然外形已经压扁或破损，但纹理分明，与现代的竹编工艺基本一样。

Many unearthed tools have obvious signs of being used whose blades are badly worn, which tells us the miners' hard work at that time. Many unearthed bamboo tools are squashed or broken, but their texture is very clear. The bamboo basketry of those tools is much the same as that of modern times.

铜工具柜

Bronze Tool Cabinets

在铁器时代之前，采矿生产所用的采掘工具全部是青铜制作的。例如铜斧、铜锛、铜镢、铜铲等。还有用于雕凿井框用的铜凿。

Before the Iron Age, all the mining tools are made of bronze, such as bronze ax, bronze adze, bronze hoe, bronze shovel, etc.. Bronze chisel is used to carve shaft frame.

铜斧有多种，形式不一，大小不同，最大的有30余斤，小的只有几斤。这些铜斧的使用方法与现代斧头的使用方法不同。现代斧头的斧柄是横装的，而古代铜斧的斧柄是竖装的。

There are many types of bronze axes with different shapes and sizes. The biggest one weighs over 15kg, but the small one is less than 5kg. The use of these axes is different from that of modern ones. The handle of modern ax is cross-loaded while that of ancient ax is vertically-installed.

大家也许会问，这么重的铜斧在低矮的巷道里，是怎样使用的？经专家们研究，大型直柄铜斧这样使用：在挖掘竖井时，由于铜斧是直柄，不受竖井断面小的影响，便于操作，而且铜斧重量大，凿岩能力也随之增大。在挖掘平巷时，可以将铜斧吊在平巷支护的横梁上，用手操作斧柄，向平巷的掘进面上撞击，这样非常省力，而且冲击力也很强。

You might be wondering how the heavy bronze ax is used in the low tunnel. Experts have found out the usage of bronze ax. In the process of shaft digging, because the handle of the bronze ax is straight, it is not affected by the small cross section of the shaft and easy to operate. What's more, the bronze ax is very heavy, so its drilling capacity increases. In the process of tunnel digging, the bronze ax is hung on the crossbeam of the tunnel support. Then the miners can operate the handle of the bronze ax, and strike the ax towards the cross section of the tunnel. Therefore, effort is saved and the impact force is strong.

铜锛、铜镢则是装上短柄使用，类似于现在的短柄锄头。

The bronze adze and hoe are equipped with short handles which are similar to the short-handled hoe at present.

铜斧独立柜前

In Front of an Independent Cabinet of a Bronze Ax

根据考古资料，大冶铜绿山出土的大铜斧，是目前世界上发现的最大铜斧，堪称“天下第一斧”。

According to the archaeological data, the bronze ax unearthed in Tonglushan of Daye is the largest one in the world which is the called “the world’s first axe.”

从出土的铜斧上，我们可以看到，铜斧的刃部均已磨圆，由平刃变成了弧刃，说明铜斧使用了很长时间。

The level blade of the unearthed bronze ax has been worn. Its flat blade has turned into curved one, which proves that it has been used for a long time.

这些铜制工具留给我们的不仅是作为文物的物质财富，更重要的是精神财富。因为透过铜斧我们可以看到一种精神，即不畏艰难、勇于开拓、勇于奉献的时代精神。我们的祖先，正是凭着这种精神，谱写着灿烂的历史，为人类文明和社会发展做出了不懈努力。

These bronze tools leave us not only material wealth. More importantly, they leave us spiritual wealth. Through the bronze ax, we can see a kind of spirit which is the fearlessness of hardships and the courage of exploitation and dedication. Depending on this spirit, our ancestors create a glorious history and make a great contribution to human civilization and social development.

矿井提升、排水、通风、照明

Mine Hoisting, Drainage, Ventilation, and Lighting

商周时期的矿井提升，一是采用人工提升，二是借助工具提升。例如利用杠杆原理进行提升，既可以节省人力又能加快提升速度、加大提升重量。这是根据出土文物复原的提升示意图，井口滑轮的作用是保持提升物的垂直。

In the Shang and Zhou Dynasties, there are two types of mine hoisting. One is hoisting by man and the other is hoisting by tools. For example, hoisting under the lever principle can save manpower, accelerate the speed and increase the weight. This is the sketch map of hoisting restored according to the unearthed relics. The function of the pulley at the wellhead is to keep the lift vertical.

当矿井深度低于地下水位时，则需要排水。矿井中的地下水是用木槽将水引入专设的排水巷道，并汇入竖井底部的“井底水仓”，再用木桶盛水，通过提升设备将水排出地表。

When the depth of mine is below the groundwater level, drainage is needed. Groundwater in the mine is led into a special draining tunnel through the wooden trough. It flows into the shaft sump at the bottom of the shaft. Then the water is held in a bucket, and removed to the surface by hoisting equipment.

矿井通风是利用井口高低差不同形成的气压进行自然通风。也可以在出风井的底部烧一堆火，当空气受热后即可产生对流，达到通风的目的。

Mine ventilation is achieved by natural ventilation which makes use of pressure formed by different height of the wellheads. Ventilation is also achieved by a fire at the bottom of a shaft, because heated air generates convection.

在古矿井的发掘中，发现了大量遗存的竹签残段，这是古代用于井下照明的遗物。竹签扎成火把，亮度大、烟量小、易燃烧，是古代常用的照明材料。

In the excavation of the ancient mine, a lot of remains of bamboo sticks are found which are relics of underground lighting in ancient times. Bamboo sticks are tied together to form torches which have the characteristics of high brightness and small amount of smoke. They are easy to burn, so they are usually used as the lighting materials in ancient times.

战国至秦汉时期的矿冶文化

Mining and metallurgical culture from the Warring States Period to the Qin and Han Dynasties

从公元前 475 年起，我国历史进入战国时期，与此同时，青铜时代也逐渐向铁器时代过渡。这一历史性的变革，为矿冶文化的发展提供了条件。由于铁制工具的凿岩能力远胜于铜制工具，从而提高了矿山的生产效率，推动了采矿技术的进步。

Since 475 BC, China entered into the Warring States Period. Meanwhile, the Bronze Age gradually transitioned to the Iron Age. This is a historical change which provides the conditions for the development of mining and metallurgical culture. As the drilling power of iron tools is much stronger than that of bronze tools, efficiency of mine production is improved and progress of mining technology is promoted.

战国秦汉时期的井巷开拓除了前面我们已经看到的竖井、平巷以外，新出现了一种阶梯式斜井。这种斜井是由多级浅井和多级短巷组成，适合在次生富集带内探矿和采矿，也可以作为上下平巷间的联络通道。

From the Warring States Period to the Qin and Han Dynasties, a kind of stepped inclined shaft appeared, except for the shafts and tunnels in the previous time. The inclined shaft was composed of multi-level shallow shaft and multi-level short tunnel which is suitable for prospecting and mining in secondary enrichment zone. It is also used as a connecting passage between the upper and lower tunnels.

由于铁制工具用于矿山生产，工具的凿岩能力增强，因此，井巷开拓的断面也随之增大。竖井断面一般都在 1 米见方左右。平巷最大的断面达到 1. 6 米高、1. 95 米宽。我们在 1 号展厅穿越的平巷，就是以此为根据而复原制作的。

As the iron tools were used in mine production, the drilling power was increased. Therefore, the cross section of shaft and tunnel was also increased. Usually, the cross section of a shaft was around 1 square meter. The largest cross section of a tunnel was 1. 6 meters high and 1. 95 meters wide. The tunnel in No. 1 exhibition hall is restored according to the tunnel of this period.

井巷断面的增大，地应力的改变也愈大，从而对井巷支护的要求也愈高。以前所用的间隔式方框支护法已不能确保开拓井巷的安全。于是，竖井出现了密集式搭接方框支护，就是将坑木的两端砍成台阶状，每四根搭接为一组，一组一组层层叠压，完成竖井支护。这种支护形式在现代采矿学上称为“垛盘结构”。

The larger the cross section of shaft and tunnel is, the stronger the crustal stress is. Thus, there are higher requirements for the support of shaft and tunnel. The previous segmented frame supporting can't ensure the safety of the extension of shaft and tunnel. Then in the shaft, intensive connected frame support appeared which is to hew two ends of the mine timber into steps, lap four as a group, pile and press in groups. Then the shaft is well supported. This kind of supporting is called "buttress plate structure" in modern mining science.

在铜绿山遗址发掘以前，大学教科书是用一个英国十八世纪的矿井资料来讲解“垛盘结构”的。考古资料证实，我国早在两千多年前就掌握了这种支护技术。

Before the excavation of Tonglushan site, in the university textbooks, “buttress plate structure” is introduced by quoting documents of a British mine in the 18th century. Archaeological materials confirm that Chinese people have mastered this supporting technique for more than two thousand years.

这时的平巷支护也有了很大进步。其方法是用一根带杈的立柱，一根横梁，一根地枕木和一根内撑木组成一组完全支护棚架。这种完全支护棚架可以有效地承受顶压、侧压和地鼓。

At that time, tunnel supporting also developed a lot. The method is to put a bifurcated pillar, a crossbeam, a ground wood sleeper, and an inner support wood together to build up a set of fully supporting scaffold. This structure can effectively resist top pressure, side pressure and ground pressure.

战国秦汉时期的生产工具

Production Tools from the Warring States Period to the Qin and Han Dynasties

战国秦汉时期的古矿井中，铁制工具已经全部取代了铜制工具。器型也有了新的变化。这是铁斧、铁锤、铁耙、凹字形铁锄、铁钻。从出土的铁斧可以看出，当时仍采用直柄，直柄的顶端由于受铁锤击打，木质纤维已外卷。斧柄顶端还扎有一层竹，用以延长使用时间。

From the Warring States Period to the Qin and Han Dynasties, iron tools have completely replaced bronze tools in ancient mines. The shape of the tools also changed. These are iron ax, iron hammer, iron rake, concave iron hoe and iron drill. From the unearthed iron ax, we see that straight handle was still used at that time. At the top of the straight handle, wood fiber was curled outward because of strike by iron hammer. The top of the ax handle was bound with a layer of bamboo, which can extend the usage time of the ax.

这是战国秦汉时期矿井中出土的木铲、木槌、木锹。这些木制工具与早期矿井中使用的木制工具相比，没有大的变化。直到现代，这一类工具仍在使用。

These are wooden shovel, wooden mallet, and wooden spade unearthed in mines from the Warring States Period to the Qin and Han Dynasties. They are almost the same as those used in the earlier mines. Until modern times, this kind of tools is still in use.

采矿方法展板
Exhibition Boards of Mining Methods

战国以前的采矿方法，一般都是一层一层由上而下逐层开采，井巷一般都开凿在矿体以内，井巷开拓的过程也是采矿过程。因此，井巷十分密集。

Before the Warring States Period, the mining method is to mine from top to bottom and layer by layer. The shafts and tunnels are usually dug within the ore body. The process of the extension of shafts and tunnels is also the mining process. So the shafts and tunnels are densely distributed.

到战国时，已由以往的“下向式开采”改为“上向式开采”。这种开采方法是先将竖井开拓在矿体或矿体底盘围岩中，再开“石门”进入矿体，然后由下向上，分层开采。将上层开采中的废石和贫矿充填到下层采矿区。这样既保证了上层开采的安全，又减少了大量废石的运输。这种上向式水平分层充填开采技术是我国古代采矿技术的一次飞跃。直到现在，这种采矿方法仍在沿用。

During the Warring States Period, the former "downward mining" has been replaced by "upward mining". This mining method is to dig a shaft within the ore body or in the rocks of the bottom, open a cross tunnel to enter the ore body, and mine from bottom to top, layer by layer. Waste rocks and low-grade ores of the upper layer are used to fill the mined-out area in the lower layer, which ensures the safety of the upper mining and reduces transportation of a large number of waste rocks. The upward horizontal layering backfill mining is a leap in Chinese ancient mining technology which is still in use up to now.

矿井提升

Mine Hoisting

战国秦汉时期的矿井提升，由于开采深度可以达60余米，所以一般都采用分段提升。在考古发掘中出土了一件木绞车车轴，还发现了用于提升的绳索、木钩、平衡石锤等器物。

From the Warring States Period to the Qin and Han Dynasties, the mining depth is more than 60 meters, so segmented hoisting is often adopted in mining. In the archaeological excavation, an axle of a wooden winch is unearthed. Other implements of mine hoisting are also discovered, such as ropes, wooden hook, balanced stone hammer, etc..

木绞车上凿有两排用于安装手柄和木条的卯眼。绞车装上手柄后可操作转动。装上木条后，可将立柱上的绳套套入其中一根木条，即可将绞车制动。

In order to install handles and wood strips, two rows of mortises are chiseled on the wooden winch. After the handles are installed, the wooden winch can be operated to rotate. After the wood strips are installed, the noose on the pillar is set into one of the wood strips, which helps the winch to brake.

平衡石锤的作用是提升矿石时在绳索的另一端挂上与提升重量相近的平衡石锤，这样提升时就比较省力。

A balanced stone hammer functions in the following way. When it is hung on the other end of the rope and has the similar weight as that of the hoisting ores, effort will be saved in the process of hoisting.

4号展厅：黄石早期的冶炼技术

Early Smelting Technology of Huangshi in No. 4 Exhibition Hall

根据考古资料考证，黄石地区已发现古代冶炼遗址57处。这些冶炼遗址一般都处在矿区周围，说明古代是就地采矿，就地筑炉炼铜，因为这样可以减少矿石的运输。通过对大冶铜绿山冶炼遗址的考古发掘，我们对距今2700多年前的中国古代冶炼技术有了比较清楚的认识。

According to archaeological materials, 57 ancient smelting sites have been found in Huangshi which are located around the mine. It indicates that in ancient times, ores are smelted in the neighboring areas of a mine, which can ease the pressure of transportation of ores. After the archaeological excavation of Daye Tonglushan smelting site, we have a clearer understanding of Chinese ancient smelting technology more than 2700 years ago.

在此之前，由于没有考古资料，国外有学者认为，中国青铜文化中所使用的铜是从国外进口的，提出了“中国青铜文化外来说”的观点。国内的一些著名学者在论及中国青铜时代铜的来源问题时，也只能引用国外的考古资料用以说明。

In the past, because of the absence of archaeological materials, some foreign scholars claim that copper in Chinese bronze culture is imported from abroad. They put forward the viewpoint that Chinese bronze culture is borrowed. When some famous domestic scholars talk about the origin of copper in the Chinese Bronze Age, they only cite the foreign archaeological documents in their explanation.

铜绿山古铜矿遗址的发现和发掘是对“中国青铜文化外来说”的否定。说明中国青铜时代不仅能够采铜，还能冶铜，而且当时采冶技术处于世界的领先水平。

The discovery and excavation of Tonglushan Ancient Copper Mine Site denies the viewpoint that Chinese bronze culture is borrowed. It proves that in the Chinese Bronze Age, copper was already mined and smelted. At that time, the mining and smelting technology is at the world's leading level.

春秋早期炼炉的结构及功能

Structure and Function of Smelting Furnaces in the Early Spring and Autumn Period

铜绿山古铜矿遗址的发掘，前后共清理出十座西周至春秋早期的鼓风炼铜竖炉，由炉基、炉缸、炉身三部分组成。

In Tonglushan Ancient Copper Mine Site, ten blast furnaces for smelting copper are cleared up which were built from the Western Zhou Dynasty to the early Spring and Autumn Period. A furnace is composed of base, vat, and body.

炉基部分设有风沟，风沟内有垫石用以支撑缸底。风沟的作用是使炉缸与地面隔离，利于保持炉温。当放渣或放铜时，风沟内可以燃烧木炭，防止炉缸内的铜液和渣液冻结，以达到顺利排渣放铜的目的。

A wind ditch is installed in the furnace base. The pad stones in the wind ditch are used to support the furnace bottom. The wind ditch is used to isolate the furnace vat from the ground, which is helpful to maintain the furnace temperature. When slag or copper is discharged, charcoals are burnt in the wind ditch to prevent the liquid copper and slag from freezing. Then slag and copper can be discharged successfully.

炉缸呈椭圆形，缸壁上残留多层矿渣。炉缸的前壁开有“金门”。“金门”是炼渣和铜液的排放口。由于炼渣的比重较金属铜轻，炼渣浮在铜液之上，只须在金门上方捅一小孔，渣即可流出。每冶炼一次，要经过多次排渣，只有当缸底的铜液达到一定数量时才放铜。需要放铜时，在“金门”下方捅一小孔，铜液即可流出。

The furnace vat shapes in oval. Multilayer slags are left over on the vat wall. “Golden door” is opened on the front wall of the vat which is the discharge port of slag and liquid copper. As the specific gravity of slag is less than that of copper, slag floats on the liquid copper. Just prick a small hole at the top of the “golden door”, slag can flow out. Several times of slag discharge are required in each time of smelting. Only when the liquid copper at the vat bottom reaches a certain amount can copper be discharged. If necessary, a small hole is pricked at the bottom of the “golden door”, then the liquid copper flows out.

炉缸上沿的炉壁设有两个对称的鼓风口。鼓风时，保证氧气在炉内循环，氧在冶炼中可以提高炉温，也有利于矿石在炉内的还原反应，将金属铜从矿石中还原出来。

There are two symmetric tuyeres in the furnace wall of the upper edge of the vat. When blasting, oxygen circulates inside the furnace. Oxygen raises the furnace temperature in the process of smelting and is also beneficial to the reduction reaction of ores in the furnace. Then cooper is reduced from the ores.

炉身是承装炉料的地方，冶炼中木炭、矿石和熔剂等依次从炉口加入。随着温度的增加，矿石由固体变为半熔体，直到全部熔化，同时，金属铜也逐渐从矿石中分离出来。

The furnace charge is loaded in the body. In the process of smelting, charcoals, ores, and solvents are added from the furnace mouth. As the temperature increases, ores turn into semi melts from solids. In the end, ores are melted completely. Meanwhile, copper is gradually isolated from the ores.

我们现在看到的是古代冶炼场景的复原景观，有助于大家对古代冶炼过程的了解和认识。

This is the restoration of the ancient smelting scene which helps us to understand the ancient smelting process.

战国时期炼炉的结构及功能

Structure and Function of Smelting Furnaces in the Warring States Period

在铜绿山镇的柯锡太村，考古工作者还发现了两座战国时期的炼炉。这两座炼炉，虽然保存不甚完好，但仍然可以看出它们的结构和前期炼炉有相同或相似的地方，应该是在前期炼炉的基础上发展而来的产物。其不同点在于前期炼炉的筑炉材料是用黏土、石英砂等夯筑的，而战国时期的炼炉则是用土坯砖砌筑的。土坯砖上还带有子母口，可以使炉体更坚固。

In Kexitai Village of Tonglushan Town, archaeologists find two smelting furnaces of the Warring States Period. Although they are not well-preserved, it is still clear that their structure is the same or similar as that of the early ones. It seems that they may develop on the basis of the early ones. Their difference lies in their building materials. The early smelting furnaces are rammed by clay, quartz sand and so on while the smelting furnaces in the Warring States Period are built by adobe bricks. On the adobe bricks, there is some special structure which strengthens the furnace body.

冶炼的辅助设施展板

Exhibition Boards of Auxiliary Facilities of Smelting

在冶炼遗址的考古发掘中，不仅发现了古代炼炉，而且在炼炉周围还发现了与冶炼生产有关的辅助设施，如：工作台、碎料台、和泥池、筛分场等。

In the archaeological excavation of the smelting site, not only ancient smelting furnaces are discovered, but auxiliary facilities are also found around, such as worktable, crushing table, mixing pool, screening field and so on which are related to smelting production.

工作台高出地表且紧靠炉体，便于冶炼工匠加料和鼓风。碎料台是破碎矿石的地方。和泥池是搅拌黏土和高岭土等耐火材料的土坑，搅拌好的耐火材料用于修补因冶炼而熔蚀的炉缸内壁。在耐火材料中还要加一定数量的铁矿粉，以增加炉壁的强度。筛分场就是筛分铁矿粉的场所。

The worktable is above the ground surface and close to the furnace body, so it is convenient for the smelting workers to feed ores and to blast. The crushing table is the place for crushing ores. The mixing pool is an earthen pit where clay, kaolin and other refractories are stirred. The stirred refractories are used to repair the inner wall of the vat which is corroded by smelting. A certain amount of iron ore powder should be added in the refractories in order to increase the intensity of the furnace wall. The screening field is the place to screen iron ore powder.

冶炼遗址文化层剖面

A Profile of Cultural Layers in the Smelting Site

这里展示的是冶炼遗址文化层的剖面。每一层文化层里面包含有不同时代的陶器残片。陶片具有明显的时代特征，用以确定文化层的时代。

This is a profile of cultural layers in the smelting site. Each cultural layer contains remains of pottery of different periods. These pottery fragments have obvious characteristics of their times which are used to determine the era of cultural layers.

炼炉的时代就是依据它所在的文化层来确定的。发掘资料说明，清理出土的炼炉，炉基坐落在西周文化层之上，而炼炉在春秋文化层中。因此，考古工作者将炼炉的时代确定为春秋早期。

The era of the smelting furnace is determined by its cultural layer. According to the excavation documents, the furnace base of the unearthed smelting furnace is located on the cultural layer of the Western Zhou Dynasty. As the smelting furnace is located on the cultural layer of the Spring and Autumn Period, archaeologists claim that the era of the smelting furnace is the Early Spring and Autumn Period.

立柜中陈列的是冶炼遗址中出土的陶器，这是陶鬲、陶瓮和陶豆。

Potteries unearthed in the smelting site are displayed in the cabinet, among which there are pottery li-pots, pottery pots, and pottery beans.

冶炼原料和燃料

Raw Materials and Fuels for Smelting

黄石地区早期炼铜，一般选用含铜品位高的氧化铜矿，如：孔雀石、蓝铜矿、赤铜矿等。

In Huangshi, copper oxide ores with high-grade copper are selected as raw materials in the early copper smelting period, among which there are malachite, azurite, cuprite, etc..

燃料是木炭。块状木炭燃烧温度在1200℃以上，机械强度高，透氧性好，利于氧在炉内循环。木炭在冶炼中不仅作为燃料，而且参与炉内的化学反应，利于矿石中铜的还原。

The fuel for smelting is charcoal. The combustion temperature of the charcoal lumps is above 1200 centigrade. Their mechanical intensity is high and the oxygen permeability is good. These characteristics are helpful for oxygen to circulate in the furnace. The charcoal is not only used as the fuel for smelting, but is also involved in chemical reaction in the furnace, which is beneficial to the reduction of copper in ores.

炉料的加工和整粒技术

Processing and Granulation Technology of the Furnace Charge

采得的矿石，大小不一，入炉前需要进行加工，即将大块矿石在石砧上砸成小块，粉状矿物则须团成小球，然后才能入炉。这样可以保证炉内透气性好，有利于氧在炉内的循环，也有利于炉内物料受热均匀，加快还原反应的速度。

Different sizes of ores need to be processed before they are added to the furnace. Large lumps of ores are smashed into small pieces on a stone anvil, and powdery minerals are rolled into small balls. Then they are added to the furnace. This process ensures good permeability in the furnace, which is beneficial for oxygen to circulate in the furnace, and for materials to be evenly heated in the furnace. Therefore, the reduction reaction speeds up.

配矿、造渣与炉温控制

Ore Blending, Slag Forming and Furnace Temperature Control

这里陈列的是古代炼渣。这种炼渣仅铜绿山遗址内就有 40 多万吨。这些炼渣呈薄片状，表面光滑，上有波纹，这说明渣的流动性良好。经过测试，渣的熔点在 1200℃左右。这一温度高于铜的熔点（1083℃）而低于铁的熔点（1450℃左右），很适于矿石中铜铁的分离。

Ancient slag is displayed here. There is more than 400,000 tons of slag in Tonglushan site which shapes in flake. Its surface is smooth and has ripples on it. All these indicate that its fluidity is good. It is tested that the melting point of the slag is about 1,200 centigrade which is higher than that of copper (1,083 centigrade) and lower than that of iron (1,450 centigrade). So it is quite suitable to separate copper from iron in the ores.

数百个渣样的分析表明，渣含铜量一般小于 0.7%，而含铁量高达 30%~50%，这说明矿石中的铜得到较充分的还原，而铁仍保留在渣中。这是我国古代配矿、造渣及炉温控制技术的具体体现。

Analysis of hundreds of slag samples demonstrates that the copper content in the slag is less than 0.7 percent while the iron content is up to 30 to 50 percent, which indicates that copper in the ores is reduced fully while iron is still preserved in the slag. This is the proof of technology of ore blending, slag forming and furnace temperature control in ancient China.

铜锭展柜

Showcase of Copper Ingots

这里陈列的是铜绿山古铜矿遗址出土的两块粗铜，经检测分析，铜的纯度已达93%以上。圆形饼状铜锭是在大冶湖边出土的，出土地点紧邻铜绿山。分析认为，这些铜锭很可能是当时装船外运时不慎落入水中而保留到现在的。

Two pieces of crude copper are displayed here which are unearthed in Tonglushan Ancient Copper Mine Site. Detection and analysis show that the purity of copper has reached over 93 percent. The round-cake-shaped copper ingots are unearthed on the bank of Daye Lake which is next to Tonglushan. Analysis suggests that these copper ingots are likely to fall into the water accidentally when they are shipped. So they are preserved until now.

这里陈列的长条形铜锭，是在大冶市金湖镇茅陈垴遗址发现的，共有96件。茅陈垴遗址距铜绿山约4公里，同时也是一处商周时期的冶炼遗址，因此这批铜锭也应该是同时期冶炼产品。

Here is the long-bared copper ingot which is found in Maochennao site of Jinhu Town in Daye. There are 96 copper ingots in total. Maochennao site is about 4 kilometers away from Tonglushan which is also a smelting site in the Shang and Zhou Dynasties. Therefore, these copper ingots may be the smelting products in the same period.

铜的去向之谜

The Mystery of the Whereabouts of Copper

根据遗存的古代炼渣数量分析，仅铜绿山一地，古代至少生产了约十万吨粗铜。黄石地区发现的古炼渣至少有数百万吨，依此推算，古代生产的粗铜不会少于百万吨。

According to the amount of the ancient slag, at least 100,000 tons of crude copper have been produced in Tonglushan in ancient times. At least millions of tons of ancient slag have been found in Huangshi. By estimation, more than 1,000,000 tons of crude copper have been produced here.

那么，大量的铜运到哪里去了呢？我们从考古资料和文献资料中可以得到答案。

Then, where is the large amount of copper? We can find the answer in the archaeological materials and the literature materials.

首先，我们看看商代的情况。

First, let's start from the Shang Dynasty.

1974 年，在武汉市东郊的盘龙城，发现了一处商代中期的城址，城址中还发现有宫殿建筑。经过多年的考古发掘，出土了一大批青铜器、陶器和玉器。还出土了一批用于熔铜的陶制坩埚、孔雀石、木炭等遗物。

In 1974, a city site of the Middle Shang Dynasty was found in Panlong City in the eastern suburb of Wuhan where some palaces were discovered. Through years of archaeological excavation, a lot of bronze wares, potteries and jades were unearthed. Besides, a number of earthen crucibles have been excavated which were used to melt copper. Malachite, charcoal, and other remains were also found.

商王朝为什么会远离中原，到长江边上修筑这座城池，而且规模宏大，这引起了学术界的广泛关注。经过研究，学者们普遍认为，盘龙城是商王朝为掠取江南丰富的矿产资源而设立的城堡。这座城堡既是一个军事据点，也是管理南方矿冶生产的中心，同时也是掠取南方矿产资源的转运站。

The Yangtze River is far away from the Central Plains. Why was the large-scaled city built along the Yangtze River in the Shang Dynasty? This has drawn great concern in academic circles. After analysis, scholars generally believe that Panlong City is a castle of the Shang Dynasty which is built to plunder the rich mineral resources in the southern areas of the Yangtze River. This castle is the military stronghold as well as the management center of mining and metallurgy of the south. Meanwhile, it is also the transfer station of the mineral resources plundered in the south.

当周王朝取代了商王朝以后，周代的统治者同样也想占有江南铜材的生产基地。为此，周王室多次以各种借口向南征战，文献资料和青铜器铭文对此多有记载。

After the Zhou Dynasty replaced the Shang Dynasty, the rulers of the Zhou Dynasty also wanted to possess the production base of copper in the south of the Yangtze River. As a result, the Zhou rulers went on southward expeditions for many times. Many records about this are discovered in the literature materials and on the bronze inscriptions.

例如，西周昭王时期的青铜器“过伯簋”上面的铭文铸有：“过伯从王伐反荆，俘金，用作宝尊彝。”古代称铜为金。意思是说，过伯跟随周昭王征伐南方的荆楚，俘获了铜，铸造这件青铜礼器作为纪念。此外簋、驭簋也有类似的铭文记载。这说明西周时，江南的铜有不少都运往中原，供贵族享用。

For example, the following inscriptions are found on “Guobo Gui” which is a bronze ware of the Western Zhou Dynasty. “Guobo followed the king to fight against Jingchu in the south, plundered copper, and made a bronze ritual vessel as souvenirs.” Copper is called gold in ancient times. There are similar inscriptions on other bronze wares, such as Gui and Yugui. This indicates that in the Western Zhou Dynasty, large amounts of copper in the south of the Yangtze River are transported to the Central Plains which are enjoyed by the nobles.

西周晚期，随着周王朝的衰落，地处荆山一带的楚国逐渐强盛，其势力已扩张到了鄂东南，目的也是为了控制鄂东南的矿产资源。

In the late Western Zhou Dynasty, with the decline of the Zhou Dynasty, the State of Chu became stronger. Chu was located in Jingshan area, but its influence had expanded to the southeast of Hubei in order to control the mineral resources there.

史学界认为，楚国经过几百年的经营，之所以能够成为雄踞南方的大国，主要原因就是拥有丰富的矿产资源，从而提高了楚国的经济实力和军事实力。从出土的文物和文献记载中也可以看出，楚国生产的铜材，不仅能满足本国的需要，而且还将铜或者铜器作为礼品赠送给其他诸侯国。

After hundreds of years' development, the State of Chu became the dominant power in the south. Historians believe that the main reason is that it possesses rich mineral resources. So its economic power and military power was greatly improved. It is also recorded in the cultural relics and literature that the copper materials of Chu can not only meet its own needs, the copper wares are also granted to other kingdoms as gifts.

1978 年，在湖北省随州市发现了一座曾国的墓葬，其就是著名的随州擂鼓墩曾侯乙墓。在这座墓葬中出土了一套震惊世界的青铜编钟，一共 64 件。此外还出土了大量青铜礼器和兵器。据统计，这座墓葬随葬青铜器的重量多达 10 吨。

In 1978, a tomb of Zeng State was found in Suizhou of Hubei which is the famous tomb of Marquis Yi of Zeng in Leigudun of Suizhou. In the tomb, a set of 64 bronze chimes was unearthed, which shocked the world. Besides, a large number of bronze ritual vessels and weapons were unearthed. According to the statistics, more than 10 tons of bronze wares were buried in the tomb.

经过微量元素检测，铸造青铜器的铜材均来自湖北大冶一带。在 64 件编钟的中央，还有一件镈钟，这件镈钟是楚惠王十六年赠送给曾侯乙的礼品。

After trace element detection, the raw materials of those bronze wares came from Daye of Hubei. In the center of 64 bronze chimes, there was a Fu Bell which was a gift to Marquis Yi of Zeng from King Hui of

Chu in his sixteen years.

据《左传》记载，楚国曾经把铜赠送给郑国，并约定郑国不得用铜铸造兵器。这说明楚国当时的铜产量很多，不仅能满足本国需要而且还有“出口”。

According to *Zuo Zhuan*, the ruler of Chu State granted copper to Zheng State. They agreed that Zheng State couldn't cast weapons from copper. This indicates that Chu State produced a lot of copper, which not only met the domestic needs, but was also exported to other countries at that time.

古城址——矿冶生产的管理中心

Ancient City Site—Management Center of Mining and Metallurgy Production

黄石地区，除了发现众多的古代矿冶遗存外，还发现了三座古代城址。这些矿冶遗存都分布在古城址的周围。研究人员认为，这三座古城应是管理矿冶生产的中心，同时也是铜材的集散地。

In Huangshi, three ancient city sites are also discovered, besides many remains of ancient mining and metallurgy. These remains are all distributed around the city sites. According to the researchers, the three ancient sites are the management center of mining and metallurgy production as well as the collection and distribution center of copper materials.

铜材运输线路图

Transportation Route Map of Copper Materials

根据以上我们展示的资料不难看出，先秦时期黄石、大冶、阳新地区生产了大量粗铜。但到目前为止，这里却没有发现一处铸造遗址，这说明这些粗铜都外运到了其他地方。这里展示的是先秦时期铜材运输线路图，可分为东南西北四条线路。

Based on the above exhibition, it is easy to see that large amounts of crude copper were produced in Huangshi, Daye and Yangxin in the Pre-Qin Period. However, until now, no casting sites are discovered in the three cities, which proves that the crude copper is delivered to other places. Here is the transportation route map of copper materials in the Pre-Qin Period. There are four routes of transportation which are the north route, the south route, the east route and the west route.

其一为北线，由铜绿山装船起运，经大冶湖进入长江，沿江而上到达盘龙城，再经过府河过随枣走廊，穿过桐柏山和大别山的隘口进入中原，到达商朝的都城。此线的另一条线路是到盘龙城后经汉水逆流而上，可到关中地区，最终到达周王朝的都城洛邑。

The first is the north route which starts from Tonglushan, through Daye Lake, into the Yangtze River, along the River to Panlong City, through Fu River and Sui Zao Corridor, across the pass of Tongbai Mountain and Dabie Mountain, into the Central Plains. At last, it arrives at the capital city of the Shang Dynasty. Another route is to sail upstream after arriving at Panlong City, along the Han River up to the Guanzhong Area. At last, it arrives at Luoyi which is the capital city of the Zhou Dynasty.

其二是西线，由大冶湖进入长江后，沿长江往西溯江而上可以到达楚国的都城郢（今荆州附近）。

The second is the west route which starts from Daye Lake to the Yangtze River, along the river up to the west to Ying which is the capital city of Chu State (Now it is the area near Jingzhou).

其三是东线，沿长江顺流而下，可以到达吴、越等国。

The third is the east route which sails along the Yangtze River down to Wu State, Yue State, etc..

其四是南线，由长江进入洞庭湖，可以到达湖南。

The fourth is the south route which sails along the Yangtze River, into Dongting Lake. At last, it arrives in Hunan Province.

三国至明代的矿冶文化

Mining and Metallurgical Culture from the Three Kingdoms Period to the Ming Dynasty

三国至明代，黄石矿冶文化持续发展。三国时，吴王孙权采武昌铜、铁，做千口剑、万口刀。三国时的武昌，就是现在的鄂州市。而开采铜、铁的地方就在黄石的铁山。这里展示的几件铁兵器，是在鄂州市郊一座三国时期的墓葬中出土的铁剑、铁削、环首铁刀、铁戟。

From the Three Kingdoms Period to the Ming Dynasty, Huangshi mining and metallurgical culture continued to develop. During the Three Kingdoms Period, Sunquan, the king of Wu State, made a large number of swords and knives with cooper and iron from Wuchang which is Ezhou at present. The above copper and iron is mined in Tieshan of Huangshi. These iron weapons were found in a tomb of the Three Kingdoms Period in the suburb of Ezhou. Among them there are iron swords, iron files, iron knives with round head and iron halberds.

据《太平环宇记》记载，两晋南北朝时，铁山地区仍在“置炉烹炼”。考古调查资料显示，铁山地区堆积着大量古代炼渣，有的厚达十余米，数量多达百万吨。这些炉渣一部分为先秦时期的遗存，也有魏晋南北朝时期的遗存。这是铁山地区古代炼渣分布图，其分布范围几乎涵盖了整个大冶铁矿区。

It is recorded in *Taiping Geographical Records* that smelting furnaces were built in Tieshan from the Western and Eastern Jin to the Southern and Northern Dynasties. It is shown in the archaeological materials that there is a lot of ancient slag in Tieshan which is more than ten meters thick and about one million tons heavy. This slag is the remains of the Pre-Qin Period, the Wei Dynasty, the Jin Dynasty, the Northern and Southern Dynasties. This is the distribution map of the ancient slag in Tieshan which covers almost the whole area of Daye Iron Mine.

隋代时，隋文帝下诏在白雉山置十炉铸钱。因此这里也就成为了全国四大钱监之一。隋代发行的钱币“五铢”钱由于钱文字样和风格与此前发行的“五铢”钱不完全一样，因此俗称“隋五铢”。这是“隋五铢”放大的样品。

In the Sui Dynasty, Emperor Wen ordered to set ten furnaces to cast money in Baizhi Mountain which was one of the four supervising institutions of coinage at that time. The Sui Dynasty issued “wuzhu” money, but its typeface and style was not the same as the previous “wuzhu”. So it was called “wuzhu of Sui.” This is the enlarged sample of it.

继隋代以后，唐代也在铁山设有十炉铸钱。只是铸造的钱币为“开元通宝”。而且在钱的背面铸有一“鄂”字。当时每炉每年铸钱三千三百缗（千文为缗），用铜二万一千二百斤，十炉合计，每年用于铸钱的铜料应在二十万斤以上。

After the Sui Dynasty, ten furnaces were also built in Tieshan which were used to cast money for the Tang Dynasty. The coins of the Tang Dynasty were called “kaiyuantongbao”, at the back of which the character “鄂” (E in pinyin) was cast. At that time, each furnace cast 3,300 strings of coins. One string was 1000 Wen. For one furnace, more than ten thousand kilograms of copper were needed. Based on this calculation, every year more than one hundred thousand kilograms of copper were needed for ten furnaces.

宋代的矿业及钱监

Mining Industry and Supervising Institutions of Coinage in the Song Dynasty

据《大冶县志》记载，宋乾德五年（公元 967 年），南唐国主李煜，升青山场，并析武昌三乡与之合并，新置一县，取“大兴炉冶”之意，定县名为“大冶”。

It is recorded in *County Annals of Daye* that in 967, Li Yu, the ruler of Southern Tang State, combined Qingshanchang with the three towns of Wuchang. And he set up a new county named Daye whose meaning is large-scaled furnace-metallurgy.

又据《宋史·地理志》记载：“兴国军大冶有富民钱监、铜场及磁湖铁务。”这说明宋代黄石地区的矿冶业仍十分发达。1978 年在大冶铜绿镇铁屎包发现了一处冶炼遗址，清理出了 17 座炼炉。这里展示的是宋代炼炉模型和炼炉出土的照片。

It is recorded in *Geographical Records in History of the Song Dynasty* that “There are Fumin Supervising Institution of Coinage, copper field and Cihu iron office in Xingguojun Town of Daye County.” This indicates that mining and metallurgy industry in Huangshi area was well developed in the Song Dynasty. In 1978, a smelting site was found in Tieshibao of Daye Tonglu Town where about 17 smelting furnaces were unearthed. Here is the model of the smelting furnace of the Song Dynasty and the photos of the unearthed smelting furnaces.

关于“磁湖铁务”，有学者推测应在铁山或磁湖附近。

Some scholars assume that Cihu Iron Office may be located in Tieshan town, or near Cihu Lake.

关于“富民钱监”的位置，由于缺乏考古资料，目前尚难断定。但它的起始时间和终结时间是有据可查的。据《宋史·食货志》记载，富民监始建于宋神宗熙宁四年（公元1071年），宋宁宗嘉定五年（公元1212年）并于汉阳监，时间长达140余年。富民监的设置无疑对宋代市场经济的发展发挥了重要作用。

But it is hard to decide the location of Fumin Supervising Institution of Coinage, because there isn't any archaeological material about it. But its opening time and closing time is well documented. It is recorded in *Annals of Agricultural Production and Currency Circulation of the History of the Song Dynasty* that Fumin Supervising Institution of Coinage was built in 1071. In 1212, it was merged with Hanyang Supervising Institution of Coinage. So it has a history of more than 140 years. Fumin Supervising Institution of Coinage played a vital role in the development of market economy of the Song Dynasty.

宋代钱窖

Money Cellars of Song Dynasty

黄石地区不仅矿产资源丰富，而且又是一处战略要地。这里紧邻长江中游，水陆交通方便，素有“楚尾吴头”之称，历来是兵家的必争之地。

Huangshi is not only rich in mineral resources, but is also an important strategic region. It is next to the middle reaches of the Yangtze River. So both water and land transportation is convenient. It is located at the end of Chu State and at the beginning of Wu State which is a place of military importance all the time.

市区内有一陡峭的山峰，直立江边，这就是古今著名的西塞山。古往今来，很多文人墨客都在这里留下了不朽的诗篇。西塞山闻名于世还有一个原因就是这里曾六次发现大型钱窖。

There is a steep mountain standing along the Yangtze River in the urban area of Huangshi which is the famous Xisai Mountain. Many men of letters have composed immortal poems about the mountain. Another reason for its fame is that large money cellars have been found there for six times.

据《大冶县志》记载，明清两代，这里曾三次发现窖藏，其中清乾隆年间发现一钱窖，坎土长二三里，挖掘时间长达数月。

It is recorded in *County Annals of Daye* that, from the Ming Dynasty to the Qing Dynasty, money cellars were found for three times in Xisai Mountain. During the reign of Qianlong Emperor, a large money cellar was found which was excavated for several months. The earth of the excavation extended more than one thousand kilometers.

1938 年，日本占领黄石前夕发现一窖，尚未发掘，黄石沦陷，出土铜钱均被日本人强迫当地农民装船运走。

In 1938, a money cellar was found, but was not excavated. After a while, Japan occupied Huangshi. Japanese army forced the local farmers to ship the unearthed copper coins to Japan.

1955 年，大冶钢厂在西塞山取土时，发现一银窖，出土银锭 292 件，共重 133.38 公斤。这里展示的是出土银锭的一部分。

In 1955, a silver cellar was found in Xisai Mountain when workers of Daye Steel Plant carried soil there. About 292 silver ingots were unearthed which weighed 133.38kg in total. These are some of the unearthed silver ingots.

1967 年冬，黄石为加固西塞山区段的长江堤防，取土时又发现一大型钱窖，出土铜钱约三十万斤。这是我国已知藏量最多的钱币窖藏。这批铜钱不仅数量大，而且钱币的种类也很多，上自西汉“半两”，下迄南宋“淳祐通宝”，其间一千余年各时代的钱币几乎都有。有些钱币还是很难得的珍品。这里陈列的是出土钱币的部分样品。

In the winter of 1967, another large money cellar was found when workers carried soil to reinforce the Yangtze River embankment of Xisai Mountain. About 150,000 kilograms' copper coins were unearthed which is the coin cellar with the largest known reserves. There is not only a large amount of copper coins, but also a lot of variety of copper coins which include the coins of all the ages in more than 1000 years. The earliest coins are "banliang" in the Western Han Dynasty and the latest ones are "Chun You Tong Bao" in the Southern Song Dynasty. Some of the coins are rare treasures. These are some samples of the unearthed coins.

汉冶萍时期的矿冶文化

Mining and Metallurgical Culture in the Han-Ye-Ping Period

汉冶萍煤铁厂矿股份有限公司，由汉阳铁厂、大冶铁矿、萍乡煤矿共同组成。它是中国近代史上首家用新式机械设备进行大规模生产的钢铁煤联合企业。汉冶萍公司的前身是湖北铁政局，由湖广总督张之洞于清光绪十六年（公元1890年）创办。

Han-Ye-Ping Coal and Iron Factory and Mine Co. Ltd. consist of Hanyang Iron Plant, Daye Iron Mine and Pingxiang Coal Mine which is the first joint venture of steel, iron and coal in modern China. New machinery and equipment are applied to its large scale production. It is formerly known as Hubei Iron Council which was founded by Zhang Zhidong in 1890 who was the governor of Hu-Guang at that time.

这幅油画和张之洞塑像是根据张之洞视察汉阳铁厂的照片制作。这里展示的照片是官办时期汉阳铁厂、大冶铁矿、黄石王三石煤矿的情景。

The oil painting and the Statue of Zhang Zhidong are designed according to his photos which were taken during his visit to Hanyang Iron

Plant. These photos display the scenes of Hanyang Iron Plant, Daye Iron Mine, Huangshi Wangsanshi Coal Mine in the government-run period.

光绪二十二年（公元1896年），官办期的湖北铁政局下属的厂矿因经费困难，张之洞委托盛宣怀招商承办。光绪三十四年（1908年），盛宣怀把汉阳铁厂、大冶铁矿和江西萍乡煤矿合并，组成汉冶萍煤铁厂矿有限公司。汉冶萍公司的创办，在中国近代工业史上占有重要地位，被誉为“中国近代钢铁工业的摇篮”。

In 1896, the factories and mines of Hubei Iron Council met financial difficulties. So Zhang Zhidong entrusted Sheng Xuanhuai to invite investment. In 1908, Sheng Xuanhuai merged Hanyang Iron Plant, Daye Iron Mine and Pingxiang Coal Mine into Han-Ye-Ping Coal and Iron Factory and Mine Co. Ltd.. The founding of Han-Ye-Ping Company occupies an important position in the history of China's modern industry. It is known as “the cradle of China's modern iron and steel industry.”

黄石矿冶文化的再度辉煌

Another Prosperity of Huangshi Mining and Metallurgical Culture

1949年前黄石市为大冶县所辖的石黄镇，1949年5月15日，石黄镇解放。鉴于黄石地区蕴藏有丰富的矿产资源和历史悠久的矿冶业，中华人民共和国成立不久，原中原临时人民政府决定将石黄镇从大冶县划出，成立石灰窑工业特区，后来又更名为大冶工矿特区。

Before 1949, Huangshi was Shihuang Town governed by Daye County. On May 15 of 1949, Shihuang Town was liberated. As this region is rich in mineral resources and has a long history of mining and metallurgy industry, shortly after the founding of People's Republic of China, Shihuang Town was drawn from Daye County. The former Central Plains Provisional People's Government decided to establish Shihuiyao

Industrial Special Region. Later it was renamed Daye Industrial and Mining Special Region.

1950 年 7 月 8 日，中南军政委员会根据湖北省人民政府的请示，决定改大冶工矿特区为省辖市，定名黄石市，并呈报中央人民政府政务院核备。1950 年 8 月 21 日，中央人民政府政务院核准成立湖北省辖黄石市。

On July 8 of 1950, according to the instruction of Hubei Provincial People's Government, Central South Military and Administrative Commission decided to change Daye Industrial and Mining Special Region into Huangshi City which is a provincial city of Hubei. This decision was submitted to the Government Administration Council of the Central People's Government for approval. On August 21 of 1950, Government Administration Council authorized the establishment of Hubei Provincial Huangshi City.

这里陈列的是关于黄石建市的档案资料的复印件。从这些档案资料中我们可以看出，设立省辖黄石市的理由，最重要的一点就是："该区系我省著名的工矿区，铁、煤、石灰石等产量丰富，对我省将来工业建设之重要，原料及动力的供给，系一巨大的来源，发展前途颇大。"

These are the copies of the files about the establishment of Huangshi City. From these files, we can see the most important reason for the establishment is that Huangshi is a famous industrial and mining area in Hubei which is rich in iron, coal, limestone, etc.. It is very important for the future industrial development of Hubei because it is a great source for the supply of raw materials and power. So Huangshi has a promising future.

关于黄石市的定名，当时也有几种意见，其中有"石黄市"，有"大冶市"，有"黄石市"，但最终经中央批准定名为黄石市。

About the name of Huangshi City, there are several opinions which are "Shihuang City", "Daye City" and "Huangshi City". Finally, the name "Huangshi City" is approved by Central People's Government.

黄石市建市后，党和政府极为重视黄石的建设和发展。1950年，国家还处在国民经济恢复时期，即投资1.5亿元改建、新建了一批重工业企业，相继有大冶钢厂、大冶铁矿、新冶铜矿等30个项目开工建设，并陆续投产。

After the establishment of Huangshi City, the Party and the Government attached great importance to its construction and development. In 1950, China was still in the period of national economic recovery. About 150 million yuan was invested to reconstruct and construct a group of heavy industries. About 30 projects started construction and were put into production which include Daye Steel Plant, Daye Iron Mine, Xinye Copper Mine and other projects.

1953年和1958年毛泽东主席两次视察黄石，极大地推动了黄石矿冶业的发展。

In 1953 and 1958, Chairman Mao Zedong inspected Huangshi twice, which greatly promotes the development of mining and metallurgy industries in Huangshi.

工矿企业

Industrial and Mining Enterprises

您现在来到了我市几家大型现代工矿企业的展示部分，也是黄石矿冶文化再度辉煌的展示部分。

This is the demonstration of several large modern industrial and mining enterprises which is also the demonstration of the glory of Huangshi mining and metallurgical culture.

首先，向大家介绍的是大冶铁矿。该矿坐落于黄石市铁山区，有铁门槛、龙洞、尖林山、象鼻山、狮子山和尖山6个矿体。

At first, let's introduce Daye Iron Mine. It is located in Tieshan District of Huangshi city which includes six ore bodies which are Tiemenkan, Longdong, Jianlinshan, Xiangbishan, Shizishan and Jianshan.

下面展柜里陈列的是大冶铁矿的主要矿产品，有铜精矿、酸性氧化球团矿、铁精矿、硫精矿、氧化矿（平炉矿）、气孔状磁铁矿、块状磁铁矿。

In the showcases are the main mineral products of Daye Iron Mine. They are copper concentrates, oxidizing acidic pellets, iron concentrates, sulfur concentrates, oxide ores (open hearth ores), vesicular magnetite and lump magnetite.

现在请大家关注一下中间的这张大幅照片，这就是大冶铁矿拥有世界第一高度边坡的矿坑。历经百余年的开采，它的高度达到了 400 多米。

Now please look at this large photo in the middle. It is the world's highest side slope in Daye Iron Mine which is more than 400 meters high and has a mining history of over 100 years.

接下来向大家介绍的是湖北新冶钢有限公司（简称新冶钢），它是中国现存最早的钢铁企业，其前身大冶铁厂是清末汉冶萍煤铁厂矿有限公司的组成部分。新冶钢历史悠久，有中国“钢铁工业的摇篮”之称。

Next, let's introduce Hubei Xinyegang Steel Co., Ltd. (Xinyegang for short). It is China's earliest steel company whose predecessor Daye Iron Plant is the component of Han-Ye-Ping Coal and Iron Factory and Mine Co., Ltd.. It has a long history, so it is called China's "cradle of the steel industry."

2004 年，香港中信泰富投资有限公司出资收购了冶钢集团有限公司钢铁主业资产，组建了我市最大的港商投资企业——湖北新冶钢有限公司。

In 2004, Hong Kong CITIC Pacific Investment Co., Ltd. purchased the main iron and steel industry assets of Daye Iron and Steel Group Co., Ltd.. Then Huangshi's largest enterprise invested by HongKong business comes into being which is Hubei Xinyegang Steel Co. , Ltd. .

这一部分介绍的是历尽沧桑，再创辉煌的黄石工矿集团。

In this section, let's introduce Huangshi Industrial and Mining Group. It suffers a lot in the past and creates a bright future now.

追溯历史，黄石煤炭已开采460多年。公元1540年《大冶县志》曾记载：“煤炭出章山，道仕袱二里。”真正形成一定规模的开采有近百年历史。

The history of coal mining in Huangshi is over 460 years. It is recorded in *Daye County Annals* that in 1540, coal mining of Zhangshan reaches one kilometer to Daoshifu. A certain scale of coal mining has a history of nearly 100 years.

1889年，湖广总督张之洞派员到黄石发布“煤斤示”，鼓励地方兴办煤矿。当地人士于1909年在黄荆山北麓桐梓堡创办富源煤矿公司（黄石矿务局前身）。1916年在黄思湾创办富华煤矿。1924年在黄荆山柯家湾创办了利华煤矿。

In 1889, Zhang Zhidong, the governor of Hu-Guang, sent officials to Huangshi to release the bulletin that he encouraged local coal mining. In 1909, the local residents founded Fuyuan Coal Company in Tongzibao at the northern slope of Huangjing Mountain which later became Huangshi Mining Bureau. In 1916, Fuhua Coal Mine was founded in Huangsiwan. In 1924, Lihua Coal Mine was founded in Kejiawan of Huangjing Mountain.

1936年富源、富华两矿合并为源华煤矿。二十世纪三十年代，源华、利华两矿最高年产量到达37万吨，在全国10省21个主要煤矿中，分别排在第16位和17位。

In 1936, Fuyuan Coal Mine and Fuhua Coal Mine were merged into Yuanhua Coal Mine. In the 1930s, the highest annual output of Yuanhua Coal Mine and Lihua Coal Mine reached 370 thousand tons which ranked

No. 16 and No. 17 among China's 21 major coal mines of 10 provinces.

这是 1936 年源华煤矿公司办公楼。这是 1909 年创办的富源煤矿。那是 1924 年创办的利华煤矿一井——新东井。

This photo is the office building of Yuanhua Coal Company in 1936. This is Fuyuan Coal Mine founded in 1909. And that is No. 1 shaft (new east shaft) of Lihua Coal Mine founded in 1924.

抗日战争爆发后，在日寇的掠夺和国民党的统治下，煤矿衰败，至 1949 年前，黄石地区的年产量仅 10 余万吨。

After the Anti-Japanese War broke out, the coal mine declined because of the plunder of Japanese aggressors and the rule of Kuomintang. Before 1949, the annual coal output of Huangshi area was only 100 thousand tons.

广大矿工也只能是当牛做马，被称为“窿花子”。“石灰窑，煤炭山，做窿如进鬼门关。”“少来混个嘴，老了去讨米，三病二痛，江里一蹦。”这两首歌谣就是黄石煤矿工人苦难生活的真实写照。

Most miners had no choice but to work hard who were known as the "Longhuazi (beggars)." Some folk songs truly portrayed the suffering life of Huangshi coal miners. It is said in one folk song that if you work for the mine, you will enter the gate of hell. Another song says that when the miners are young, they just muddle along; when they are old, they have to beg; when they are ill, they have no choice but to commit suicide.

1949 年以前，源华煤矿工人在井下作业的场景是脚穿草鞋，头巾当矿帽，手锤打炮眼。

This is the photo of the working conditions of Yuanhua coal miners before 1949. At that time, they wore straw shoes, took scarves as mining hats and stroke blast-holes with hand hammers when they worked underground.

哪里有压迫，哪里就有反抗。黄石地区最早的中共党组织——富源、富华两个党小组带领广大矿工与封建把头、国民党反动派展开了一系列的英勇斗争。中国的保尔·柯察金——吴运铎同志就是从源华机电车间走上革命道路的。

Where there is oppression, there is resistance. Two party groups of Fuyuan and Fuhua are among the earliest Chinese communist party organizations in Huangshi region. They led the miners to launch a series of heroic struggles against the feudal head and the Kuomintang reactionaries. Wu Yunduo once worked in Yuanhua mechanical and electrical workshop. Later he went on to the revolutionary road who is called China's Paul Korchagin.

照片中坐在椅子上的就是有“中国的保尔·柯察金”之称的吴运铎同志。这是他于1988年4月28日为黄石矿务局建井八十周年题的词——“把光和热献给人类”。

This is the photo of Wu Yunduo sitting in a chair. This is his inscription on April 28 of 1988 which is the 80th anniversary of the mine built by Huangshi Mining Bureau. It is said in the inscription that "to dedicate the light and heat to humankind."

中华人民共和国成立后，源华和利华煤矿成为全省组建的第一个省辖地级市，即黄石市的五大厂矿中的其中两个，为湖北省和鄂东南地区的经济建设做出了重要贡献。

After the founding of People's Republic of China, Yuanhua and Lihua Coal Mines become the two of the five factories in Huangshi. They have made great contributions to the economic development of Hubei province, especially Southeast Hubei.

进入21世纪，黄石矿务局下放到黄石市管理后，矿务局实施改制。2004年5月底，50位股东出资组建成立了黄石工矿（集团）有限公司，并以新的姿态展现在世人面前。

In the 21st century, Huangshi Mining Bureau is put under the administration of Huangshi. Then it begins to reconstruct its organization. At the end of May of 2004, 50 shareholders invested to establish Huangshi Industrial and Mining Group Co. , Ltd. which displays a new appearance to the world.

黄石工矿集团步入了快速发展的新时期，并取得了较好的业绩，为湖北省的中部崛起和黄石市的跨越式大发展做出了积极贡献，成为湖北省煤炭开采行业龙头企业。

Huangshi Industrial and Mining Group Co. , Ltd. enters a new period of rapid development and makes great achievements, which contributes a lot to the rise of Hubei Province and to the fast development of Huangshi. It has become the leading enterprise of coal mining industry in Hubei Province.

请大家跟我往这边走，现在呈现在我们面前的是大冶有色金属公司的展示部分。大冶有色金属公司是湖北省重点骨干企业。公司始创于 1953 年，是国家“一五”时期建设的 156 个重点项目之一。

Please follow me. In front of us is the part of Daye Nonferrous Metals Group Holdings Co. , Ltd.. It is the key enterprise in Hubei Province. The company was founded in 1953 which is one of the 156 key national projects during “the first five-year period.”

经过 50 多年的发展，如今的大冶有色金属公司全面落实科学发展观，牢固树立“以市场为导向，以效益为中心”的经营理念和“一流铜业，国际品牌”的发展目标。展柜里陈列的是该公司提供的展品，有阴极铜、黄金、白银……

After 50 years’ development, the company implements the Scientific Outlook on Development, and establishes its business philosophy of being “market-oriented and efficiency-centered.” Its development goals are to become “the first-class copper industry and an international brand.” The exhibits in the showcases are provided by the company, among which are copper cathodes, gold, silver, etc..

最后给大家介绍的是百年华新。

At last, let's introduce Huaxin with a history of one hundred years.

华新水泥股份有限公司始创于1907年，是我国水泥行业“12强”中唯一具有百年历史的龙头企业，被誉为中国水泥工业的摇篮。1993年，公司成为中国建材行业第一家A、B股上市公司；1999年，与全球最大的水泥制造商之一的瑞士HOLCIM集团结为战略伙伴关系。

Huaxin Cement Co., Ltd. was founded in 1907 which has a history over one hundred years. It is the leading one among the "Top 12" cement enterprises in China which is known as China's cradle of the cement industry. In 1993, it became China's first A, B share listed company in building materials industry. In 1999, it built a strategic partnership with Swiss HOLCIM Group which is one of the world's largest cement manufacturers.

截止到2008年，公司在湖北、江苏、湖南、云南、西藏、河南、四川等地拥有30余个水泥生产基地，企业综合实力位居国内同行业前列。

By 2008, it has more than 30 cement production bases which are distributed in Hubei, Jiangsu, Hunan, Yunnan, Tibet, Henan, Sichuan, etc.. Its comprehensive strength is in the forefront of the domestic cement industry.

这里陈列的有华新建厂时清政府的批文；还有华新分别于1914年、1947年、1954年、1993年发行的股票；这是石灰石，是生产水泥的原料；这是华新生产的高标号水泥。

This is the approval of Huaxin construction from the Qing government. These are the shares issued by Huaxin in 1914, 1947, 1954 and 1993. This is limestone which is the raw material of cement. That is the high grade cement produced by Huaxin.

到此，《天地一洪炉——黄石矿冶文化展》的参观就全部结束了。

Now, our visit of Huangshi Mining and Metallurgical Culture Exhibition is over.

第二节　铜绿山古铜矿遗址中英文解说词
Chinese and English Tour Guide Manual of Tonglushan Ancient Copper Mine Site

大门口
At the Main Entrance

各位朋友，大家好！欢迎大家来到铜绿山古铜矿遗址参观考察。

Ladies and gentlemen, welcome to Tonglushan Ancient Copper Mine Site.

众所周知，大冶是华夏青铜文化的发祥地，素有“百里黄金地，江南聚宝盆”的美誉。境内矿产资源丰富，已发现和探明金属矿产 12 种，非金属矿产 30 种。3000 多年前的殷商时期，华夏祖先在这里采炼青铜，创造了光辉灿烂的青铜文明，铜绿山古铜矿遗址被称为继秦始皇兵马俑之后的“世界第九大奇迹”。

As we all know, Daye is the birthplace of Chinese bronze culture which is known as the treasure bowl in the south of the Yangtze River. There are abundant mineral resources, among which about 12 metallic minerals and 30 non-metallic minerals have been discovered and explored. More than 3000 years ago, Chinese ancestors mined and smelted copper here since the Yin and Shang Dynasties. They created the splendid bronze culture, which is the reason that Tonglushan Ancient Copper Mine Site is called "the world's ninth wonder", just after Emperor Qin's Terracotta Warriors.

铜绿山古铜矿遗址位于湖北省大冶市城西3公里处，交通便利。遗址保护区范围东至三里七湖西岸，西至铜山村，北至长流港南侧，南至铜绿山矿铁路线，面积约为555.7公顷。

Tonglushan Ancient Copper Mine Site lies 3 kilometers west of Daye City of Hubei Province. Its protection zone covers an area of 555.7 hectares which is easily accessible on every direction. It stretches to the west bank of Sanliqi Lake on the east, Tongshan Village on the west, the South of Changliu Harbor on the north and the railway of Tonglushan Mine on the south.

铜绿山古铜矿遗址于1973年被发现和发掘，是一处以采矿遗址和冶炼遗址为核心的古代矿冶遗址。铜绿山古铜矿采掘始于商代，经西周、春秋战国延续至汉代，延续时间长达千余年，距今3300余年，贯穿了整个青铜时代。

Tonglushan Ancient Copper Mine Site was discovered and excavated in 1973 which is a site of ancient mining and smelting. Its mining dates back to the Shang Dynasty, about 3300 years ago. Since then, it lasted a period of nearly 1000 years, from the Xizhou Dynasty, the Spring and Autumn Period, and the Warring States Period to the Han Dynasty which ran throughout the whole Bronze Age,

它是中国迄今发现的古矿遗址中采掘年代久远、规模最大、保存最完整、冶炼工艺水平最高、文化内涵最丰富、持续生产时间最长的一处古铜矿遗址，代表了中国青铜时代采矿、冶炼技术的最高成就。它的发现发掘，揭示了我国青铜文化的独立起源，填补了我国古代科学技术发展史上的一段空白。

So far, it is the oldest, the largest-scale and the best-preserved historic site of ancient copper mine with the most advanced smelting technique level, the richest cultural connotation and the longest continuous production time. It represents the greatest achievement in copper mining and smelting technology of the Bronze Age in China. Its discovery and excavation proves the independent origin of Chinese bronze culture and fills the gaps in Chinese history of ancient science and technology development.

中国著名考古学家夏鼐对此遗址评价为："这是中国古代青铜器研究的一个新领域，也是中国考古学新开辟的一个领域，是中国矿冶考古的诞生地，是中华民族的骄傲。"

The famous Chinese archaeologist Xia Nai speaks highly of the site: "It is a new realm in Chinese ancient bronze research and Chinese archaeology, and it is the birthplace of Chinese mining and metallurgy archaeology. Therefore, it is the pride of Chinese people."

鉴于其突出且独特的价值，1982 年国务院将铜绿山古铜矿遗址列为第二批全国重点文物保护单位。1984 年在 7 号矿体 1 号点发掘原址上建成铜绿山古铜矿遗址博物馆并对外开放。1994 年国家文物局将铜绿山古铜矿遗址列入《世界文化遗产名录》预备清单。

Because of its prominent research value, Tonglushan Ancient Copper Mine Site has attracted much attention. In 1982, it was included in the list of the second batch of key cultural relic's protection units by the State Council. In 1984, the Museum of Tonglushan Ancient Copper Mine Site was built on No. 1 mining site of No. 7 ore body and was opened to the visitors. In 1994, National Cultural Relics Bureau put the site in The Tentative List of World Cultural Heritage.

2001 年，铜绿山古铜矿遗址被评为我国 20 世纪 100 项重大考古发现之一，并成为湖北省爱国主义教育基地。2011 年，国家文物局批准了《铜绿山古铜矿遗址考古工作计划》（2011—2015）。2012 年 7 月，《大冶市铜绿山古铜矿遗址保护规划》被湖北省政府公布实施。2012 年 11 月，以铜绿山古铜矿遗址为核心的“黄石矿冶工业遗产片区”被国家列入《中国世界文化遗产预备名单》。同年，被中国科协授予全国科普教育基地。

In 2001, it was awarded as one of the 100 great archaeological discoveries in 20th century which is also the patriotism education base in Hubei Province. In 2011, National Cultural Relics Bureau approved *The Archeological Work Plan (2011—2015) of Tonglushan Ancient Copper Mine Site*. In July of 2012, *The Protection Scheme of Tonglushan Ancient Copper Mine Site in Daye* was announced and implemented by Hubei provincial government. In November of 2012, “the Hunangshi Mining and Metallurgy Heritage Area” was listed on *The World Cultural Heritage Tentative List of China* which was centered on Tonglushan Ancient Copper Mine Site. In the same year, it was awarded the National Science Education Base by the China Association for Science and Technology.

2013 年 7 月，被国家公布为“十二五”时期全国重大遗址。2013 年 11 月，铜绿山国家考古遗址公园正式被国家公布立项，铜绿山新馆建设方案也得到国家批复。

In July of 2013, it was announced as the Chinese important relics in the period of 12th Five-year Plan. In November of 2013, Tonglushan National Archaeological Site Park was announced by the State. The building plan of Tonglushan new museum was also approved by the State.

遗址厅门口

At the Entrance of the Site Hall

铜绿山古铜矿遗址是“全国大型遗址文物保护的典范”，充分体现了中央到地方各级党委、政府对文物保护工作的高度重视，也体现了全社会对文物保护工作的关心。

Tonglushan Ancient Copper Mine Site has set an example for national large-scale relic's protection, which demonstrates the great concern of all ranks of administrations for the relic's protection. The whole society also shows care for the heritage conservation work.

铜绿山有 12 个矿体，面积两平方公里，基本上都被古人进行过不同深度的开采。

There are 12 ore bodies in Tonglushan which cover two square kilometers and have all been exploited by the ancient miners.

一方面，遗址的规模很大，有着丰富的矿冶遗存，具有极高的历史研究价值；但另一方面，国家建设急需矿产资源，铜绿山矿的铜矿储量丰富，是全国“状元矿”，对国家经济建设非常重要。因此，这些遗址无法进行全部保留。

On the one hand, the site has a large scale and wealthy relics of mining and metallurgy and possesses a high value for historical research. On the other hand, the mine is rich in copper ore reserves which is known as the "National Champion Mine." China is in urgent need of mineral resources, so the mine is very important for the national economic construction. Therefore, it is impossible to protect all the sites.

如何解决这一突出矛盾，矿山生产部门和文物保护部门进行了长达 8 年的多次探讨和磋商。最后，按照矿山生产兼顾文物保护的原则，1991 年 8 月，国务院下发了《国务院关于湖北省大冶铜绿山古铜矿遗址保护方案的批复》，同意将已开采 70 万土石方、采矿量达日产 400 吨的 7 号矿体永久保留。现在我们就是在 7 号矿体上面行走。

In order to solve the prominent contradiction, Mine Production Departments and Cultural Relics Protection Departments carried on discussions and consultations for several times in eight years. At last, they decided to take both production and protection into account. In August of 1991, The State Council issued *The Approval of the Protection*

Scheme of Tonglushan Ancient Copper Mine Site in Daye of Hubei. It is agreed that the No. 7 ore body is preserved for ever which has been mined 700,000 cubic meters of earth and stones and whose mining capacity has been up to 400 tons per day. Now we are walking on it.

我们面前看到的遗址博物馆，里面就是一处春秋时期的古矿井遗址，于 1979 年至 1980 年由中国社会科学院考古研究所发掘。镶嵌在遗址馆正前方的“铜绿山古铜矿遗址”八个鎏金大字系我国著名考古专家夏鼐先生的亲笔题词。大家可以在此拍照留念。

There is an ancient pit of the Spring and Autumn Period in the site museum which was excavated by the Institute of Archaeology of Chinese Academy of Social Sciences from 1979 to 1980. The eight golden Chinese characters “铜绿山古铜矿遗址（Tonglushan Ancient Copper Mine Site）” are written by Xia Nai, the famous archaeologist in China. These characters are inlaid in front of the site museum. We can take photos here.

遗址大厅

The Site Hall

展现在我们面前的是一处春秋时期井下采矿遗址。7 号矿体原名铜锣山，山顶高度为海拔 91. 9 米，我们现在所处的位置位于山北坡。古地表井口高程为海拔 72. 8 米，现在的地平面高程为 54. 3 米，上部已被剥离。

In front of us is the underground mining site of the Spring and Autumn Period. The No. 7 ore body is originally called Tongluoshan which is at an altitude of 91. 9 meters. Now we are standing at the north side of the mountain. The altitude of the ancient wellhead is 72. 8 meters. Because its upper part is removed, now the altitude is 54. 3 meters.

在已揭露的 430m^2 范围内，这些井巷纵横交错，层层叠压，记录了古代工匠们在矿体中开拓井巷、采掘矿石的情景。美国麻省理工学院教授、国际知名科技权威史密斯到了这里无限感慨地说："我在这里看到了世界其他地方看不到的东西，这在我一生中是永远不会忘记的。"

In the 430m^2 exposed areas, shafts and tunnels are crisscrossed, which records the process of excavation and mining of the ancient miners. Mr. Smith, the professor of Massachusetts Institute of Technology and the renowned authority in international science and technology, once claimed: "I will never forget what I have seen here, because it is peerless and unique in the world. "

古人用竖井、平巷、斜井、盲井开采地下矿藏，深度一般达 20 ~ 30 米。那么，古代井下采矿要解决的问题很多，古人是怎样做到的呢?

The ancient miners exploited the underground minerals by digging shafts, tunnels, inclined shafts and blind shafts. The digging depth is about 20 or 30 meters underground. Then many problems should be solved for the underground mining. How do the ancient miners solve all the problems?

首先是支护问题。为了保证地下采掘正常运行与操作安全，古代矿工发明和发展了一整套木构支护技术。支架是在井下边掘进边安装的。

The first problem is supporting. To ensure the production and safety of underground mining, the ancient miners invented and developed a system of wood supporting techniques. The frames were installed simultaneously in the process of excavating.

春秋以前的竖井支护由两根榫木和两根卯木杆件组成方框，在框架与围岩间用木棍、竹笆背护，以防止围岩塌落。矿井净断面一般为 60 厘米× 60 厘米。

Before the Spring and Autumn Period, the shaft was supported by a square frame which is composed of two tenon wood and two mortise wood. In addition, the wooden sticks and bamboo fence were inserted into the gap between the frame and the surrounding rocks in order to prevent the surrounding rocks from falling. In general, the net cross section of the shaft was 60cm long and 60cm wide.

经 2700 多年的地壳运动和挤压变形，以至于我们现在看到的这处春秋时期的矿井给人一种无法进入竖井的感觉。为了再现当年古矿井原貌，我们在遗址厅东面拐角处，用钢筋水泥按原矿井的大小 1∶1 比例复原了一段井巷，大家可以仔细看看。

After 2700 years' crustal movement, the shaft was deformed by extrusion. So it seems difficult to enter into the shaft of the Spring and Autumn Period. In order to reproduce the original appearance of the ancient mine, we restore a section of shaft and tunnel with steel and cement at the east corner of the site hall which is as big as the original one. We can have a look here.

古人从地表至地下凿竖井，井底凿平巷，巷底凿盲井，上下连贯，井巷相通。狭窄的巷道仅足容身，而人只能在里面侧身曲臂地作业，古代矿工所处的艰苦环境不言而喻。

The ancient miners dug the shaft from the surface to the underground. Then they dug the tunnel at the bottom of the shaft and dug the blind shaft at the end of the tunnel. The tunnels and the shafts were interlinked with each other. So it was well connected from the top to the bottom and from the shafts to the tunnels. Both the shafts and the tunnels were so narrow that only one person could stay there. When the miners work in the mine, they should lean their bodies and bend their arms. So we can imagine their tough working conditions.

其次是井下通风、照明和排水问题。

Next are the problems of underground ventilation, lighting and drainage.

根据井下有风墙遗存来推测，古人在井下作业主要是利用井口高低气压差自然通风。

Judging from the remains of the ventilation wall, we can infer that the ancient miners rely on natural ventilation. They make use of air pressure difference of the wellheads.

由于是自然通风，所以井下氧气稀薄，为此矿工们经过摸索试验，选择用燃点低、浓烟少的竹子削成片，三五根扎成一把做照明用。发掘出土物中的大量未燃尽竹片就是佐证。

Just because of natural ventilation, the oxygen in the shaft is very limited. To solve the problem, the miners take several tests. At last, they choose to cut bamboo into chips because its burning point is low and it releases a little smoke. They tie three or five chips of bamboo into a bunch, and then fire it for lighting. This is proved by a number of unburned bamboo chips unearthed in the remains.

铜绿山地下水位高，古矿井大多低于潜水位 20 米以下，矿井中有大量地下水渗出，为保证采矿工作的正常进行，工匠们又发明了水槽和水沟排水。

In Tonglushan area, the underground water level is high. Most of the ancient mines are 20 meters below the phreatic level. So a large number of groundwater seeps into the mine. To ensure the normal operation of mining, the miners invent water sinks and water ditches to drain the water.

水槽是一根较粗的原木对剖，掏空后铺在两个平巷之间。水沟一般是在废弃的平巷底部挖出窄小的沟，并在沟的两边和底部铺上木板，使地下水顺利地沿水槽、水沟汇集到水仓，然后用木桶把积水提吊出井外，完成整个排水过程。

The sink is made of a thick log which is cut into two equal parts which are hollowed out and put between two tunnels. The narrow ditches are dug at the bottom of the discarded tunnels. The wooden boards are laid at both sides and the bottom of the ditch, so that the groundwater flows to the water sump through the sinks and the ditches. Finally, the water is carried out of the mine by wooden buckets. Then the whole process of drainage is over.

我们的古人就是这样成功解决了井下开采所需要的全部技术。正如夏鼐先生所言："这是中华民族的瑰宝，是中华民族的骄傲。"

That's how the ancient miners solve all the problems in underground mining. Just as Xia Nai says, "The mining technology is the treasure of China and the pride of Chinese nation."

陈列厅

The Exhibition Hall

这里依次展示的有：

What displays in the exhibition hall are as follows:

（1）古人找矿的方法。

（1）The methods to prospect of the ancient miners.

一是根据地质地貌找矿。《管子·地数》记载："上有丹砂者，下有黄金；上有磁石者，下有铜金；上有陵石者，下有铅锡赤铜；上有赭者，下有铁，此山之见荣。"

The first method is to prospect according to the geological features. It is recorded in *Land and Amount* of *Guanzi* that "If there is cinnabar above, there is gold below; the magnetite above, the copper and gold below; the ling stone above, the lead, tin and red copper below; the ochre above, the iron below. This is the appearance of ores in the mountain."

二是根据植物找矿。在铜绿山，一到秋天，漫山遍野盛开着紫红色的铜草花。铜草花，又名"海州香薷"，是一种寻找铜矿的指示植物。草和矿的关系是，有铜矿的地方不一定有铜草花，但有铜草花的地方一定有铜矿。在铜绿山，一年四季都有不同的喜铜植物盛开，如鸭跖草、蝇子草等，把整个铜绿山装扮得格外美丽。

The second method is to prospect according to the plants. The purple red copper flowers are in full bloom in autumn all over Tonglushan. The copper flower is also called "Haizhou Elsholtzia" which is an indicator plant to find copper ores. The relationship between copper flower and copper ore is that: if there is copper ore, there is not necessarily copper flower; however, if there is copper flower, there is copper ore for sure. In Tonglushan, many plants are closely related to copper ores, such as dayflowers and silene gallica which grow in all seasons. So they dress up Tonglushan and form a beautiful landscape.

（2）铜绿山古铜矿遗址出土的采矿工具。

（2）Mining tools unearthed from Tonglushan Ancient Copper Mine Site.

铜绿山出土的采矿工具计300余件，按质地可分为木、竹、青铜、铁质工具等四大类；按用途可分为探矿、挖掘、装载、选矿、排水、提升、装运工具等七大类。出土的这些工具表明，它们的专业化程度较高，基本上包括了当时手工开采所需的全部工具。

There are about 300 mining tools unearthed in Tonglushan. According to the raw materials, they are divided into wood tools, bamboo tools, bronze tools and iron tools. According to the use, they are divided into prospecting tools, digging tools, loading tools, ore-dressing tools, draining tools, hoisting tools and transporting tools. These tools are characterized with high degree of specialization which include all the tools needed in mining and exploiting at that time.

（3）幻影成像系统。

（3）Phantom imaging system.

幻影成像系统利用现在的高科技手段，用动感的形式向大家生动、逼真地再现古人找矿、采矿、探矿、运输、提升以及炼矿的整个过程。

The high-tech means are used in phantom imaging system which vividly reproduces the whole process of ore prospecting, mining, exploring, transporting, hoisting and smelting of the ancient miners.

（4）复原的战国至汉代井下采矿遗址。

（4）Restoration of the underground mining site from the Warring States Period to the Han Dynasty.

随着社会生产力和科学技术的发展，到了战国至汉代，井下采矿环境明显得到改善。矿井支护已从早期的榫卯式支护过渡发展到搭接式支护，即由两根带叉口的丫字形立柱、一根地梁、一根内撑木和一根横梁五件组合而成棚式支护，它能够有效地承受矿井的侧压、顶压和底压。

From the Warring States Period to the Han Dynasty, social productivity developed and science and technology made a great progress. So the environment of underground mining was greatly improved. The mine supporting developed from the earlier tenon mortise structure to the lap joint structure. That is the shed supporting structure which is composed of two Y-shaped columns, one ground beam, one inside log and one crossbeam. This structure effectively bears the side pressure, top pressure and bottom pressure.

这个时期的矿井净断面一般是130厘米×150厘米，最大的平巷宽度达190厘米，高达160厘米。

At that time, the net cross section of a shaft was 130cm wide and 150cm high. The largest horizontal tunnel was 190cm wide and 160cm high.

在这里，大家可以下去体验一下，切身感受一下我们祖先这一伟大的创举。

Now let's go down to the mining site to have a personal experience of ancient miners.

冶炼馆

The Smelting Hall

在铜绿山矿区，除了在地下发现、发掘了大量古代采矿遗存之外，在地表还发现了大量古代炼渣，其分布面积约 14 万平方米，估计达 50 万~60 万吨，炼渣内还夹有大量红烧土和残破的炉壁。经分析表明，这些炼渣为冶铜生产的遗物，由此说明，古代不仅在这里开采铜矿，而且还在这里将所采矿石冶炼成粗铜。

In Tonglushan Mine, besides a large number of the underground mining remains, a lot of ancient slag has been found on the surface which weighs about 500,000 or 600,000 tons, and scatters in an area of about 140,000 square meters. A great number of red clay and some broken furnace walls are mixed in the slag. The analysis shows that the slag is the remains of copper smelting, which implies that in the ancient times, copper ores are not only mined here but also smelted into crude copper.

铜绿山东北坡（11 号矿体）是当时重要的冶炼场所。从 1976 年开始，考古工作者重点对该处冶炼遗址进行发掘，先后发现 10 座残存的西周晚期到春秋早期（距今 2800 年左右）的炼铜竖炉及一批冶炼遗物。另外还在柯锡太村发现了 2 座战国时期的冶炼炉。

The smelting site of No. 11 mine is on the northeast side of Tonglushan which is an important smelting place at that time. The archaeologists focus on the excavation of this smelting site since 1976. They find ten copper smelting furnaces and a number of smelting relics which belong to the period from the late Western Zhou Dynasty to the early Spring and Autumn Period, about 2800 years ago. Moreover, another two smelting furnaces of the Warring States Period are found in

Kexitai Village.

为了研究古代炼铜技术，考古工作者、铜绿山矿及科研单位按竖炉结构及材料 1∶1 复原，与大冶有色金属公司的冶炼技术人员合作，并成功地进行了模拟试验。

In order to study the ancient copper smelting technology, archaeologists, Tonglushan Mine and other research institutes reconstruct the shaft furnace whose size, structure and materials are all the same as the original one. With the help of smelting technicians from Daye Nonferrous Metals Group Holdings Co., Ltd., a simulation test is carried out successfully.

下面介绍一下竖炉的构筑和功能。竖炉由炉基、炉缸、炉身三部分组成。

Now let me introduce the structure and function of the shaft furnace. A shaft furnace is composed of the base, the vat and the body.

炉基是炼炉的基础。筑炉前首先在地表挖一椭圆形浅沟，坑内用石块和红色黏土夯实，夯层之上用红色黏土夯筑“T”形风沟。风沟之上再筑炉缸，使炉缸不直接与地表接触，有利于防潮保温，而且在排渣或放铜的过程中，风沟内还可燃烧木炭，以保持炉缸内的温度，防止炉缸冻结，保证渣液或铜液的顺利排放。风沟内，在炉缸的底部还垫有石块，起稳固炉基的作用。

Furnace base is the foundation of smelting furnace. An oval shallow trench is dug before building the furnace. Stones and red clay are tamped in the trench. Then a T-shaped wind ditch is built with the red clay. The vat is built above the wind ditch. So it doesn't directly connect to the surface of the earth, which is beneficial to protect against moisture and preserve heat. In the process of slag or copper discharge, charcoal is burned inside the wind ditch, which can preserve the temperature in the vat in order to keep the vat from freezing. So the smooth discharge of liquid slag and copper is ensured. Stones are filled at the bottom of the vat, which firms up the furnace base.

炉缸是炼炉的冶炼区，架设在炉基的风沟之上，一般呈椭圆形。炉缸上沿的长轴两端各设有管状鼓风口，它是鼓风器向炉内送风增氧的通道，氧气能够助燃，并能增强冶炼中的氧化还原反应。炉缸前壁下部设有拱形“金门”，金门的设置用于开炉点火，排渣放铜。

Furnace vat is the smelting area of the furnace which is built on the wind ditch of the furnace base. It is often in oval shape. On the top of the vat is a long axis with two tubular tuyeres at each end which is the passage for a blower to send oxygen into the furnace. Oxygen can boost combustion and enhance the oxidation-reduction reaction in the process of smelting. The arched “golden door” is at the lower side of the front wall of the vat which is the place to light fire and release copper and slag.

炉身处在炼炉上部，入炉的物料（矿石、木炭、溶剂等）首先需要在炉身内预热，然后进入炉缸冶炼。

Furnace body is the upper part of the smelting furnace. At first, ores, charcoals, solvents and other materials are preheated in the furnace body. Then they are smelted in the vat.

发掘出土的炼炉，炉身均已坍塌。根据炉身坍塌的炉身残块堆积数量推算，复原的炉高，从缸底到炉顶约为 1.5 米。这一高度适合冶炼工人从炉顶投入冶炼物料。

The body of the unearthed smelting furnace always falls down. According to the number of the remains of the collapsed body, the restored furnace is about 1.5 meters high from the bottom to the top. This is a suitable height for the smelters to put the materials into the furnace from the top.

再介绍一下冶炼的辅助设施。主要有工作台、碎料台、和泥池、筛分场等。工作台的作用：一是架设和操作鼓风设备；二是便于工匠添加冶炼物料。碎料台用于矿石的破碎和筑炉材料的碾磨。和泥池用于黏土、高岭土等补炉材料的拌和，亦可用于粉状矿物的团粒。筛分场主要是对采出的矿石进行筛选，块粒状矿物可直接入炉，而粉粒状矿物则须团成小球才能入炉冶炼。

Now, let's introduce the auxiliary facilities of smelting which are worktable, crushing table, mixing pool, screening field, etc.. The first function of the worktable is to set up and operate the blast equipment. The second is for the workers to add the smelting materials. The crushing table is used to crush the ores and grind the furnace building materials. The mixing pool is used to mix the materials for the furnace repair, such as clay and kaolin. It is also used to pellet the powdery mineral. The screening field is mainly used to screen ores. Clumpy ores are put into the furnace directly, while powdery ores should be rolled into small balls before putting into the furnace to smelt.

根据发掘资料表明，铜绿山早期冶铜的矿石主要是在氧化富集带开采的氧化铜矿，如：孔雀石、赤铜矿、蓝铜矿等单一铜矿，但更多的入炉矿石则是铜铁共生的氧化矿。

According to the excavation documents, in Tonglushan, the ores for early copper smelting are mainly copper oxide ores which are explored in the oxidation enrichment zone, such as malachite, cuprite and azurite. But most of the ores for smelting are oxide ores of copper and iron.

铜绿山春秋早期冶铜所用的燃料是木炭，木炭易于燃烧，能够达到矿石熔炼的高温。同时，木炭还和氧一起参与炉内的还原反应，使矿石中提炼的金属还原。

In the early Spring and Autumn Period, in Tonglushan, the fuel used for smelting is charcoal which is easy to burn and can reach the high temperature for smelting the ores. What's more, charcoal and oxygen join together in reduction reaction in the furnace, which helps the refined metal reduces from the ores.

我们再来了解一下古代冶铜的技术成就：

Now let's have a look at the technological achievements of ancient copper smelting.

（1）造渣与配矿技术。冶炼过程实际上是造渣过程，渣形越好，说明冶炼技术越高。铜绿山矿区遗存着数十万吨古代炼渣，这些炼渣呈薄片状，表面光滑，上有波纹，说明渣的流动性好。数百个渣样的分析表明，渣的成分合理，硅酸度合适，这反映了我国古代已成功地运用了配矿技术。

（1）Technology of slag forming and ore blending. The process of smelting is actually the process of slag forming. Better-shaped slag indicates higher smelting technology. There are hundreds of thousands of tons of ancient slag remained in Tonglushan which is flake-shaped. It has a smooth surface with ripples, which shows that the fluidity of the slag is good. The analysis of hundreds of slag samples indicates that the composition of the slag is reasonable and the silicic acid degree is appropriate, which reflects the successful application of ore blending technology in ancient China.

（2）炉温控制技术。铜绿山出土的炼铜竖炉，采用的是炉内加热，这在冶金技术上是一次飞跃。经测试，渣熔点在1200摄氏度左右，这一温度很适合铜的冶炼。如果炉温过低，铜离子岿然不动；炉温过高，矿石中的铁也开始溶解，影响铜的纯度。

（2）Technology of furnace temperature control. The copper smelting furnaces unearthed in Tonglushan heat the ores inside the furnace, which is a great leap in smelting technology. According to the tests, slag melting point is about 1,200℃, which is a suitable temperature for copper smelting. If the temperature is lower, the copper ions cannot be melted;

if the temperature is higher, the iron in the ores will also be melted, which will affect the purity of the copper.

研究人员先后采集了数百个渣样进行分析化验。结果表明：炼渣平均含铜量在 0.7% 左右，而铁含量高达 30% ~50% 。由此看出，矿石中的铜得到了较充分的还原。这是我国古代炉温控制技术的具体表现。

The researchers have collected hundreds of slag samples for tests and analysis. The results show that the average content of copper in the slag is about 0.7% , while the content of iron is up to 30% or 50% , which indicates that the copper in the ores is fully reduced. This represents the technology of furnace temperature control in ancient China.

（3）冶铜技术。通过对铜绿山古铜矿遗址遗存的炉渣进行分析测试表明，铜绿山古铜矿遗址存在两种冶炼技术，即除了采用冶炼氧化矿石的“氧化铜—铜”工艺外，最迟在春秋早期已经掌握了“硫化矿—冰铜—铜”的工艺。经过上述工艺，生产出的粗铜，纯度已达到 93% 以上。

（3）Technology of copper smelting. According to the tests and analysis of the slag in Tonglushan Ancient Copper Mine Site, there are two kinds of smelting techniques. One is to smelt oxide ores to get copper from copper oxide. The other is to smelt sulfide ores to get copper from copper matte. The latter is mastered no later than the early Spring and Autumn Period. As a result of these techniques, the purity of the smelted crude copper is higher than 93% .

据测算，铜绿山矿至少生产了 10 万吨以上的粗铜，为当时社会经济及文化发展做出了巨大贡献。据考证，随州曾侯乙墓出土的编钟、盘龙城出土的大量青铜器以及河南安阳出土的司母戊大方鼎等都用的是铜绿山的铜。同时，铜绿山的铜为楚国供应了大量制造兵器和礼器的原料，为楚国的发展和壮大奠定了坚实的基础。

It is estimated that Tonglushan Mine produced more than 100,000 tons of crude copper, which contributed a lot to the economic and cultural development of the society at that time. According to the research, the copper of Tonglushan was used as the raw material for many famous bronze wares, among which are the set of chime bells unearthed from the tomb of Marquis Yi of Zeng in Suizhou, the bronze wares unearthed from Panlongcheng, the Simuwu big square tripod unearthed in Anyang of Henan Province, etc.. Moreover, the copper of Tonglushan was also used as the raw material for abundant weapons and ritual vessels of Chu State, which laid down a solid foundation for the development and expansion of the country.

总之，铜绿山古铜矿的发现归纳起来具有如下几点重要意义：

All in all, the discovery of Tonglushan Ancient Copper Mine Site is of great importance in the following aspects:

（1）它为中国古代发达的青铜时代找到了一个十分重要的原料产地，证明了中国青铜时代的历史是一部独立的、完整的历史；

Firstly, it is an important place of the raw material in the Bronze Age of ancient China, which proves the history of Chinese Bronze Age is independent and complete;

（2）它向世人提供了一个证明古代先民掌握高水平采冶工艺富有说服力的实例；

Secondly, it offers persuasive evidence which confirms that Chinese ancient people have mastered the advanced mining and smelting technology;

（3）铜绿山古铜矿的发现与研究，向世人证明当时的冶炼技术达到了很高的水准；

Thirdly, the discovery and research of the site proves the high standard of the smelting technology in ancient China;

（4）它的发现说明，当时在青铜冶铸技术方面的成就还直接影响了中国铁器时代的发展；

Fourthly, its discovery indicates that the achievements in bronze smelting and casting technology have a direct influence on the development of the Iron Age in China;

（5）铜绿山古铜矿的发现，还为中国考古学开创了一个学科分支——矿冶考古学。

Lastly, the discovery of the site establishes a new branch of Chinese archaeology which is mining and metallurgy archaeology.

今天，它已成为传播历史知识、弘扬民族文化、进行爱国主义教育、科普教育的一个重要基地，它也是留给子孙后代的珍贵礼物，让我们子子孙孙共享这份优秀的历史文化遗产！

Nowadays, the site has become an important base to disseminate historical knowledge, to promote national culture and to carry out patriotism education and popular science education. It's a precious gift to Chinese descendants. All the generations may share this marvelous historical and cultural heritage.

最后，值得一提的是：经过省考古队在铜绿山片区进行的新一轮考古发掘以及对原来出土的陶片进行整理等情况表明，铜绿山古铜矿的起始年代可能要推至夏朝，专家正在对这一结论进行论证。

At last, it is worth mentioning that the beginning of Tonglushan Ancient Copper Mine may be traced back to the Xia Dynasty. The viewpoint is based on a new round of archaeological excavation of Tonglushan and the research of the unearthed pottery pieces, which is conducted by Hubei archaeological team. Some experts are trying to prove their conclusion.

朋友们，我们的导览到此结束，解说中如还有不清楚的地方，敬请提出宝贵意见和建议。祝您旅途愉快并真诚欢迎大家下次再来铜绿山古铜矿遗址参观！

Ladies and gentlemen, our tour is coming to the end. Please give us your valuable comments and suggestions. Wish you a happy journey! Warmly welcome you to visit Tonglushan Ancient Copper Mine Site next time!

第三节　大冶铁矿博物馆中英文解说词

Chinese and English Tour Guide Manual of Daye Iron Mine Museum

早上好！/下午好！欢迎大家参观大冶铁矿博物馆。

Good morning! /afternoon! Welcome to Daye Iron Mine Museum.

大冶铁矿是我国首批、湖北省唯一一家国家矿山公园的一部分，博物馆是其中的看点之一。首先向大家简单介绍大冶铁矿的历史。

Daye Iron Mine is a part of the national mine park which is among the China's first batch and is the only one in Hubei Province. This museum is one of the sceneries. First, I will briefly introduce the history of Daye Iron Mine.

大冶铁矿从公元226年三国吴大帝开采至今已经有1700多年的历史。

Daye Iron Mine has a history of over 1700 years whose mining history started from 226 in the Three Kingdoms Period. At that time, this area was under the reign of Wu State.

中华人民共和国成立后，从1958年7月1日大规模机械化开采至2004年，大冶铁矿已成功剥离废石3.7亿吨，生产矿石1.3亿吨。如果用这里剥离的废石铺路，可以从这里铺一条通往月球的大路；如果用这里的矿石炼成钢轨，可铺成220条京九铁路。

After the founding of the People's Republic of China, Daye Iron Mine starts large scale mechanized mining from July 1st of 1958. By 2004, 370 million tons of waste rocks have been stripped and 130 million tons of ores have been produced. If the waste rocks are used to pave roads, we can build a road to the moon; if the ores are smelted into rails, we can build 220 railways from Beijing to Kowloon.

大冶铁矿是日本最早开始掠夺中国铁矿的一座矿山；是张之洞创办的众多洋务企业中唯一保留下来的一座铁矿；是毛泽东主席视察过的唯一一座铁矿；是中国人雇聘外国矿师用地质科学勘得的第一座铁矿；是中国第一家用机器开采的大型露天铁矿；是汉冶萍公司的一个主要组成部分。

Daye Iron Mine is the first mine plundered by Japanese and the only survivor of numerous enterprises founded by Zhang Zhidong in the Westernization Movement which is inspected by Chairman Mao. It's also the first iron mine explored by foreign mining experts with the help of geological sciences and the first large open pit iron mine in China that adopts machines to mining. It's a major component of Han-Ye-Ping Company.

在大冶铁矿爆发过中国唯一一次以胜利告终的下陆大罢工；组建过中国第一支大型地质勘探队 429 队，并组成中国第一批女地质队员；运用现代力学治理稳定了世界第一高陡边坡；兴建了亚洲第一硬岩复垦基地。所以说，大冶铁矿有着丰富的矿产资源，更有着悠久的人文历史。

A famous strike, Xialu Strike, breaks out in Daye Iron Mine, which is the only one ended in victory. The Mine forms the first large-scale geological prospecting team which is the 429 Prospecting Team. China's first female geological team is composed here, too. There is the world's No. 1 high steep side slope which is stabilized by the use of modern mechanics. And Asia's first hard rock reclamation base is also constructed here. Therefore, Daye Iron Mine not only possesses rich mineral resources, but also has a long humanistic history.

目前博物馆共设 8 个展厅，集中展现珍贵历史图片资料 635 幅，矿物标本 483 个。首先请大家看沙盘。

There are 8 exhibition halls in the museum where 635 precious historical pictures and 483 mineral specimens are displayed. First, let's look at the sand table.

从这个沙盘我们可以看出，大冶铁矿地处群山之间，宛如盆地。俗语说：靠山吃山，靠水吃水。正是这富饶的矿山养育了我们矿山四代人。

From the sand table, we can see Daye Iron Mine lies among the mountains which looks like a basin. As the saying goes, if you live near a mountain, you live on the mountain; if you live by the water, you live on the water. It is the rich mine that has brought up four generations.

大家细看，这个沙盘主要分两大区域，一个是我们的矿区，一个是我们的家属区。我们可以看到张之洞文化广场、铁矿办公大楼等。大家看到的那一排排整齐的楼房，就是我们的家属区。

The sand table is divided into two areas which are the family area and the mining area. We can see Zhang Zhidong Culture Square and the Mine office buildings there. Those rows of buildings are the family area.

我着重讲一下矿区，大家看，这个橘黄色闪灯的呈梯田状的地方就是亚洲第一采坑——大冶铁矿东露天采坑。这个具有 114 年机械开采历史的东露天采坑东西跨度为 2400 米，南北跨度为 900 米，上下落差为 444 米，形成了亚洲第一边坡。现场的景色颇为壮观。

Now let's look at the mining area. The terraced place with orange flash is the Asia's first mining pit which is the East Open Mining Pit of Daye Iron Mine. It has a history of mechanical mining for 114 years which has an east-west span of 2,400 meters, a north-south span of 900 meters and a drop of 444 meters. It is the first side slope in Asia whose scene is quite spectacular.

大冶铁矿矿床有 6 个主矿体，从我的右手边自西往东依次为铁门坎、龙洞、尖林山、象鼻山、狮子山、尖山矿体。在采场东边是著名的佛教圣地“三楚第一山”——东方山。佛教文化与矿山文化浑然一体，遥相呼应！

There are six main ore bodies in Daye Iron Deposit. On my right side, from west to east, they are Tiemenkan, Longdong, Jianlinshan, Xiangbishan, Shizishan and Jianshan. There is Dongfangshan in the east of the mining pit which is a famous Buddhist resort. So the Buddhist culture and the mine culture are integrated into a whole. They echo each other!

大家再看这片茂密的树林，还有西边光彩山那片树林，这就是亚洲最大的硬岩复垦基地，总绿化面积为247万平方米，这是在石头缝里栽种出来的一片绿地。大冶铁矿采矿剥离了3.7亿吨废石，堆积在周围占据了大量的绿地。大冶铁矿人用20多年的时间绿化复垦，使这里绿树成荫、鸟语花香，成为矿山人休闲的好去处。

Now let's look at the dense forest and Guangcaishan in the west. This is Asia's biggest hard rock reclamation base whose total green area is 2.47 million square meters. It is a piece of green life planted in the rock seam. About 370 million tons of waste rocks are stripped from Daye Iron Mine which pile up to occupy a lot of green space. It takes the residents of Daye Iron Mine more than 20 years to finish the reclamation. Now it is full of trees, birds and flowers. So it becomes a good place for leisure.

大家再看，除了东露天采坑，矿区西边还有一个小采坑，中间一道山梁，看这情景像不像一根扁担挑着一对箩筐呢？

Besides the East Open Mining Pit, there is a small mining pit in the west of the mine, in the middle of which there is a bridge. Doesn't it look like a shoulder pole with a pair of baskets?

这其中有一段美丽的传说：铁山有一个“得道湾”，当年八仙之一铁拐李未得道之时，曾受仙人指点，如果他炼就一副九龙铁拐便可成仙。

There is a beautiful legend which is about an immortal in a village of Tieshan whose name is Tieguai Li. He is one of the Eight Immortals. Before he became immortal, he was enlightened by another immortal who said that if he refined a nine-dragon iron crutch, he could become immortal.

他找啊找，翻山越岭，历经千辛万苦。当他云游到铁山时，看此处青藤绕古树，奇花异草，九道溪流直泄而下，猿猴在山谷啼叫，百鸟在山林里歌唱。铁拐李异常兴奋，自语道，此处正是炼拐绝好之处。

So he tried to look for the material to refine iron crutch. He crossed mountains and experienced many hardships. When he arrived at Tieshan, he felt extremely excited. There were vines around old trees, exotic flowers, and rare herbs. Nine streams were falling straight down, apes were crowing in the valley, and birds were singing in the wood. He said to himself that this was the right place to refine his crutch.

于是他筑起八卦炉，每天用箩筐和扁担到山上采些赤橙黄绿青蓝紫的泥土和宝石。他烧啊烧啊，足足烧了九九八十一天。一根铁拐"腾"地从炉口中冲了出来，铁拐杖映着霞光，瑞气腾腾，可以呼风唤雨。铁拐李从此得道，腾云驾雾而去，把那箩筐与扁担留在人间，故形成此景。

Then he built the eight trigrams furnace. Every day, he climbed the mountains to collect colored soils and gems with baskets and shoulder pole. He burnt for 81 days. Finally, an iron crutch rushed out from the furnace which reflected rays and looked bling. It had the magic to control the forces of nature and to do anything as you like. Since then, he became an immortal, flew away and left the baskets and the shoulder pole behind. That is why the present landscape came into being.

现在，大家请随我进入第一展厅——矿床展。大家看到走廊上悬挂着一幅幅精美的矿石图片，这上面有 14 种形状各异、色彩斑驳的矿石。这些矿石在展厅都有实物，关于它们的用途及形成，我将一一介绍。

Now please follow me to the first exhibition hall where there is a mineral deposit exhibition. Beautiful pictures of ores are hung in the corridor, among which are 14 kinds of colorful ores with different shapes. They are all exhibited in the mineral deposit hall. I will introduce their functions and formations one by one.

这里是大冶铁矿在全国的位置图，可以看出大冶铁矿地处鄂东南，长江黄金水道和京广、武九铁路的交汇地带。地理位置承东启西，扼南控北，面向鄂东南及鄂赣皖豫四边地区。

This is Daye Iron Mine in the map of China which is located in the southeast of Hubei Province. The Yangtze River, Beijing-Guangzhou Railway and Wuhan-Jiujiang Railway are interlinked here. In geography, it connects the east and the west, the south and the north which faces the southeast of Hubei Province and the surrounding areas of Hubei, Jiangxi, Anhui, and Henan.

大冶铁矿矿床有 6 个主矿体，自西往东依次为铁门坎、龙洞、尖林山、象鼻山、狮子山、尖山矿体。除尖林山隐伏矿体外，其余矿体均露出地表，因此在尖林山采取的是井下开采。整个矿床全长约 5 千米，宽为 500 米，面积 2.5 平方千米。

Daye Iron Deposit consists of six main ore bodies which are Tiemenkan, Longdong, Jianlinshan, Xiangbishan, Shizishan and Jianshan from the west to the east. The ore body of Jianlinshan is hidden. All the other five ore bodies are exposed on the surface. So underground mining is adopted in Jianlinshan. The whole mineral deposit stretches five kilometers long and five hundred meters wide whose area is 2.5 square kilometers.

在这个展厅里，大家可看到区域地层系统表、区域地质构造图、区域主要侵入体特征一览表、区域六大岩体图、产于三叠纪大冶群的鱼化石和第四纪前东方剑齿象牙化石照片、铁山铁铜矿床的剖面图、铁山铁铜矿床形态、产状和规模表、铁山铁铜矿床地质图。

In this exhibition hall, we can see the regional stratigraphic system table, the map of regional geological structure, the list of the regional main intrusive bodies' features, the diagram of the six regional rock bodies, the pictures of the fish fossil of Triassic Daye Group and the ivory fossil of former oriental stegodon in Quaternary, the sectional view of iron copper deposit in Tieshan, the table of morphology, occurrence and size of iron copper deposit in Tieshan, and the geological map of iron copper deposit in Tieshan.

大冶铁矿的矿体产于岩体与大冶组灰岩接触带。矿石分布在氧化带与原生带，因而矿石的分类有所不同。铁矿石的化学组成特点是富铁、高硫、低磷，并伴生铜、钴、金等有益元素，是一个经济价值很高的铁铜矿床。

The ore body of Daye Iron Mine exists in the contact zone of rock body and limestone. The ores are distributed in the oxidation zone and the original zone. So the classification of ores is different. The chemical composition of iron ores has the following characteristics which are rich in iron, high in sulfur, and low in phosphate. They are accompanying with some beneficial elements, such as copper, cobalt and gold. This is an iron copper deposit of high economic value.

这是岩石室。大家可以看到大部分泛白色的石头，也有许多是大家在平时不经意看到的石头，但它们是怎么形成的呢？大冶铁矿为什么会有这么多的岩石呢？那么岩石与矿石之间有何区别呢？在之前我反复提到了“矿床”一词，矿床又是什么呢？

This is the rock room. Most rocks are whitish. Many are commonly seen in our life. How are they formed? Why is Daye Iron Mine rich in so many rocks? What is the difference between rock and ore? I have mentioned mineral deposit several times. Then what's mineral deposit?

我做一个简单的介绍。

Now I will explain all this briefly.

首先，由一种或者几种矿物组成的集合体叫岩石；而在岩石形成过程中，一些有用的矿物在地壳中或地表富集起来，达到工农业利用的要求，就是矿产。在一定地质作用下，矿产的富集地段是矿床。

At first, rock is the aggregate of one mineral or several minerals. In the process of its formation, some useful minerals concentrate in the earth crust or surface. When they are rich enough to meet the requirements of industry and agriculture use, ores come into being. Under certain geological effect, ores are accumulated. Then a mineral deposit is formed.

矿石是指某种元素的含量达到一定数值之上的岩石，比如：铁矿石的含铁量要在30%以上才有工业开采价值。岩石只是普通的地表沉积物，通常是矽元素占绝大多数含量，虽然也有一些金属元素，可是因为含量太低不符合开采要求。它们的区别是：矿石一定是岩石，岩石包括矿石，但是岩石不一定是矿石，而矿床又是更大的集合体。

Ore is a kind of rock whose content of some element reaches a certain level. For example, iron ores have a value of industrial mining only when the content of iron reaches over 30% . Rock is only the ordinary surface sediment whose major content is usually silicon. Although there are some metal elements in the rock, the low content does not meet the requirement of mining. To sum up, ores are certainly rocks. Rocks include ores, but rocks are not necessarily ores. A mineral deposit is a big aggregate of ores.

在铁山矿体中自西向东，主要分布为闪长岩、矽卡岩、长石、斑岩、大理岩，含石榴子大理岩等六种岩石。这些岩石都有一些形象贴切的名字，有的如刀砍状，有的如藕节状，有的如条带状、肠状等。

There are six kinds of rocks in Tieshan ore body which are diorite, skarn, feldspar, porphyry, marble, and garnet-contained marble from the west to the east. These rocks are vividly named after their shapes. Some looks like knife, some like lotus root, some like strip, and some like intestine.

岩石的主要成分是碳酸钙，我们日常最常用的可能就是这种大理岩。这种岩石是变质岩之一，因盛产于我国云南大理而得名。

The main element of rocks is calcium carbonate. The most commonly-used rocks we can see easily in our daily life may be marble which is a kind of metamorphic rock. They are rich in Dali of Yunnan Province, which is the reason for its name.

由于原岩成分不纯，因此常有各种杂质，如含有蛇纹的大理石，称“蛇纹大理岩”，白色中夹绿色花纹，磨光后非常美观，可供艺术雕刻和装饰品之用；纯洁雪白的细粒大理岩，称“汉白玉”，是一种著名的石雕材料。

Since the original rocks are not pure, they contain various impurities. Those marbles containing serpentine are called “serpentine marbles” which are white rocks with green patterns. They are very beautiful after polishing, so they are used for art carving and ornament. The snow-white marbles are called “Chinese white jades” which is a kind of raw material for stone carving.

还有一种常见的岩石就是这种闪长岩。闪长岩是一种颜色较深的岩石，多呈灰黑色、带深绿斑点的灰色或浅绿色，色率20%～35%。当暗色矿物因蚀变而绿泥石化、纤闪石化时，岩石显出不同程度的绿色色调，因此用其作为饰面石材更具美感。

Another ordinary rock is diorite which is a kind of dark-colored rock. It is mainly gray and black, usually gray with dark green spots or light green whose color ratio is from 20% to 35%. When the dark minerals are corroded in the process of chloritization and uralitization, the rock will present various degrees of green color. When it is used as the material of decorative stone, it is more beautiful.

闪长岩的物理特征是：压缩强度为130～200MPa（干）或100～160MPa（湿），抗弯强度为10～25MPa，体积密度为2.85～3.00g/cm^3，吸水率为0.4%。闪长岩往往具有独特的风格而被用作外墙饰面石材。但一般闪长岩抛光较为困难，多用以制作台阶及阳台地板。

Diorite has the following physical characteristics. When it is dry, the compressive strength is from 130MPa to 200MPa. When it is wet, the compressive strength is from 100MPa to 160MPa. Its flexural strength is from 10MPa to 25MPa. Its volume density is from 2.85g/cm^3 to 3.00g/cm^3. Its water absorption ratio is 0.4%. Because of its unique characteristics, diorite is often used as a decorative stone material of a building wall. But it is difficult to polish. So it is mainly used in steps or balcony floor.

每一种岩石都有它独特的特性，也有它独特的用途。请大家随意观看，如果有什么疑问，我可以帮助解答。

Each rock has its own features and uses. Please feel free to look around. If you have any questions, please call me.

在进入矿石室前，我们看一下这幅《鄂东南区域地质矿产图》。红色是铁矿储量，蓝色为石灰石，黑色为大理石。这里大片红色就是我们大冶铁矿所在之处，往北是程潮铁矿，西南方向是灵乡铁矿。显而易见，大冶铁矿的矿产资源是非常丰富的。

Before we go to the ore room, please look at *The Map of Geology and Mineral Resources in the Southeast of Hubei*. The red color refers to iron ore reserves, the blue refers to limestone reserves, and the black refers to marble reserves. The large red zone is the location of Daye Iron Mine. In the north of it lies Chengchao Iron Mine. And in the southwest of it lies Lingxiang Iron Mine. Obviously, Daye Iron Mine is very rich in mineral resources.

这个展室展出了镇馆之宝，即距今有 175 万年的前东方剑齿象化石。现在我们所看到的是剑齿象的牙齿，剑齿象是古代哺乳动物的一属，属长鼻目。它们的化石主要发现于亚洲和非洲上新世至更新世地层中。

The treasure of the museum is exhibited in this exhibition room which is a fossil of former oriental stegodon of 1.75 million years ago. These are the teeth of the stegodon which belongs to ancient mammal genus, proboscidea. Their fossils are often discovered in Asia and Africa from the strata of Pliocene to Pleistocene.

最大的剑齿象有 9 米多长、四五米高，体重好几十吨，以草食为主，每天食量达 10 吨至 20 吨。我国的剑齿象化石迄今为止已发现 8 种，其中以东方剑齿象多见。数十万年至数万年前，它们生活在热带及亚热带沼泽和河边的温暖地带，是继恐龙之后的“巨无霸”。

The biggest stegodon is over nine meters long, and four or five meters tall and weighs dozens of tons. They mainly feed on grass and eat ten or twenty tons every day. In China, about eight species of stegodons are discovered, among which the oriental stegodons are most common. From hundreds of thousands of years ago to tens of thousands of years ago, they lived in tropical or subtropical swamps and the warm regions of the riverside. They are the “Big Mac” after dinosaurs.

下面进入矿石室，这里收集有 93 块矿石，相比之下，与之前的岩石室有着明显区别。矿石分为两种：一种是脉石矿物，比如那边颜色亮丽的白云石、方解石、透辉石、水晶石、云母及石膏等。另一种就是矿石矿物，主要有磁铁矿、赤铁矿、黄铜矿等。

Now we come to the ore room. Ninety-three pieces of ores are collected here. The ore room is quite different from the rock room. The ores are divided into two kinds. The first are gangue minerals, including the bright-colored dolomite, calcite, diopside, crystal, mica, and gypsum, and so on. The second are ore minerals, including magnetite, hematite, chalcopyrite, and so on.

磁铁矿的颜色大部分呈黑色、褐色，而且就重量而言，同等体积下，矿石是岩石的2~3倍。有些矿石还会隐现出一些绚丽的光彩。矿石的主要成分有铁、铜、硫、磷及金、钴等稀有元素。

The color of magnetite is mainly black or brown. Under equal volume, an ore is two or three times as heavy as a rock. Some ores display brilliant color. The main components of ores are iron, copper, sulfur, phosphorus, and rare elements as gold, cobalt, etc..

矿石现在含铁品位为42%~52%，这四个比较大、形状比较有特点的磁铁矿分别为角砾状构造磁铁矿、伟晶状磁铁矿、花斑状混合矿和气管状磁铁矿。这是伟晶状磁铁矿，色黑如墨，由多个菱面组成。把手放在上面，能够感觉到一点点磁力的存在，说明这种矿石含铁量是很高的。

The iron content of the ores ranges from 42% to 52%. These four magnetite ores are relatively bigger and their shapes are more distinctive. They are brecciated magnetite, pegmatoidal magnetite, graniphyric mixed ore, and trachea magnetite. This is the pegmatoidal magnetite which is as black as ink. It is composed of several rhombs. Put your hands on it, and you will feel some faint magnetic force, which indicates that its iron content is high.

磁矿石根据所含金属量的不同，可分为低铜磁铁矿，贫铁混合矿，低铜混合矿，低铜高硫氧化矿等9种。如果以形状划分，可分为片状、纤维状、葡萄状、肾状、晶洞状、波纹状、气孔状等14类。

According to the metal content, the magnetic ores are divided into nine kinds, among which are low copper magnetite, low iron mixed ore, low copper mixed ore, low-copper high-sulfur oxide ore, etc.. In light of the shape, the ores are classified into fourteen kinds, among which are flake-shaped, fibrous-shaped, grape-shaped, kidney-shaped, geodeshaped, ripple-shaped, stoma-shaped, etc..

这里有一些色彩比较特别的矿石，比如这一块绿色矿石，非常醒目，它就是较为稀有的孔雀石。孔雀石，古称石绿、缥绿、绿青。其英文名称，源于希腊语，为“绿色”之意。她美丽的绿色与花纹，恰似孔雀羽毛，后人称为孔雀石，矿物学与美术界通用。古今中外，孔雀石以其美妙的命名带上种种神奇的色彩，象征福善、嘉庆、吉祥美好。

There are some ores with distinctive color. This eye-catching green ore is the rare malachite. In the old times, it is also named mineral green, pale green or dark green. Its English name derives from ancient Greek which means “green” . Its green color and beautiful patterns look like the feathers of a peacock. So it is later named malachite which is the same in mineralogy as in art. Malachite possesses a lot of magical color because of its amazing name. It is a symbol of fortune, kindness, and good luck in all countries.

孔雀石是基性无水碳酸铜矿物，含铜量 57.5%，是重要的铜矿石，又可制作上乘的国画颜料和艺术盆景。意大利著名画家波提切利的名画《春天》就采用了孔雀石原料，500 年来未变色。

Malachite is basic anhydrous copper carbonate whose copper content is 57.5%. It is an important copper ore which is used to make superior Chinese painting pigments and art bonsai. The famous painting *Spring* of Italian painter Botticelli uses malachite as raw material whose color does not change for 500 years.

致密者可作宝石、玉石原料，用孔雀石雕琢成的工艺品，其价值可与翡翠、玛瑙制品相媲美。北京故宫中便有孔雀石珍贵饰品，俄罗斯冬宫也有孔雀石装饰物。有的国家还将孔雀石作为国石。

Compact malachite is used as raw material for gem and jade. If the crafts are carved with malachite, their value can be compared with jade and agate products. In Beijing Forbidden City, there is precious malachite jewelry. In Russia Hermitage, there are some malachite decorations. Some countries regard malachite as their national stone.

孔雀石还可入药，我国古代把它当作珍贵的石药，明朝李时珍在《本草纲目》中有记载。

Malachite is also used as medicine. In ancient China, it is regarded as a precious stone medicine. Li Shizhen of the Ming Dynasty records this function of malachite in his *Compendium of Materia Medica*.

还有这块晶莹剔透的石膏，我们大家平时或多或少都会用到石膏。它的作用很广泛，在建筑装潢业，石膏吊顶装饰板是我国目前家装中应用最广的一种新型吊顶装饰材料。其中防潮石膏装饰板特别适用于卫生间、厨房的吊顶装饰，吸声石膏装饰板具有很强的防噪音功能，还有其他功能的石膏装饰板。

This is a piece of crystal gypsum which is often used widely in our daily life. In building and decoration industry, plaster ceiling decorative board is one of the most widely used ceiling decoration materials in China's home decoration. Moisture-proof plaster decorative board is suitable for the ceiling decoration of bathrooms and kitchens. Acoustic plaster decorative board has a strong anti-noise function. Plaster decorative board has many other functions.

在医学上，医用石膏含水硫酸钙，有软硬两种，入药者用软石膏，其功用是清热降火、止渴解渴，外用可收敛疮疡、接骨等。在工业上可用于模具、雕刻、工业原料，以及用来做豆腐。

In medicine, medical plaster contains water calcium sulfate which is divided into hard plaster and soft plaster. Soft plaster is used as medicine. For internal use, its function is to decrease heat and quench thirst; for external use, its function is to converge ulcers and to set broken bones. In industry, gypsum is used in mold and sculpture, used as raw material in industry and used to make tofu.

如果大家想了解铁山各类矿石的储量数据及各类矿石详细化学成分的话，请大家看墙面上的8幅表格。这里有铁山铁铜矿床工业类化学成分表，铁铜矿床氧化带、原生带矿石矿物成分表，氧化带、原生带矿石结构构造一览表，以及铁山铁铜矿床铁矿石储量（万吨）表等。

If you want to know the reserve data and chemical composition of all kinds of ores in Tieshan, please look at the eight tables on the wall. They are Table of Industrial Chemical Composition of Iron Copper Deposit, Table of Ore Mineral Composition in Oxidation Zone and Original Zone of Iron Copper Deposit, Table of Configuration List of Ores in Oxidation Zone and Original Zone, Table of Iron Ore Reserves of Iron Copper Deposit, etc..

请大家慢慢观赏，有什么疑问可以问我。稍后，我们将参观下一个展厅——伟人馆。

Please take the time and look around as you like. Ask me if you have any questions. Later we will visit the next exhibition hall. That is the great men hall.

现在，大家请随我走入伟人馆。上楼时，请大家注意防滑。

Now please follow me to the great men hall. Please watch your step when going upstairs.

大家请看这幅毛泽东主席的相片，当年他手上握着的就是这块矿石。这幅相片是他真人的1.8倍大。大冶铁矿是毛泽东主席生平唯一视察过的铁矿山。

Please look at the big photo of Chairman Mao. This is the ore he held when he inspected Daye Iron Mine. The photo is 1.8 times bigger than himself. As we all know, Daye Iron Mine is the only iron mine Chairman Mao inspected.

当时的具体情况是这样的，1958年9月15日上午10时40分，毛泽东主席到大冶铁矿视察。当时陪同毛泽东主席视察的有国防委员会副主席张冶中、中共湖北省委第一书记王任重、中共湖北省委书记处书记张平化，黄石市委书记杨锐等。

What happened at that time is described clearly in the introduction. At 10：40 on the morning of September 15 of 1958，Chairman Mao came to inspect Daye Iron Mine. He was accompanied by Zhang Yezhong，Wang Renzhong，Zhang Pinghua，and Yang Rui. Zhang Yezhong was the vice chairman of the National Defense Commission. Wang Renzhong was the first secretary of the CPC Hubei Provincial Party Committee. Zhang Pinghua was the secretary of the Secretariat of the CPC Hubei Provincial Party Committee. Yang Rui was the secretary of Huangshi Municipal Party Committee.

毛泽东主席来到东露天采场 180 米处下车，与迎接他的矿山负责人亲切握手后，举目环视采场，指着尖山和狮子山问："这两个山头在搞什么?"当时东露天采坑还未进行开采，回话的是当时大冶铁矿矿长陈明江："在进行剥离工程。""矿石在哪里?"毛泽东主席又问。"压在下面。"陈明江回答。"有多少矿石?""一亿零三百万吨。"陈明江说。

Chairman Mao got off his car and went to the East Open Mining Pit which is 180 meters high. He kindly shook hands with the head of the mine. Then he looked around the pit. He pointed to Jianshan and Shizishan and asked："What are they doing on those two mountains?" The East Open Mining Pit was not mined at that time. Chen Mingjiang，the manager of Daye Iron Mine，answered："They are carrying on stripping project. ""Where are the ores?" Chairman Mao asked again. "Under the ground，" Chen answered. "How many ores are explored there?" Chairman Mao asked. "103 million tons，" Chen answered.

毛泽东主席望着陈明江，风趣地说："就是这么多，不能再多一点。"事实上我们现在正在进行深度挖掘，并已勘探出地下大约 1000 米处还有 3 千多万吨矿石，直接效益可达 100 亿。可当时，陈明江可不敢估量更多的矿产，他一板一眼地回答道：“工业储量报告是这么写的。”

“That’s all? Can’t you produce a little more?” Chairman Mao asked humorously, looking at Chen Mingjiang. In fact, we are conducting deep mining now, and have explored more than 30 million tons of ores at about 1,000 meters below the ground. Its direct benefit is up to 10,000 million yuan. But at that time, Chen Mingjiang didn’t dare to estimate more than that. He replied seriously: “That’s what the industrial reserve report says.”

毛泽东主席笑了，又问矿石情况，陈明江指着一片露头矿说，那里有200多公尺厚。“哪是矿石?”毛泽东主席又问。陈明江说：“前面就是的，那里一炮放了40多吨炸药。”这时省委第一书记王任重捡起一块矿石递给毛泽东主席，当时捡起的矿石就是这块矿石。

Chairman Mao smiled, and asked about the situation of the mine. Chen pointed to an exposed mine. He told Chairman Mao that it was more than 200 meters thick. “Where are the ores?” Chairman Mao asked. Chen answered, “Right there ahead of us. Each blasting needs more than 40 tons of explosives.” At that moment, Wang Renzhong picked up a piece of ore and gave it to Chairman Mao. This piece is the right one.

毛泽东主席接过矿石，在手上掂了掂说：“品位多少?”省委书记处书记张平化说：“60%左右。”毛泽东把矿石递给张冶中，并请他介绍矿石的含铁量，什么是富矿，什么是贫矿。“矿石里面有些什么东西?”毛泽东主席又问。“有铁、铜等五种。”陈明江回答说。毛泽东主席听了，不无担忧地说：“光要铁，其他不要了?”“不，其他矿物也准备选。”陈明江说。

Chairman Mao took the piece of ore, weighed it in his hand and asked, “What is the grade of the ores?” Zhang Pinghua replied, “About 60%.” Chairman Mao passed it to Zhang Yezhong and asked Zhang to tell him the amount of iron in the ores, what a high-grade mine is and what a low-grade mine is. “What are there in the ores?” Chairman Mao asked again. “There are five kinds of minerals, such as iron, copper, etc..” Chen Mingjiang answered. Hearing that, Chairman Mao looked worried, “If we only need iron, what about the other minerals?” “Not like that, other minerals are also selected.” Chen Mingjiang answered.

主席听后好像松了一口气，随后又问到铜草花。我们大冶铁矿到了夏、秋两季，漫山遍野都会开满淡紫色的铜草花。据说这种花是有灵性的，有铜、铁的地方才会长出这种花。可以说，铜草花是我们的矿花，希望之花！

Hearing that, Chairman Mao seemed relieved. Then he asked about copper flower. In Daye Iron Mine, copper flowers blossom all over the mountains and hills in summer and autumn. The color of copper flower is pale purple. It is said that this flower is spiritual. They only grow in the places rich of copper and iron. In some sense, copper flower is the flower of the mine and the flower of hope.

随后主席具有先见性地指示，矿石里含有铜和其他稀有金属，那么开一个矿就相当于开几个矿，要综合利用。谈了十分钟后，主席到工棚里休息，经过避炮洞时，毛泽东主席指着用石头垒起的避炮洞问：“是到这里面休息？”陈明江说：“不是，还在前面，这是避炮洞。”“我也进去避避炮。”毛主席说。

Then Chairman Mao indicated with foresight that there were other rare metals in the ores besides copper. So when we explored one mine, it meant several mines were explored. Chairman Mao suggested that we should make full use of the mine. After ten minutes' talk, Chairman Mao went to have a rest in the work shed. When they passed a blaster shelter, Chairman Mao pointed to the shelter which was made of stones, and asked, “Do we have a rest here?” “No. We will have a rest in another place. This is a blaster shelter.” Chen Mingjiang answered. “Let me go into the shelter to hide from a blaster." Chairman Mao said.

于是他走进去，坐在炮药箱上，抬头观察洞顶后对陈明江说："这个洞很薄，能顶得起石头吗?"陈明江说："小石头可以顶得住，没有大石头飞到这里。"毛泽东主席点点头。在避炮洞坐了一会儿，就到前面工棚休息。工棚里放了一张藤椅和几条板凳。毛泽东主席不坐藤椅，和大家一起坐在板凳上。

Chairman Mao went into the shelter and sat on a box. He looked at the top of the shelter and said to Chen Mingjiang, "It is very thin. Is it tough enough to hide from the rocks?" Chen said, "It is enough for small rocks. Big rocks don't fly here." Chairman Mao nodded. After a while, they went to the work shed to have a rest. In the work shed, there was a wicker chair and several wood benches. Chairman Mao didn't sit on the chair. Instead, he sat on the bench with others.

当王任重、张平化、杨锐等向主席汇报大冶铁矿的建设情况和工人们解放思想创造的一个又一个新纪录时，毛泽东主席不断点头微笑。当陈明江谈到矿山在实行建设资金大包干时节省了三千多万元时，毛泽东主席赞许说："还是包干好。"

Wang Renzhong, Zhang Pinghua, and Yang Rui reported the construction of Daye Iron Mine and the achievements of the mine workers. The workers emancipated their mind and created a lot of new records. Chairman Mao kept smiling while listening. Chen Mingjiang said that the mine carried out an all-round responsibility system in the management of construction funds. As a result, more than 30 million yuan was saved. Hearing that, Chairman Mao praised, "All-round responsibility system is really good."

在工棚休息20多分钟后，毛泽东主席站起来。大家陪同主席到掌子面看电铲装汽车、电机车，穿孔机穿孔和风钻钻大块。主席一面走一面询问作业情况。工人们高呼"毛主席万岁"，有的跑来和主席握手。主席一边走，一边挥手向欢呼的工人们致意。11 时 15 分，毛泽东主席及陪同人员上车去黄石视察。

After twenty minutes' rest, Chairman Mao stood up. They went to the tunnel face where there were the electric shovels, electric locomotive, drilling rigs, and wind drills. All these machines were busy working. He asked about the work conditions while walking. The workers shouted "Long lives Chairman Mao!" Some of them ran to shake hands with him. As he walked, he waved to the cheering workers. At a quarter past eleven, Chairman Mao went to inspect Huangshi with the accompanying officials.

这就是当时工棚的样子，几条长凳，一把藤椅，地上放的就是铜草花。

This is the work shed where Chairman Mao stayed which is kept as it was at that time. There are several wood benches and a wicker chair. Some copper flowers are laid on the ground.

这边还有 1960 年董必武副主席视察大冶铁矿的照片。1930 年时任军长的彭德怀将军率红军抵达过铁山。1953 年时任中共中央政治局委员、中央人民政府副主席高岗与中共中央中南局副书记李雪峰一同到铁山视察大冶铁矿勘探工作。同年 7 月，时任中共中央中南局第三书记，主管工业建设的叶剑英到达大冶铁矿对厂房、用水、招工、运输等问题进行了详细考察。

This is the photo of Vice Chairman Dong Biwu who visited Daye Iron Mine in 1960. In 1930, Commander Peng Dehuai led the Red Army to Tieshan. In 1953, Gao Gang and Li Xuefeng came to inspect the exploration of Daye Iron Mine. At that time, Gao was the member of the Political Bureau of the CPC Central Committee and Vice Chairman of the Central People's Government. Li was the deputy secretary of the Central South Bureau of the CPC Central Committee. In July of 1953, Ye

Jianying, who was the third secretary of the Central South Bureau of the CPC Central Committee, and in charge of the industrial construction, came to Daye Iron Mine to investigate the factory buildings, water, recruitment and transportation.

具体情况，图片边的文字都有详细的说明。这边还有一些大冶铁矿制作的毛主席徽章。这就是当年避炮洞的真实再现，用几根旧枕木搭起，还有很重的油味。一般避炮洞与放炮处会相隔 200 米，所以可以抵挡一些飞溅的石子。

There are detailed illustrations beside the photos. Here are some badges of Chairman Mao made in Daye Iron Mine. This is the true representation of the blaster shelter which is built with several old wood sleepers, so it smells of heavy oil. The blaster shelter is usually 200 meters away from the blasting spot. This distance is enough to hide from the flying stones.

这是古代开采馆，走廊上有十四幅黑白相片。这些是 20 世纪二三十年代的铁山旧貌，大部分还是日本人拍下的，图片来源于日铁职员撰写的《日铁大冶回忆录》。

This is the ancient mining hall. There are fourteen black and white photos in the corridor of the ancient mining hall, which is the appearance of Tieshan in the 1920s and 1930s. Most of the pictures were taken by Japanese which are chosen from *Memoirs of Daye Iron Mine under Japanese Occupation* which was written by a Japanese clerk of that time.

公元 226 年，三国吴大帝孙权就在这里冶炼过农具和兵器。古代把采矿、冶炼的工人分为矿丁与冶户。这个展厅采用大量的玻璃钢雕塑形象逼真地反映了当时的冶炼情景。大家看这里有一个泼水的场景，古代人没有先进的机器，他们把有矿石的部分用柴火烧热，然后再泼上冷水，使它瞬间崩裂。

In 226, Sun Quan, the king of Wu State of the Three Kingdoms, once smelted agricultural tools and weapons in Tieshan. In ancient times, workers of mining and smelting were divided into mining workers and smelting workers. In this exhibition hall, lots of fiberglass sculptures are used to vividly reproduce the smelting scene of that time. This is an action of splashing water. Without advanced machines, the ancient workers usually heat parts of the ores on a fire and then splash cold water on them, which makes the ores crack in an instant.

古代诗歌中，只有李白在《秋浦歌十七首》中真实生动地再现了当时冶炼工人的情景。秋浦现今在安徽，在唐代是金与银的生产地之一。《秋浦歌十七首》是唐代伟大诗人李白的组诗作品，其中第十四首写到“炉火照天地，红星乱紫烟，赧郎明月夜，歌曲动寒川”。“赧”原指因害羞而红了脸，在这里指炉火映红了冶炼工人的脸。

Li Bai, a famous poet in the Tang Dynasty, reproduces the smelting scene of the ancient times in his *Seventeen Poems of Qiupu*, among which the fourteenth is about smelting workers. Qiupu is a district in Anhui province now. It was one of the production places of gold and silver in the Tang Dynasty. It is written in the poem that “The furnace fire lightens up the sky and the land. The red sparks flash in the purple smoke. The red-faced smelting workers work in the night of the moon. Their songs echo through the steep valley.” “Red-faced” originally means that a man’s face becomes red because of shyness. Here it refers to the smelting workers’ red faces lit up by the furnace fire.

这三堆是炉渣，据考证是古代冶炼时遗留在铁山的。其中有三国时期的，有南北宋时期的。当时的技术有限，这些炉渣还含有大量的铁、铜、硫，这类炉渣在铁山有八处。到了南宋，民族英雄岳飞曾在此炼就了“大冶之剑”以抵制金兵。到了隋唐，皇帝杨广在此浇铸钱币。

According to the researches, these three piles of slag are the smelting remains of the ancient time, some of which are left from the Three

Kingdoms Period. Others are left from the Southern and Northern Song Dynasties. Because of the limited technology, the slag still contains a large number of iron, copper and sulfur. This kind of slag is found in eight places of Tieshan. In the Southern Song Dynasty, the national hero Yue Fei forged his "Sword of Daye" to fight against the troops of Jin State. In the Sui Dynasty, Emperor Yang Guang casted coins here.

这边是近代开采史陈列馆。1890年，湖广总督张之洞与商人盛宣怀成立了官督商办的汉冶萍公司。公司由汉阳铁厂、大冶铁矿、萍乡煤矿组成，是当时亚洲最早、最大的近代钢铁联合企业，在中国的历史上存在了58年。这是当时相关的历史人物。

This is the modern mining hall. In 1890, Zhang Zhidong, the governor of Hu-Guang, and Sheng Xuanhuai, a businessman, established Han-Ye-Ping Company which was government-supervised and merchant-managed. It was composed of Hanyang Iron Plant, Daye Iron Mine and Pingxiang Coal Mine. At that time, it was the earliest and the largest modern joint venture of iron and steel in Asia which lasted for fifty-eight years in China's history. These are the relevant historical figures of that period.

这里有两根钢轨，它们是当时汉冶萍公司的产品，上面有文字记载："民国四年。"（1915年）它比现在的铁轨要高一些，宽一些，而且不容易锈蚀。这两根钢轨见证了我们中国的采矿史、冶炼史、铁路运输史。为什么这么说呢？汉冶萍当时生产的钢轨主要是供给卢（卢沟桥）汉（汉口）铁路之用。

Here are two steel rails which are the products of Han-Ye-Ping Company. We can see some written records on them. Four Chinese characters "民国四年（the fourth year of the Republic of China）" are carved on them. That is the year of 1915. At that time, the steel rails are higher and wider than the present ones which are not easy to rust away.

These two steel rails have witnessed China's history of mining, smelting and railway transportation. Why do we say so? The steel rails of Han-Ye-Ping Company were mainly used for Lu (Lugouqiao) -Han (Hankou) Railway.

铁厂投产后，轧制的钢轨分轻重两类。产品有 42.16 公斤/米、37.7 公斤/米、37.2 公斤/米、36.2 公斤/米、33.4 公斤/米等 10 种规格，其式样分中国、美国、英国、法国、比利时式。产品除供卢汉铁路外，正太、淞沪、沪宁、沪杭甬等铁路也都用了汉阳铁厂生产的钢轨。

When the company went into operation, two kinds of steel rails were produced which were the light ones and the heavy ones. The products had ten specifications, such as 42.16 kg/m, 37.7 kg/m, 37.2 kg/m, 36.2 kg/m, and 33.4 kg/m and so on. They were produced into different styles, such as Chinese style, American style, British style, French style and Belgian style. Besides Lu-Han Railway, some other railways also used the steel rails of Hanyang Iron Plant which were Zheng-Tai Railway, Song-Hu Railway, Hu-Ning Railway and Hu-Hang-Yong Railway.

由于大冶铁矿的矿石含铜，轧制的钢轨不生锈、耐用。此钢轨 1914 年 1 月 30 日在意大利首都举办的世界博览会上获得最优奖。而且当时大冶铁矿至黄石港码头的这条运矿铁路是当时黄河以南唯一的一条铁路。

Copper is contained in the ores of Daye Iron Mine, so the steel rails do not rust and are durable. This rail won the best prize at the World Expo in the capital of Italy on Jan. 30th of 1914. At that time, the railway from Daye Iron Mine to Huangshigang Dock was the only one in the south of the Yellow River which was used to transport ores.

在这里还可以看到汉冶萍发行的股票的票样。张之洞创办汉阳铁厂、大冶铁矿等厂矿，为官办企业。1896 年交盛宣怀招商承办，改官办企业为官督商办，招募商股 100 万两，年利 8 厘。

Here are the stock samples issued by Han-Ye-Ping Company at that time. Hanyang Iron Plant, Daye Iron Mine, and some other factories founded by Zhang Zhidong were government-run enterprises. In 1896, these factories were handed over to Sheng Xuanhuai to operate. He changed the government-run enterprises into government-supervised and merchant-managed ones. These enterprises collected business shares of one million liang. The annual interest was 8%.

1908 年，盛宣怀将汉阳铁厂、大冶铁矿、萍乡煤矿合并成立汉冶萍公司，改官督商办为完全商办公司。合并公司再次招募商股，老股新股合股共招股份银元两千万元，分作四十万股，每股银元五十元。最先创始股本银元三百万元为头等优先股。股票分头等优先股，二等优先股及普通股三种。

In 1908, Sheng Xuanhuai merged Hanyang Iron Plant with Daye Iron Mine and Pingxiang Coal Mine to form Han-Ye-Ping Company. The government-supervised and merchant-managed enterprise was changed into a totally merchant-managed company since then. The company collected business shares again. Together with the old shares, the company collected 20 million yuan (silver dollar) in total. The capital was divided into 400,000 shares. The price of each share was fifty yuan (silver dollar). The capital of the founding shares was three million yuan (silver dollar) which was the first-class preferred stock. The stock was divided into the first-class preferred one, the second-class preferred one and the common one.

民国初年又发行了一批股票。从 1909 年起，公司每年召开一次股东大会，每年按公司盈余情况分派股息及股东红利。

A series of stock was issued in the early years of Republic of China. Since 1909, the company held a general meeting of shareholders every year. And dividends and shareholders' bonus were distributed according to the profits of the company every year.

这些图片记载着当时发生的一切。从这些图片中我们可以看到当时的盛世繁华，也可以感受到技术的落后，从而导致最后的衰亡。

These pictures record what happened at that time, from which we can see the prosperity of the times as well as the lag of technology, which leads to the eventual decline.

汉冶萍公司还创建了砖瓦厂，这些是当时的红砖瓦，每块砖瓦上都打有汉冶萍公司的印字，青砖上的“YTK”代表着冶铁矿。还有当时采矿主任张慎国用过的锤子与铲子，他每天带着地质锤和铲子到采场圈定矿点，指挥矿工按线采矿。这边是一些盛宣怀当时创建大冶铁厂的图片，这里几本《大冶铁厂志》详细地介绍了当时的具体情况。

Han-Ye-Ping Company also founded a brick factory. These are the red bricks of that time. The name of the company was engraved on each piece of brick. “YTK” on the black bricks are the initial letters of Chinese characters“冶铁矿（yetiekuang）”. Here are a hammer and a shovel which were used by Zhang Shenguo, the director of the mine at that time. Every day, he went to the stope to circle the mining point with his hammer and shovel, and directed the miners to mine according to the circle. Here are some pictures of Daye Iron Plant founded by Sheng Xuanhuai. *The History of Daye Iron Plant* introduces the specific situations of that time in details.

三楼展示的是工人运动、日本掠夺及矿山重建。由于汉冶萍公司工作条件艰苦，工人工资低廉，工人的自发斗争经常发生，但大多数由于没有坚强的领导，都被镇压下去。

The third floor is the exhibition of workers' movement, Japanese plundering and mine reconstruction. In Han-Ye-Ping Company, the working conditions were very hard and the workers' wages were very low, so the workers often carried out spontaneous struggles. But most of the struggles were suppressed because there was no strong leadership.

1923 年，大冶铁矿运务段工人在俱乐部领导下，要求增加工资，1 月 23 日在下陆举行罢工。罢工坚持到 2 月 3 日，历时 12 天。汉冶萍公司接受了工人提出的全部条件，次日复工。这是中国第一次以胜利结束的罢工斗争。何为胜利？其一，这 12 天没有一人死亡受伤；其二，工人提出的要求都得到了解决。

In 1923, under the leadership of the club, workers from the transport section of Daye Iron Mine demanded a pay raise. They went on strike on January 23rd. The strike carried on till February 3rd. It lasted for 12 days. Finally, Han-Ye-Ping Company accepted all the terms proposed by the workers who returned to work the next day. This is the first strike ended in victory in China. Why is it a victory? There are two reasons. First, no one dies or is injured in the twelve days. Second, all the requirements raised by the workers are accepted.

1937 年，日本发动了全面侵华战争。为了发动群众起来抗击日本侵略军，同年 11 月 26 日，中国近现代音乐家冼星海带领“上海救亡演剧二队”和“武汉大学学生救亡歌咏队”来到铁山，在盛洪卿村演出《放下你的鞭子》《牺牲已到最后关头》等节目，唱响了抗日救亡歌曲。

In 1937, Japan launched a full invasion of China. In order to call on the people to fight against the Japanese invaders, on November 26, the second team of Shanghai Salvation Drama and Student Salvation Team of Wuhan University went to Tieshan which were led by a Chinese modern musician Xian Xinghai. In the village of Shenghongqing, they performed the following programs *Put Down Your Whip*, *Sacrifice Has Come to the Last Minute*, and so on which aroused the people to start the Anti-Japanese War.

这边是 1927 年成立的湖北象鼻山铁矿局，也称湖北官矿公署象鼻山铁矿，它不隶属于汉冶萍公司。象鼻山铁矿当时年产铁矿石 20 万吨左右，因无法进行提炼加工，大部分运往了日本。

This is the Bureau of Hubei Xiangbishan Iron Mine which was founded in 1927. It was also called Xiangbishan Iron Mine of Hubei Official Mining Bureau which didn't belong to Han-Ye-Ping Company. At that time, Xiangbishan Iron Mine produced 200,000 tons of iron ores every year. Because there was no technology to smelt those ores, most of them were shipped to Japan.

这个馆记录了日本对大冶铁矿矿石的掠夺情况，这是一段不能被遗忘的历史。1896 年，日本创办了第一家钢铁企业——八幡制铁所。日本虽然有较为丰富的煤矿，但无铁矿，这阻碍了其钢铁工业的发展。

This hall records how Japanese plunder the ores of Daye Iron Mine. It is a history that cannot be forgotten. In 1896, Japan established its first iron and steel enterprise— Yawata Iron Works. Japan is rich in coal ores but lack of iron ores, which obstructs the development of its iron and steel industry.

1904 年，盛宣怀以大冶铁矿矿山及全部财产作抵押，向日本兴业银行借款 300 万日元，以大冶铁矿的头等矿石分三十年偿还。1913 年，盛宣怀兴建大冶铁厂，又以汉冶萍公司全部财产作抵押，向日本借了 1500 万日元，以大冶铁矿生产的头等矿石 1500 万吨，汉阳铁厂生产的生铁 800 万吨分四十年偿还。

In 1904, Sheng Xuanhuai borrowed three million Japanese yen from the Industrial Bank of Japan. He took Daye Iron Mine and all its property as mortgage, and promised to pay back the loan with first class ores of Daye Iron Mine within 30 years. In 1913, Sheng Xuanhuai constructed Daye Iron Plant. He borrowed 15 million Japanese yen from Japan and took all the property of Han-Ye-Ping Company as mortgage. He promised to pay back the loan with 15 million tons of first class ores of Daye Iron Mine and 8 million tons of crude iron of Hanyang Iron Plant within 40 years.

从此，汉冶萍公司全部由日本人控制，日本开始正式掠夺大冶铁矿矿石。仅 1939 年到 1945 年 6 年时间，从大冶铁矿采出的优质矿石达 501 万吨，有 413 万吨运回日本。

From then on, Han-Ye-Ping Company was completely controlled by Japanese who started to plunder the ores of Daye Iron Mine. From 1939 to 1945, 5. 01 million tons of high-quality ores were produced in Daye Iron Mine. However, 4. 13 million tons of them were shipped to Japan.

这边是日本人当时用的物品，有饭盒、香槟瓶、灯火盆，以及用来装炸药的桶，还有日本人的马鞍和当时用的刺刀。当时的机构是很齐全的，有总务部、矿业部、警卫队、后勤部、医疗部，这些在《日铁回忆录》里都有记载。

These are the Japanese products used by the Japanese invaders at that time which are lunch boxes, champagne bottles, light basins, barrels used to store explosives, the Japanese saddles and bayonets. The company is fully equipped with institutions including general affairs department, ministry of mining, guard unit, logistics department and medical department, which is recorded in the *Memoirs of Iron Mine of Japan*.

这边就是“重建开采”馆。1949 年 5 月 12 日，铁山解放。1952 年，中央地质工作指导委员会在铁山组建中国第一支大型地质勘探队——429 勘探队，并在这里诞生了中国第一批女地质队员。当时投入了 70 余台钻机，同时在灵乡、金山店、铜绿山、程潮进行全面勘探。

This is the mine reconstruction hall. On May 12 of 1949, Tieshan was liberated. In 1952, the Central Geological Work Steering Committee established China’s first large-scale geological prospecting team in Tieshan which was the 429 Prospecting Team. China’s first group of female geological team members was born here. More than 70 drilling rigs were put into use. Full explorations were carried out simultaneously in the areas of Lingxiang, Jinshandian, Tonglushan and Chengchao.

1958 年 7 月 1 日，东露天采场投入生产。到 1960 年，大冶铁矿年产矿石 290 万吨，成为全国十大铁矿生产基地之一。

On July 1st of 1958, East Open Mining Pit was put into production. In 1960, Daye Iron Mine had an annual output of 2.9 million tons of ores which became one of the top ten iron ore production bases in China.

四楼是深部开采、非矿产业、矿山科技。到了 20 世纪 90 年代，大冶铁矿露天采场矿石储量日渐减少，经济效益下降。因此，又兴建了铁门坎地下采场、龙洞地下采场二期工程、尖林山地下采场二期工程、东露天地下采场。还兴建了球团厂，对矿石进行深加工，使之仍保持较高的经济效益，延长矿山的服务年限。

The fourth floor is the exhibition of deep mining, non-mining industries, and mining technology. In the 1990s, the ore reserves of the open mining pit in Daye Iron Mine decreased gradually, so the economic benefits declined. Then several projects were constructed which include Tiemenkan underground stope, the second phase project of Longdong underground stope, the second phase project of Jianlinshan underground stope, and the underground stope of the east open pit. The pellet plants were also established for the deep processing of the ores. By means of these measures, the economic benefits of the mines kept relatively high and their length of service was prolonged.

这边是我们的非矿产业，包括铜材厂生产的铜线圈，还有托辊、电机，以及中日合资的美丽服装厂生产的“美丽牌服装”。

These are the non-mining industries which include the copper coils, rollers and electrical motors produced by the copper plant, and the beautiful garments produced by Meili Garment Factory, a Sino-Japanese joint venture.

这些是历年大冶铁矿获得的荣誉，到 20 世纪末，大冶铁矿共获得国家科技进步一等奖 1 项、二等奖 2 项、发明奖 12 项、科技攻关项目 159 项等。这边是历年省部级以上领导来大冶铁矿指导工作的一些图片，以及他们的题词、墨宝，请大家随意参观。

这次讲解到此结束，谢谢！

These are the honors of Daye Iron Mine in the past years. By the end of the 20th century, Daye Iron Mine has won a first prize of National Science and Technology Progress Award, two second prizes, and twelve prizes of Invention Award. 159 key scientific and technological research projects are achieved. Here are the pictures of some leaders who come to Daye Iron Mine to guide the work. These are their inscriptions and calligraphy. Please feel free to visit.

That's all about the introduction of Daye Iron Mine Museum. Thank you!

第四节 黄石国家矿山公园中英文解说词

Chinese and English Tour Guide Manual of Huangshi National Mine Park

各位游客朋友们，欢迎您来到美丽的黄石观光游览。这里是黄石市铁山区，现在我们将要游览的景点是国家4A级风景旅游区，同时也是湖北省两大工业旅游示范点之一——湖北黄石国家矿山公园。

Ladies and gentlemen, welcome to Huangshi. Now we are in Tieshan district of Huangshi. Let's visit Huangshi National Mine Park which is a 4A Scenic Tourist Area in China and one of the two industrial tourism demonstration sites of Hubei Province.

2005年，黄石国家矿山公园成为国土资源部审批的第一批矿山公园。三年前的4月22日，也就是世界地球日的这一天，黄石国家矿山公园开园，成为国土资源部审批的第一批28家矿山公园中首家开园的国家级矿山公园。

In 2005, Huangshi National Mine Park was approved by Ministry of Land and Resources which was one of the first batch 28 mine parks. On April 22nd of 2002, the World Earth Day, Huangshi National Mine Park was open, which was the first national mine park open to the tourists.

现在矗立在我们面前的这个标志性建筑物，是黄石国家矿山公园的主碑。主碑最上端是黄石国家矿山公园的标志。这座主碑总重100吨，高30米，里面有11个铁箱子，分别装载着大冶铁矿所产的各种各样的矿石。大冶铁矿矿产资源丰富，是矿石储量巨大的国有大型矿山。

There is a tall landmark building in front of us which is the main stele of Huangshi National Mine Park. At the top of it, there is a logo which is the symbol of the Park. The main stele is 100 tons heavy and 30 meters high. There are eleven iron boxes in it. Different kinds of ores are put into the boxes. These ores are produced by Daye Iron Mine. The Mine is rich in mineral resources and is a large state-owned one with great ore reserves.

这座主碑总重量 100 吨，寓意着大冶铁矿是一座有着一百多年现代开采历史的矿山。它的采矿史可以追溯到公元 226 年，也就是中国历史上的三国时代。事实上，它的采矿史就有 1790 年。在一千多年前，古代的先民就是在我们参观的这个地方，也就是大冶铁矿矿山这个地方进行采矿冶铁活动的。

The 100-ton-weight of the main stele means that Daye Iron Mine has a modern mining history of more than 100 years which can be dated back to the year of 226. That is the Three Kingdoms Period in Chinese history. In fact, it has a mining history of about 1790 years. A thousand years ago, the local residents began to mine and smelt in the areas of Daye Iron Mine.

在主碑的身后，有一座具有楚风韵的建筑群，这里就是游客服务中心，里面设有商场、休息厅、医疗室、咨询处等服务设施，为每一位游客提供便利。走进大厅，木质结构的屋顶，清雅而不失华丽。大厅正中间的前台咨询工作人员除了为游客提供优质的咨询服务外，还为游客精心准备了矿冶文化的宣传资料。

Behind the main stele is a building complex with Chu charm which is the tourist service center. Inside there are some service facilities which are the shopping mall, the lounge, the medical room, the information desk, etc.. These facilities provide convenience for the tourists. Entering the hall, we see the elegant and gorgeous wooden roof. In the middle of the hall, there is the information desk. The staff members provide qualified consulting services and prepare publicity materials of mining and metallurgical culture for the tourists.

咨询处的左边设有矿冶文化纪念品专柜，专柜中最为引人注目的是一些奇形怪状的石头。可别小看了这些石头，这些石头都是浑然天成的矿物晶体，形态各异、姿态万千，有孔雀石、蓝铜矿、萤石、水晶石等。挑一块喜欢的矿物晶体带回家，送给朋友或自己珍藏，都是非常惬意的。

On the left of the information desk is the special souvenir counter of mining and metallurgical culture. Some odd stones are most striking which are the natural mineral crystals. They have different shapes and styles, among which there are malachite, azurite, fluorite, rock crystals, etc.. Pick up a piece of mineral crystal as you like and take it home. Whether you send it to your friend or preserve it by yourself, it is a real pleasure.

入口的右侧，播放着由中央电视台著名主持人任志宏配音解说的《炉火照天地》矿冶文化专题片。他那浑厚而具有磁性的声音，将矿山美好画卷慢慢铺开，娓娓述说着矿山的发展变迁。

On the right of the entrance, the feature film of mining and metallurgical culture is broadcasted whose name is *The Furnace Fire Lightens up the Sky and the Land*. It is dubbed and narrated by Ren Zhihong, the famous host in CCTV. He introduces the beautiful scene of the mines and their development and changes.

在大厅进门的右侧，摆放着一块天然的紫水晶洞石，足有一人多高。这块紫水晶洞石产于巴西，里面一个一个的紫水晶，晶莹剔透。紫水晶神秘而浪漫，是唯一的紫色系宝石，其色泽由浅紫色到深紫色各有不同。传说紫水晶有镇定安神功效，我国的《博物要览》中说，紫水晶“色如葡萄，光盈可爱”，这种如葡萄般的紫色是由于水晶中所含微量氧化铁所致。

On the right of the hall, there is a natural amethyst stone which is as high as a man. Such a big amethyst stone is made in Brazil, in which each amethyst is crystal clear. Amethyst looks mysterious and romantic which is the only jewel of purple color. Its color varies from light purple to dark purple. It's said that amethyst has the effect to keep calm. According to the Chinese book *An Overview of All the Things in the World*, the amethyst looks like grapes which is shining and lovely. Its color originates from trace amounts of iron oxide in it.

大冶铁矿也产有紫水晶，除了紫水晶之外，还产有许多其他的矿物晶体。接下来请游客朋友们随我一起去参观矿物晶体奇石展，其中以孔雀石最为漂亮。孔雀石的颜色酷似孔雀羽毛上的斑点，中国古代称为“绿青”“石绿”或“青琅玕”，是一种古老的玉料。

Apart from amethyst, Daye Iron Mine produces many other mineral crystals. Next, please follow me to visit the exhibition of mineral crystals and odd stones, among which malachite is the prettiest one. Malachite is a kind of jade material whose color is similar to the spots of the feather of a peacock. In ancient China, it is named as lvqing, shilv or qinglanggan.

世上没有两块一样的孔雀石。这种充满纹理的石头就有这种好处，每一块都有独一无二的魅力。判断孔雀石品质的依据主要就是它的颜色和纹理，纹理越细腻，颜色越鲜艳，品质就越上乘。

There is no identical malachite in the world. Malachite is full of textures. Each one is of unique charm. The quality of malachite is mainly determined by its color and texture. The smoother the texture, the brighter the color, and the superior the quality.

看完奇石展，穿过游客服务大厅，请游客朋友们随我一同前往黄石国家矿山公园一个最重要的组成部分——工业博览园，进行观光游览。刚才我给大家介绍了一个小常识，即黄石国家矿山公园是全国工业旅游示范点。目前湖北省只有两家全国工业旅游示范点，另外一家就是三峡大坝工业园。

Now, please follow me to visit the Industrial Expo Park which is the most important part of Huangshi National Mine Park. Just now, I told you that Huangshi National Mine Park was the national industrial tourism demonstration site. There are two demonstration sites in Hubei Province. The other one is the Three Gorges Dam Industrial Park.

不知道现场的游客朋友们，有没有去过三峡工业园。三峡工业园一个最显著的标志，就是把修建三峡大坝时使用的大型设备，在陈列场上进行陈列，同时通过一些雕塑进行展示，以告诉大家三峡大坝是如何建成的，而且告诉我们三峡大坝的修建者们经历了一些什么样的磨难，才把这个世界第一的水利工程展示在世人面前。

Now I will introduce the Three Gorges Dam Industrial Park in a few words. Its most striking symbol is the large equipment which was used in the construction of the Three Gorges Dam. In the showground, they are displayed in sculptures which tell us how the Three Gorges Dam is constructed and how many hardships the builders have gone through in the construction. As we know, the Three Gorges Dam is the largest hydraulic engineering project in the world.

黄石国家矿山公园与三峡大坝工业园有着异曲同工之妙。工业博览园和三峡大坝工业园的设计风格是一样的，即通过一些采矿设备的展示，向大家讲述矿山的发展变迁。请大家随我一起往前走，现在这里陈列着一些大大小小的采矿设备。这些采矿设备都是从 1952 年东露天采场进行大规模机械化开采时就一直使用到现在的大型设备。

Huangshi National Mine Park is designed in the same way, in which the design and style of the Industrial Expo Park is the same as that of the Three Gorges Dam Industrial Park. These mining machines tell us the development and changes of the Mine. Please move forward and look at the mining equipments of different shapes and sizes. These large equipments are still in use since the large scale mechanization of East Open Mining Pit in 1952.

过一会儿，我将带领各位游客朋友穿过一条特别的小路，去看一个外形像鳄鱼的运输设备。我们右边就是马上要经过的这条小路，上面所铺设的这些圆柱状的东西可不是一般的石头，它们是从地底下最深处达八九百米的地方凿上来的。它们就是这个地方的岩芯。大冶铁矿是温家宝总理亲批的，作为全国十家危机矿山之一，特批进行深部勘探，而这些岩芯就是当时深部勘探钻探出来的岩芯。

After a while, we will pass through a special path to see the transportation equipment which looks like a crocodile. Now we come to the path on the right side. Some particular cylindrical rocks are laid on the path. They are not ordinary stones. They are drilled from the underground of 800 or 900 meters deep which are the cores of this area. Daye Iron Mine is one of the ten mines in crisis situation. The former Prime Minister Wen Jiabao approved its deep exploration. And these cores were drilled through deep exploration at that time.

走过岩芯路，游客朋友们可以看到，在我们的右边，有一台形似鳄鱼的运输机车。这是一台电力机车，它是双向运输的。这种电力机车目前仍然在大冶铁矿运作。当年在东露天采坑里，它就像一条链子一样，穿梭于采坑当中，非常好看。

Walking through the path, we see the crocodile-shaped transport locomotive on our right which is an electric one. It is used to transport ores in two directions. This type of electric locomotive is still working in Daye Iron Mine. In the past, it came and went in the mining pit which looked like a chain in the East Open Mining Pit.

有必要给大家特别介绍的是我们左手边的这台设备，它的名字叫“爬犁机”。它是从苏联进口的，它有一个绰号叫“清道夫”。为什么呢？这与它的功能有关，这个“爬犁机”专门用来清理铁路上运输时散落的矿石。

它把大块的矿石清理干净以后，为电力机车的顺利运行打下坚实的基础。

Now I will introduce the equipment on our left whose name is sledge machine. It is imported from Soviet Union whose nickname is "street sweeper" which relates to its function. It is used to clean up the ores on the railway whose job is laying a solid foundation for the safe operation of electric locomotive.

黄石国家矿山公园工业博览园里有一些非常有代表性的工业雕塑。这些雕塑都是大冶铁矿人运用自己的智慧，并且通过自己的双手制作完成的。右手边这组用汽油桶、链条、皮带运输机的托辊支架做成的雕塑，它的名字叫“掠夺”。

Some representative industrial sculptures are exhibited in the Industrial Expo Park which are manufactured by the workers of Daye Iron Mine who make full use of their wisdom and their hands. This group of sculptures on the right is called "plunder" which is made of petrol barrels, chains, and roller support of belt conveyor.

日本曾经对中华民族犯下了滔天罪行，对中国进行了长达十余年的侵略活动。1938 至 1945 年期间，日本在大冶铁矿进行掠采，掠走的矿石高达 500 多万吨。这段屈辱的历史，时刻激励着中华民族一定要自强不息，一定要奋发图强。

The Japanese have committed great crimes against the Chinese nation. They have carried out over 10 years of aggression against China. From 1938 to 1945, the Japanese conducted predatory mining in Daye Iron Mine. More than five million tons of ores were shipped to Japan. The history of humiliation always inspires the Chinese nation to strive to become stronger and stronger.

中华人民共和国成立之后，毛主席就提出一手抓工业，一手抓农业。这个口号提出以后，全国就开始了大兴工业这条道路。当时在大冶铁矿这个东露天采场就形成了灯火通明、热火朝天的生产场景，矿山人发挥守山吃、伴山眠的精神，进行夜以继日的开采作业，为新中国的钢铁工业打下坚实的基础。

After the founding of People's Republic of China, Chairman Mao called on the whole nation to attach importance to both industry and agriculture. Then the whole country began to focus on industrial development. At that time, workers of Daye Iron Mine conducted ore mining day and night. A vigorous production scene appeared in the East Open Mining Pit. This laid a solid foundation for Chinese steel industry.

游客朋友们现在请看我右手边的这个庞然大物，它可不是小孩子在动画片里看到的变形金刚，它的名字叫电铲，是一种大型的铲运机。它是通过柴油和电力进行工作的，它前面的铲斗一次能装四吨的矿石，是非常厉害的大型采掘设备。

Now please look at the big equipment on our right. It is not the transformer in cartoons. Its name is electric shovel which is driven by diesel and electricity. A shovel can load four tons of ores. It is a large and powerful mining equipment.

东露天采坑边坡通过转孔、填充炸药、放炮之后，会有一些大块的矿石散落下来。通过这样的电铲，把这些经过改炮后的矿石，一铲一铲地运送到刚才看到的这些装载设备上，然后再通过这些形似鳄鱼的设备将矿石再运送到堆矿场，最后在选矿车间进行破碎工艺处理，将大块矿石改成小块矿石，从而变成一种矿泥。

The workers drill holes, fill explosives and blast on the side slope of the East Open Mining Pit. Then some large pieces of ores fall down. The electric shovel transports the ores to the loading equipment, through which the ores are carried onto the crocodile-shaped equipment and transported to the field of ores. Then they are taken to the mineral processing workshop where the large pieces of ores are crushed into small ones. At last, they are made into a kind of sludge.

现在继续参观，在我的左手边，游客朋友可以看到两台黄色设备，其中右手边的这台设备，它的名字叫“伟步客矿用自卸汽车”，俗称 50B，为什么这样称呼它呢？因为这台机车的载重量达 50 吨。尤其值得一提的是它的轮胎，现场的朋友一定想去和它比试一下，看看这轮胎到底有多高？我可以告诉大家，姚明比它高一点，除了姚明以外，估计没有多少人比它高。这个轮胎的直径达两米，我相信一般人的身高是不能跟它相比的。

Now let's go forward. There are two yellow devices on my left. The device on the right is Weibuke Auto-unloading Mining Vehicle which is commonly known as 50B. The reason for its name is that the load capacity of this locomotive is 50 tons whose tires are worth mentioning. You may wonder how tall they are. Yao Ming is a little taller than it. Only a few people may have a height of that. The diameter of the tire is two meters. The average person's height cannot compare with it.

还有装在它车斗里的白色圆柱体，与刚才我带领大家穿过的那条小路所用的岩芯是同一种，都是我们进行深部勘探凿出来的岩芯。在我右手边的这台设备我们称它为日式装载机。

The white cylinder is installed in the equipment which is the same as the cores of the path we just go through. They are taken out through deep drilling. The device on the right is called Japanese loader.

这两台设备工作的时候，是一起配合作业的。在采场，当年有 50B 出现的地方，在它的不远处就一定会有这种装载机。

They cooperate with each other and form a very close partnership. When the two devices are working together, they also cooperate with each other. Where there is a 50B, there is a loader nearby.

这种装载机和电铲所起到的作用是一样的，它把经过放炮、改炮后的矿石全部运送到伟步客矿用自卸车里，然后这个伟步客自卸车托运着这些矿石，沿着这个环线路行驶，最终把它所装载的这些矿石运送到黑色双向的电机车上，再运送到选矿车间去。这个 50B 是从美国进口的。

The loader's role is the same as that of the electric shovel. After ores are blasted, they are delivered to Weibuke Auto-unloading Mining Vehicle. Then the vehicle runs on the ring road to transport the ores to the black two-way electric locomotive. At last the ores are sent to the mineral processing workshop. The device 50B is imported from the USA.

一会儿我们要参观的这个露天采坑，已经经过了50多年的大规模机械化开采。在这里服役的设备一共有三代。刚才我介绍的这台50B型装载机车是第三代。现在游客朋友们顺着我手指的前方，可以看到一台非常旧的绿色的机车，而在它的右前方还有一台黄色的机车，这两台机车是矿山最早使用的运输装载机车，属于第一代。在工业博览园里还有第二代运输装载机车，它们就是位于我们左手边的黄色机车和绿色机车。

Later, we continue to visit an open mining pit which has a history of more than 50 years of large scale mechanized mining. There are three generations of equipment in the mining pit. The loader 50B belongs to the third generation. Now you can see an old green locomotive ahead of us. On its right, there is another yellow one. These two locomotives are the earliest loading locomotives in the mine which belong to the first generation. In the Industrial Expo Park, there are also loading locomotives of the second generation which are the yellow and green ones on our left.

我介绍的这些运输设备，不知道游客朋友们发现了没有，随着时代的变迁，矿山所使用的这些设备也是越来越先进。在工业博览园里，这些设备虽然不复往日的喧嚣，默默地停放在这里，但是一台台机车就像一首首赞歌，谱写着不同时代的风采，呈现给大家的是昔日的辉煌。

It is a fact that the mining equipment becomes more and more advanced with the changing time. In the Industrial Expo Park, all the equipment stays there silently. Each locomotive is a symbol of its time. They display the styles of different times and present their glory of the past.

这里我给大家介绍一下大冶铁矿及铁山采矿的历史。最早古人在这里采矿可以追溯到公元 226 年，距今已有 1790 余年的历史。而有历史记载的采用比较先进的机械对铁山进行钻探开采，就不得不提到张之洞！

Now I will introduce the mining history of Daye Iron Mine and Tieshan. The earliest time of mining dated back to 226 which has a history of about 1790 years. There are historical records of drilling and mining with advanced machines in Tieshan. Zhang Zhidong is an important figure in this aspect.

张之洞当时聘请英国著名的工匠师郭师敦来铁山进行勘探，郭师敦来到铁山后，发现象鼻山一带有品位非常高的矿石显露于地表。张之洞当时是中国洋务运动的代表，他当时就从国外进口了一些大型的机械化设备，从此开始了机械化的开采活动。郭师敦可以说是矿山采用先进设备探矿的第一人，在他之后我们就要提到 429 地质队。

At that time, Zhang Zhidong invited Guo Shidun, a famous British craftsman, to carry out exploration in Tieshan. When Guo came here, he found some high-grade ores were exposed on the surface in the area of Xiangbishan. Zhang Zhidong was one of the representatives of the Westernization Movement of China. He imported some large scale mechanized equipment from abroad. Since then, mechanized mining activities began in the mine. Guo is said to be the first to conduct exploration with advanced equipment. Next the Geological Team 429 should be mentioned.

一会儿我们将去的地方就是芯动乐园，来到芯动乐园我就给大家介绍 429 地质队勘探的历史。走到芯动乐园的入口，在我们身后，游客朋友可以看到一个半圆形的岩石造型景观，这都是由深部勘探凿出来的岩芯制作的。这些岩芯粗细有不同，颜色有深浅，为什么会呈现这种状态呢？

This is the Core Amusement Park. When we come here, I will talk about the exploration history of the Geological Team 429. Please follow me to the entrance of the Park. You can see a semicircular rock modeling landscape behind us which is made of the cores drilled by deep exploration. The cores are in different sizes and different colors. What is the reason for their appearance?

这里我给大家介绍一些深部探矿的知识，那么大冶铁矿深部探矿是如何操作的呢？在大冶铁矿的矿山里，钻探队员们通过地表的颜色初步判断有矿石，于是就安装一台钻机，当钻机工作时，钻孔钻到地下的岩层，再将岩层中的岩石取出来，取出来的就是岩芯。

Here, I will introduce some knowledge about deep exploration. How deep exploration is conducted in Daye Iron Mine? In the Mine, the drilling team makes a preliminary judgment of ore according to the colors of the surface. Then they install a drilling rig. When the rig is drilling into the underground rock strata, some rocks are taken out. These rocks are the cores.

大家看到每一块岩芯都标有一些数据，这些数据就是取出这块岩芯钻杆钻的次数以及所钻到地下的深度。不同的深度取出来的岩芯都是不同的，通过分析岩芯的颜色和成分，可以了解地下有没有矿物。我们看到的一些白色的岩芯就是大理岩，当钻机继续往下钻，陆续钻出的岩芯，颜色和成分就会发生变化，经过化验，就可以了解是否含有矿物。

As you see, there are some data labeled on each core. These data are about the drilling time and drilling depth. Cores are different as they are taken from different depth. By analyzing the color and composition of the cores, we know whether there are minerals underground. Those white cores are marbles. When the drilling rig continues to drill, more cores are taken out. Their colors and composition change too. After test, whether there are minerals can be determined.

然后钻机还会接着往下钻，这时取出来的岩芯，颜色变成黑色或者褐色，这就是含矿的岩芯了。此时钻机还会继续钻，直到钻探取出来的岩芯是岩石时，就可以了解这一段矿脉的厚度是多少。知道了矿脉的厚度，那么整个矿脉的面积有多大呢？于是钻探队员会在周围的不同地界进行多次钻探，根据钻探取出来的岩芯做数据分析，这样矿脉的面积就一目了然。这就是深部勘探的整个过程。

Then, the rig drills deeper. The color of the cores becomes black or brown. These are the cores containing minerals. At this moment, the rig will continue to drill till the cores are rocks. Then the thickness of the vein is found out. But there is another question. What is the area of the vein? In order to find the answer, the drilling team drill many times at different places. They conduct data analysis based on the cores. Therefore, the area of the vein becomes clear. That is the whole process of deep exploration.

现在我们一起往前走。中华人民共和国成立之后，在大冶铁矿成立了中国第一支地质勘探队——429 地质队。429 地质队在矿山破解了尖山无矿之谜。这个尖山无矿之谜，是指在大冶铁矿的矿床当中所含的一个隐藏的矿体，一直以来未被人们发现。直至 429 地质队成立之后，在矿山勘探探得尖山矿石储量丰富，至少可以开采五十年。这一发现在当时曾经轰动全国，报纸杂志争相报道此事。

Now please follow me ahead. After the founding of the People's Republic of China, the first geological prospecting team was founded in Daye Iron Mine which was Geological Team 429. They broke the mystery of the absence of ores in Jianshan which is a hidden ore body in the mineral deposits of Daye Iron Mine. But it has never been discovered. After the founding of Geological Team 429, they carried out exploration in Jianshan and found out that the ore reserves of Jianshan are rich enough to be drilled for at least 50 years. This news became sensational nationwide. Newspapers and magazines rushed to report it.

游客朋友们随我一起拾级而上，在我们的左手边，细心的游客会发现这里有一些用小岩芯制作的五线谱音乐墙。这上面是采用大冶铁矿所产的铜做成的音符，顺着这些音符的律动，我们仿佛看到当年地质队员们满怀着激情，忙碌在矿山的每一寸土地上，谱写着一曲曲动人的地质之歌！

Please follow me to upstairs. On our left, there is a music wall which is made of small cores. The musical notes are made of copper produced by Daye Iron Mine. The melodies of these notes remind us of the drilling team's passion. It seems that they are still busy with their work in the mine. At the same time, they are composing vigorous songs of geology.

我提醒游客朋友们，在观景的时候，要注意安全！请靠里面的路走，继续我们的地质之旅！芯动乐园给大家展示的是工人们利用自己的聪明才智，把这些岩芯制作成别致新颖的雕塑。现在我们来到的是芯动乐园的主景区，感兴趣的朋友们，可以在这里合影留念。

Be careful when appreciating the beautiful scenery. Please walk inside. Let's continue our geological journey. The Core Amusement Park displays how the workers make use of their wisdom to change the cores into novel sculptures. Now we come to the main scenic area of the Core Amusement Park. If you like, you can take photos here.

现在我给大家介绍古人是如何探矿的。古人的探矿方法大致有三种途径，第一种途径是通过传说故事找矿。根据一些先民的记载，判断哪里会有矿石。第二种途径是通过颜色的辨认找矿。刚才给大家介绍过，铁矿经过氧化后会呈现一种黑色，铜矿会呈现一种绿色，所以古人通过土壤颜色判断是否有矿，同时判断是一种什么样的矿石。

Now I will explain how ancient people prospect the ores. Generally, there are three methods to prospect. The first method is to follow the legends. That is to judge the location of the ores according to ancestors' records. The second method is to identify the colors of the ground. After oxidization, iron ores turn black and copper ores turn green. Therefore, according to the colors of the ground, the ancestors decide whether there are ores or not and what kind of ores there are.

第三种途径是通过植物找矿。在铁山有一种植物叫铜草花，这里矿石储量非常丰富，除了金、银、钴、硫等，还伴生铜矿，那么有铜矿的地方，地面就一定会有铜草花生长，因为铜草花在富含铜元素的土壤里才能存活。所以古人非常聪明，知道找到铜草花，就一定会找到铜矿。

The third method is to follow plants. In Tieshan, there is a plant called copper flower. This area is rich in ore reserves. Besides gold, silver, cobalt, and sulfur, there are also copper ores. Where there are copper ores, there are copper flowers. Copper flowers can only survive in the soil rich of copper elements. Ancestors are so wise that they know if they find copper flowers, they can discover copper ores.

这个芯韵广场形似八卦，八卦分别象征自然界的八种物质，即天、地、雷、风、水、火、山、泽，它们是万物衍生的物质基础。这个芯韵广场造型独特，非常值得游客朋友们一游。大家可以拍照留念！

The Xinyun Square looks like the Eight Trigrams which symbolize the eight substances in nature in Chinese philosophy. They are the sky, the earth, the thunder, the wind, the water, the fire, the mountain, and the river which are the material basis of everything in the world. The Square is in a unique shape which is worth visiting. You can take photos here.

五分钟后我们继续沿台阶而上，很多朋友到过黄石国家矿山公园，那么它最主要的亮点是什么呢？我们能看到什么跟别的地方不一样的吗？在这里，我可以给游客朋友们介绍一下，在黄石国家矿山公园，各位将看到一个“世界之最”和“两个亚洲之最”。“世界之最”指的就是世界第一高陡边坡的采坑，那游客朋友们就会问，这个世界第一高陡边坡在哪里呢？

We continue to step up. Many people have come to Huangshi National Mine Park. What is the most striking scene in the Park? What is unique here? Now let me introduce one "Top of the World" and two "Tops of Asia" in the Park. One "Top of the World" refers to the mining pit with the world's No. 1 high steep side slope. Then where is the world's No. 1 high steep side slope?

其实现在就可以告诉大家，我们恰好正在坑里走。这个采坑是经过了几代人的努力，花了五十年的时间，运用了一些大规模的现代化机械设备进行开采而形成的。相信游客朋友来这里之前对此已有一定的了解。这个采坑是一个阶梯状的采坑。

To tell the truth, we are just walking in the mining pit. It takes several generations 50 years to explore the mine with large scale modern mechanical equipment. Some of us may know a little about the step-like mining pit.

现在所游览的这个层面，就是世界第一高陡边坡中的一个掌子面，我们现在正从下面的边坡往上面边坡行走。现在我们已经在坑里了，这样一个阶梯状掌子面的每一个台阶的高度是十二米，宽度是三十米。我们可以来到栏杆边上，看一下这个东露天采坑的全貌。

Now we are walking in one of the tunnel faces of the world's No. 1 high steep side slope. We are walking from a lower side slope to a higher one. Now we are totally within the pit. Each step of such a step-like tunnel face is 12 meters high and 30 meters wide. If we come near to the railings, we can see the general view of the East Open Mining Pit.

这里游客朋友会发现一些牛粪，这对于矿山来说也是宝贝。为什么这样说呢？因为这里原来是采矿工业区，完全没有植被，矿山人整整花了二十年时间，在这里进行大规模的绿化复垦。通过这些年的努力，现在这里形成了亚洲最大的硬岩复垦基地，就是刚才给大家提到的矿山公园的第二大亮点。

We can see some cow dung here which is precious for the mine. Why do we say so? In the past, the mine is an industrial area. There is no vegetation because of mining. After 20 years of large scale afforestation and reclamation, the largest hard rock reclamation base of Asia comes into being which is the second spotlight of the mine park.

通过复垦这一环保举措，这里的生态环境大大改善，吸引了不少的小动物在这里栖息生活。正是因为这个复垦林，大冶铁矿曾经获得全国绿化先进单位。这在全国所有冶金行业矿山当中是首屈一指的。游客朋友们，现在我们来这里看看，这里有一些用岩芯做的竖琴雕塑，喜欢的朋友可以在这里拍照留念。

Through the environmental protection measures of reclamation, the ecological environment here has greatly improved. Many animals are attracted to inhabit here. Daye Iron Mine wins the honor of the national advanced afforestation unit because of the reclamation forest which is second to none among all the mines in metallurgical and mining industry. Now let's come here to have a look. There are some harp sculptures made of cores. You can take photos here if you like.

一会儿我们即将前往当年 429 地质队勘探的一个遗址，也是毛泽东主席来到大冶铁矿视察的一个掌子面。我们继续往前走，这里有一个地球模型，如果我们把地球解剖成四个等分，就会看到地球分地壳、地核、地幔三部分，越往里面地心温度越高，越往里面硬度越密。

Next we will go to visit a mining site left by Geological Team 429 which is also the tunnel face inspected by Chairman Mao when he came to Daye Iron Mine. Let's go forward. Here is an earth model. If we divide the earth in a quarter way, we can see the crust, the core, and the mantle. The more you go inside, the higher the temperature is and the denser the hardness is.

现在我们看到的这个钻机，就是 429 地质队在这里留下来的一个遗迹，这个绝对是真品。它是如何工作的呢？通过悬挂在上方的钻头，一个套着一个，就像我们的音乐指挥棒一样伸缩自如，在钻探的时候，加水来润滑，以降低温度，钻探的探头是合金的，密度比一般的石头要大，所以工作的时候就不会发生磨损的现象。因为中间是空心的，所以可以直接把地下的岩石，也就是我们之前看到的岩芯，取出来。

This drilling rig is the real original one left by Geological Team 429. How does it work? The bits are hung on the top of the rig one by one which are flexible like a music baton. In the process of drilling, water is added to lubricate the machine and to bring down the temperature. As the bits are made of alloy, the density is higher than the ordinary stones. Therefore, they are resistant to abrasion. The bits are hollow in the middle, so rocks can be taken out directly from underground which are the cores we saw just now.

游客朋友们，我们现在所参观的地方，也曾经是一代伟人毛泽东主席视察大冶铁矿时所停留的一个掌子面。我们可以站在这边栏杆旁的平台，驻足观望矿山，细细品味当年毛泽东主席视察大冶铁矿时的喜悦心情。这里是一个很好的观测点，你在这里可以看到芯韵广场，还可以看到东露天采场坑底的情况。

This tunnel face is where Chairman Mao visited when he inspected Daye Iron Mine. Let's stand on this platform beside the railings. We can appreciate the scene of the whole mine and share the joy and happiness as Chairman Mao did. This is a good observation spot where you can see both the Xinyun Square and the East Open Mining Pit.

当年毛主席视察大冶铁矿时，我们所站的这一个掌子面下面还是深埋在地下的矿体，还没有被开采出来。当时这里还是山体，还没有形成一层一层的边坡状。一些大型的开采设备经过一层一层的剥离式作业，从上往下开采。那么现在我们游客朋友们再看，从 1958 年到现在几十年过去了，呈现在我们眼前的就是这样一个人类奇迹。

When Chairman Mao inspected Daye Iron Mine, the ore body was deeply buried below the present tunnel face which was not explored yet.

Here was still mountain instead of layers of side slope. The large scale mining equipment carried out stripping operation layer by layer, by which the exploration advanced from top to bottom. Since 1958, a few decades have passed. Now a miracle of human beings is present in front of us.

大家都听说过“愚公移山”这个典故，那么现在游客朋友们看到的就是矿山版的“愚公移山”。矿山人发扬“守山吃、伴山眠”的精神，用了五十多年的时间，把这一奇迹展示在世人面前。

In China, there is a famous allusion about Yugong who managed to remove the mountains by hand. What we see now is a similar version as the allusion. The miners spent fifty years removing the mountains of the mine, which has been a miracle in the world.

我们顺着台阶往上走，就会看到这里有一个木式建筑。这个木式建筑就是黄石国家矿山公园的游客参与的项目——“天坑飞索”。这个“天坑飞索”目前是华中地区最长的飞索，全长446米，最大落差38米。在国家旅游建设项目中有明文规定，全国的飞索不得超过500米，所以这个飞索被称为华中地区最长的飞索。

Walking along the steps, we will see a wooden building which is the pit ropeway. This is the tourist participating project in Huangshi National Mine Park. It is the longest ropeway in central China which is 446 meters long and whose maximum drop is 38 meters. In the national tourism construction projects, it is stipulated that the length of ropeway cannot exceed 500 meters. Therefore, this is the longest one in central China.

刚才我介绍了许多矿冶文化知识，现在游客朋友们可以亲身体验一下“天坑飞索”的惊险刺激。在畅游天坑之旅中，我相信游客朋友们一定会流连忘返。游客朋友们现在可以看到铁山的全景，铁山是全国面积最小的行政区，人口7万，也是全国唯一的一个因矿建区的地方。站在这里可以看到铁山目前最高的楼盘，二十六层商用住宅楼。

Just now I have introduced some knowledge about mining and

metallurgical culture. Now you can experience the thrill of the pit ropeway. On the ropeway you can see the panorama of Tieshan which is the smallest administrative region in China. It has a population of 70,000 and is the only administrative region constructed on the basis of the mine. If we stand here, we can see the highest building of Tieshan which is a 26-storey commercial residential building.

如果不是因为东露天采坑闭坑了，游客朋友们是不可能看到这座高楼的。因为在东露天采坑闭坑之前，这里经常会放大炮，放一次炮就相当于发生了一次 3.7 级的地震，所以铁山没有高楼就是这个原因。后来随着生产的逐步转型，铁山才出现了一些高高低低的住宅楼。

If the East Open Mining Pit is not closed, we cannot see the tall building. Before that, blasting was often carried out. One blasting is equivalent to a 3.7 magnitude earthquake, so there isn't tall building at that time. Later, after the gradual transformation of production, high residential buildings appear in Tieshan.

说着说着，我们就来到了“天坑飞索”。这里有游客须知，有心脏病和高血压的朋友一定要仔细阅读，建议大家根据自己的体重来选择是否参与。

Now we come to the pit ropeway. These are the instructions for visitors. If you have heart disease or high blood pressure, you must read it carefully. You'd better choose to participate in the activities of the pit ropeway based on your own weight.

游客朋友们，我将继续带领大家到达这座山的山顶。这里有一个气象观测点，它有一个测风速的风速标、一个测风向的风向标、一个温度计，一个量雨桶。为什么在这里建气象观测点呢？因为当时在矿山组织生产，需要掌握一些天气数据，以避免一些安全事故的发生，从而保证矿山开采井然有序地进行。

This is the top of the mountain. Here is a meteorological observation spot which includes a wind speed indicator, a wind direction indicator, a thermometer and a rain indicating bucket. Why is the meteorological observation spot built here? At that time, when the mine production was organized, the weather information should be obtained. Then safety accidents may be avoided and orderly exploration may be ensured.

游客朋友可以看到这里有一个圆筒状的不锈钢物体，这就是量雨桶。每到下雨的时候，这里就会储存一些雨水。通过对储存的雨水做一个数据分析，了解雨季的降雨量，那么雨季的生产就可以安全进行了。在量雨桶的旁边，有一个小箱子，这个就是温度箱，用来测量地表温度。现在我们可以看到风向标和风速标在随风摆动，似乎在欢迎远道而来的朋友！

This is a cylindrical stainless steel bucket which is used to measure the amount of rain. Every time when it rains, water will be stored in the bucket. The amount of rainfall in the rainy season is calculated through the data analysis of the stored rain. Then the safety of the mine production in the rainy season is ensured. Beside the rain indicating bucket, there is a small box which is the temperature box. It is used to measure the surface temperature. The wind speed indicator and the wind direction indicator are swinging in the wind which seem to welcome us.

参观完气象观测点，我们就沿着这条蜿蜒的小路，前往矿山公园的另外一个“亚洲第一”参观——亚洲第一硬岩复垦林。这个亚洲第一硬岩复垦林最初的时候，都是一些开采之后遗留下来的废石。后来，日积月累形成了一个废石堆场，侵占了大量的绿地，也污染了矿山的环境。

After the visit of meteorological observation spot, let’s go along the winding path to visit another “top of Asia” which is Asia’s largest hard rock reclamation forest. In the past, this was a place full of waste rocks left by mine exploration. Gradually a waste rock field was formed. A lot of green space was occupied. And the environment of the mine was also polluted.

于是矿山人就对废石堆场进行绿化复垦，也就是人工运土堆砌在这片废石当中，使它慢慢形成土壤植被，再种植槐树。经过二十年时间和几代矿山人的努力，昔日的废石堆场变成了绿树成荫的槐树林。游客朋友们可曾领略过槐花的妩媚和奇香呢？

Therefore, the miners began to carry out afforestation and reclamation in the waste rock field. Soil was transported and piled up in the field. Gradually, vegetation grew in the soil. Then locust trees were planted. Several generations of miners have made great effort to improve the environment. After twenty years, the waste rock field becomes a forest of locust trees. Have you enjoyed the charm and fragrance of sophora japonica?

我们长久地在城市青灰色的天空中生活，何不期盼着能回归自然，在槐林中漫步，呼吸一下自然的空气，慰藉一下自己蒙满尘嚣的心灵？置身于槐林之中，眼前是一望无际的绿色槐林，春分时节，蜂飞蝶舞，令人陶醉。槐树枝头垂满盛开的槐花，一团团，一簇簇，如同美女的笑靥，纯美中洋溢着一种纯真的韵味，采一枝嗅一下，槐香四溢，芬芳沁人心脾，让人陶醉。相信到那时游客一定会有意想不到的收获！

We live under the grey sky of the city for a long time, so we are eager to return to nature. If we can walk in the forest of locust trees and breathe the fresh air, we will feel relieved and comfortable. In spring, there are bees and butterflies in the forest of locust trees which are in full blossom. The pure flavor is filled with pure beauty. Pick a flower of the locust tree and have a smell, through which the trip to the forest of locust trees really deserves. There are unexpected results waiting for us.

现在我们来到了天坑观景平台，站在这里我们可以看到东露天采坑的坑底。这个观景平台也是欣赏天坑的一个最佳观赏点。从空中俯视东露天采坑的横截面，它的外形形似一个宝葫芦，我们现在所处的这个地方，就是宝葫芦的底部。天坑观景平台距离最大的边坡角最近，最大的边坡角达到 60 度，但依然稳固，非常难得。

Now we get to the viewing platform of the pit where we can see the bottom of the East Open Mining Pit. This platform is also the best observation spot of the pit. Looking down from the sky, the East Open Mining Pit looks like a gourd. Now we are at the bottom of the gourd. The viewing platform is close to the largest side slope whose angle is 60°, but it is still stable.

东露天采坑为什么称为世界第一呢？其实世界第一并不是指它的面积，因为面积最大的人工采坑在美国的明尼苏达州，它的面积比这个采坑大三倍，但东露天采坑为什么能称世界第一呢？这个采坑深度达到 444 米，它最陡的地方达到 60 度，也就是最大的边坡角达到 60 度，但它依然巍然矗立。

Why is the East Open Mining Pit the No. 1 in the world? It does not refer to its area. The mining pit covering the largest area in the Minnesota State in the USA is three times as large as this one. The East Open Mining Pit is called the No. 1 in the world because its depth is 444 meters, and the steepest place reaches 60°. That is to say, the largest slope angle is 60°. But it still stands there firmly.

矿山人对这座山体实施挂网支护、喷浆支护、挂杆支护等保护措施，才保存了现在较为完好的、稳固的山体。我们现在所看到的这个采坑，岩石疏松的地方采用先挂网、再喷浆的方式进行支护，以保持坡面的稳固，所以这里称得上是世界第一高陡边坡，这个采坑就称得上亚洲第一了。

The miners make use of suspended net support, gunite support and suspended rod support to protect the mountain. So it keeps relatively sound and stable until now. In the loose place, the suspended net support is adopted first. Then the gunite support is followed. These measures ensure the stability of the side slope. So the high steep side slope is No. 1 in the world. And the mining pit is No. 1 in Asia.

这边大家可以看到水泥的痕迹，这里就是经过喷浆支护作业的一个层面。边坡支护高处和低处不同，尤其是越到底部支护会越密集。在这个采坑当中，我们可以看到远处有一个滑体，这就是著名的 F9 滑体。这个名字是根据这座采坑的坐标图来命名的，它所处的位置就是 F9，因此而得名。

We can see the place with cement here which is the layer of gunite support. The slope support on the high level is different from the low level. The deeper it goes to the bottom, the denser is the support. In this mining pit, we can see a landslide in the distance which is the famous landslide F9. It is named according to the coordinate figure of the mining pit.

刚才介绍了几种常用的矿山支护方式，这些支护方式曾经获得国家科技进步一等奖，那为什么还会出现滑坡呢？这是因为整个露天采坑原来是由三座山体组成的，分别是象鼻山、狮子山、尖山三座山体。我们看到的这个滑坡，正好就是这两座山体接缝的地方，所以容易垮塌。

We have introduced several supporting methods of the mine. These methods once won the first prize of National Science and Technology Progress Award. Why is there still landslide? Originally, the East Open Mining Pit consists of 3 mountains which are Xiangbishan, Shizishan and Jianshan. The landslide is the joint place between two mountains, so it is easy to fall down.

现在我们走到栏杆边上可以看到坑底，有游客朋友会问，坑底为什么不会积水？其实在这里每四层就会有一个截洪沟，现在游客朋友顺着我手指的地方就可以看到截洪沟，截洪沟底部还建立了泵站，进行抽水作业。在东露天采坑有文字记载的积水有三次，每一次积水坑底都会形成一个小潭。最近的一次积水就是 1998 年的那次大洪水，当时把这个坑底都淹没了。

Now let's go to the railings to see the bottom of the mining pit. Maybe you will ask me a question why there isn't water at the bottom?

Actually there is a flood ditch every four layers and a pump station at the bottom which is used to pump the water of the ditch. It is recorded that there are three times of water accumulation in the East Open Mining Pit, at the bottom of which there is a small pond. The nearest time of water accumulation is the flood of 1998 when the bottom of the pit was flooded.

我们现在看到的采坑已经闭坑了，但有游客朋友会问，为什么还有一些设备在这里运作呢？这是因为 2003 年以前，这里仍然有大规模的机械化露天开采，而在这之后，随着采坑的矿石储量减少，分布也不是很集中，如果再进行大规模的机械化开采，它的工业成本会很高，所以现在进行的都是小规模的人工开采。

Just now, I told you that the mining pit is closed. Why is the equipment still operating here? Before 2003, large scale mechanized surface mining was carried out here. Since then, the ore reserves reduced and their distribution was not concentrated. If large scale mechanized surface mining is still adopted, the industrial cost will be high. So only small scale artificial mining is carried on.

想继续了解采坑的其他情况，请大家跟随我沿着旅游步道前往观礼台参观。我们经常说“走路不观景，观景不走路”，这句话是提醒游客朋友们注意安全。沿途我们会看到一些用废旧的材料做成的围栏，接下来我们还将经过一座利用废弃旧枕木搭建的悬空小桥。

If you want to know more about the pit, please follow me along the tourist trails to the viewing platform. Be careful while walking and sightseeing. Along the way we will see the fence made of waste materials. After a while, we will pass a small dangling bridge which is built by abandoned old wood sleeper.

我们现在就到了这座小桥，穿过小桥，沿着蜿蜒的小路，在我们的左手边，可以看到一些研究地质的朋友比较感兴趣的岩层。这里有一部分岩石比较特别，左手边呈黄红色，右手边呈黑褐色，而且它们的分界线特别明显。黄红色岩石这一边比较阳刚，黑褐色岩石这一边比较阴柔。如果我们把一边比做女人的话，另一边就像男人了。

Now we are on the small bridge. Cross the bridge and walk along the winding path. On our left, we can see the rock strata. If you are studying geology, you will be interested in it. Some of the rocks are very special. The rocks on the left side are yellow red, and those on the right side are dark brown. The dividing line is easily recognized. The yellow red rocks seem quite masculine and the dark brown ones seem relatively feminine. If we compare one side to a woman, the other side is like a man.

为什么岩石会出现红色呢？地质学者解释说，经过泥土的包裹，时间长了以后，岩石表层有气孔，泥土附着在上面，久而久之就形成了这种颜色。而这些岩石出现层层叠叠的姿态，就是因为在大自然的地壳运动和挤压后，岩石发生了氧化作用而形成黑色，这种黑色的岩石就是矿石。所以说，岩石不一定是矿石，矿石一定是岩石。

Why are the rocks red? Geologists tell us the answer. Because the rocks are wrapped by soil for a long time, a lot of air holes appear on their surface. Then the rocks change into the present color. Squeezed by the crustal movement of nature, oxidation occurs, which leads to the formation of the black rocks which are also called ores. So rocks are not necessarily ores, while ores must be rocks.

对地质感兴趣的朋友可以在这里拍照留念。接下来我们继续往前走，我给大家介绍一种凿岩的设备——牙轮钻。我们现在就可以看到当年采坑运作的第一道工序——牙轮钻布孔。这个台阶一层是十二米，为什么会是十二米呢？这是因为牙轮钻的钻头最长是十二米，所以就形成十二米一级的台阶。当年使用牙轮钻布孔工作的时候，牙轮钻从每个平面的这一头排到另一头。

If you are interested in geology, you can take photos here. Now, let's go ahead. I will introduce a kind of drilling equipment which is rock drill. Now we can see the first step of mining operation which is drilling holes by the rock drill. Each layer of the steps is 12 meters. The reason why it is designed like that depends on the length of the drill bit. Because its maximum length is 12 meters, the length of the step can't exceed that. When the rock drills work in the mining pit, they go from one end to the other of the tunnel face.

接着进行的第二道工序是放炸药。爆破工将炸药填充到钻孔里，经过严密的核算后，每天下午四点钟以后，开始放炮，这就是放排炮。所以今天游客朋友们可以看到一排排的钻孔，这就是当年放排炮留下的痕迹。随着东露天采坑闭坑，牙轮钻也“下岗”了。但发展工业旅游时，牙轮钻又派上了用场，成为主碑的重要组成部分，这相当于让它重见天日，重新为矿山做贡献！

The second step of mining operation is to fill the explosives. The blasting workers fill the holes with explosives. After strict calculation, the workers begin to blast after 4 p. m. every day. There are rows of holes left here, which is the mark of blasting. As the mining pit is closed, the rock drill is also laid off. When we develop industrial tourism, the rock drill becomes useful again. It is an important part of the main stele which comes to our sight and contributes to the mine again.

现在我们看到这里有一根铁管，这是一根从气象站上部延伸到坑底的管道。有没有朋友知道这根管道是起什么作用的呢？这是一根回填管道，现在随着矿山的资源逐步减少，矿山的开采主要以地下开采为主。讲到这里大家都会忧虑了，长期这样开采，地下的矿石终有一日会开采完，这样地下不就是空的了吗？不会发生地陷吗？

Here is an iron pipe which extends from the top of the weather station to the bottom of the pit. What is the function of this pipe? This is a backfill pipeline. As the resources of the mine gradually reduce, underground mining is mainly adopted in the mine. If the mine is explored over a long time, the ores underground may be exhausted one day. Is the underground empty then? Will the ground fall down?

其实，游客朋友们不必担心，地下开采的矿石输送到“武钢”之后会剩下一些废石，将这些废石运送到充填站，经过大型的碾碎机碾碎之后，加入混凝土搅拌，然后通过管道输送到地下开采作业区进行回填。这样既解决了地陷的隐患，同时也将废石重新利用了，所以我们刚刚看到的这根铁管就是回填管道。这边的山体中，其实有许多这样的回填管道。

Actually, what we are worried about will not happen. The ores mined underground are transported to Wuhan Iron and Steel Plant. The waste rocks left are sent to the filling station, smashed by a large crusher and mixed with concrete, and then they are sent back to the underground to backfill the mining area through the pipeline, which prevents the ground from falling down. And the waste rocks are also reused. So this iron pipe is just the backfill pipeline. Along the side of the mountain, there are many backfill pipelines.

请游客朋友们继续随我沿着旅游步道往前走。我刚才站在“宝葫芦”的底部，给大家介绍了天坑的支护，现在我们所走到的位置在“宝葫芦”的腰部。大冶铁矿矿物质丰富，岩石种类也非常多，经过地质运动、海水和陆地的变迁，这里形成了丰富的矿床。接下来我将带领大家去参观一个“奇迹”。

Please follow me along the tourist trails. Just now I introduced the support of the pit at the bottom of the “gourd.” Now we are in the waist of the “gourd.” Daye Iron Mine is rich in minerals and there are varieties of rocks. Because of the geological movement and the change of sea and land, a rich ore deposit comes into being. Next I will show you a “miracle.”

接下来我将要给大家隆重介绍一幅天然的崖画。这幅天然的崖画，可以说是大自然鬼斧神工的点睛之笔，它完全把东露天采场的现状给展示出来了。崖画整个呈现出来的外形也是一个“宝葫芦”形状，而且崖画的上半部，也就是宝葫芦的底部，正好与天坑“宝葫芦”的底部遥相呼应。天坑“宝葫芦”的出口处比较狭长，游客朋友们可以顺着我手指的方向看到天坑“宝葫芦”的出口。看完了实物，再看崖画，是否感受到了两者之间的异曲同工之妙呢？

Next I will introduce a natural cliff painting which is a real magic of nature. It fully represents the appearance of the East Open Mining Pit. The shape of the cliff painting is also like a “gourd.” The upper part of the painting is the bottom of the gourd which echoes the bottom of the mining pit. The exit of the mining pit is long and narrow. If you compare the mining pit with the cliff painting, don't you think they have a lot in common?

当然了，很多东西都是三分想，七分像。崖画中有很多形似古罗马剧场的阶梯状的东西，最为相似的就是崖画中间不同的岩石构成“天坑的底部”。发现这幅崖画的时间是 2005 年，当时矿山公园刚刚开始筹建。一个偶然的机会，人们在观礼台的尽头发现了这幅崖画。

If you make full use of your imagination, you will find the cliff painting and the mining pit are similar in many aspects. The most similar part is the “bottom of the pit” which consists of different kinds of rocks. It looks much like the staircase of ancient Roman Theater. The cliff painting was found in 2005 when the Mine Park just started to build. It is found by accident because it is at the end of the viewing platform.

最早的时候，这里有一堵矮墙，是严禁游客往下和往前走的。但就在不经意间，人们发现了这幅崖画。这幅崖画的发现更加坚定了我们建造矿山公园的信心和决心。仿佛冥冥之中，老天爷在指引着我们观崖画，看天坑。这不就是最好的导游图吗？

In the past, there was a short wall. The tourists were prohibited to go further. But the cliff painting is still found unexpectedly, which confirms our confidence and determination to build the Mine Park and promote the mine culture. It seems that the mining pit is leading us to appreciate the cliff painting. It is the best tour guide map, isn't it?

黄石国家矿山公园是首批申报的28家矿山公园中第一家开园的矿山公园，也是目前接待游客量最多的矿山公园。黄石国家矿山公园的建设经验在国土资源部被积极推广。我们继续往前走，来到观礼台最佳观赏位置。

Huangshi National Mine Park is the first to be opened among the first-approved 28 ones which has received more tourists than any other mine parks. Its experience has been promoted by the Ministry of Land and Resources. Please go ahead. We will get to the best viewing position of the viewing platform.

现在沿着时光的脉络给大家介绍天坑。最早的时候，吴大帝孙权建都在鄂州，成为吴都。为了建造自己强大的军事王国，他四处寻找制造兵器的材料。而铁山离鄂州不远，于是他就根据一些传说以及一些记载在铁山找到了制作兵器的材料，即矿石。于是他就开始在此大兴炉冶，铸造兵器，这里后来还出土了古代的炉渣。

Now I will introduce the mining pit along with the time passage. In the earliest time, Emperor Sun Quan founded the capital of Wu in Ezhou. To build up his strong military kingdom, he looked for materials to make weapons. According to the legends and historical records, he learnt that he could find the materials in Tieshan. As Tieshan was not far away from Ezhou, he started large-scaled furnace-metallurgy and cast weapons here. That's why the ancient slag is later unearthed.

说到最早的机械化开采就要提到张之洞了，当时清政府兴起洋务运动，慈禧亲批他为洋务大臣。他聘请了英国的工匠师郭师敦，探明大冶铁矿蕴藏着丰富的矿藏。他是第一个用机械化设备到这里进行开采的人。他当时建造了华中第一条铁路，利用铁路运输将矿石运送到黄石石灰窑码头，再通过码头的船将矿石运送到汉阳铁厂，建造高炉进行冶炼。

When we talk about the earliest mechanized mining, we should mention Zhang Zhidong. At that time, the Qing government started the westernization movement. He was appointed as the Foreign Minister by Empress Cixi. He hired an English craftsman Guo Shidun who found out that there were rich mineral resources in Daye Iron Mine. Zhang is the first to carry out mechanized mining here. What's more, he built the first railway in central China. Along the railway, the ores were transported to Shihuiyao dock of Huangshi. Then they were shipped to Hanyang Iron Plant where the ores were smelted in furnaces.

因为进行实体企业运作，不久就发生资金的周转问题。于是他就和当时的“红顶商人”盛宣怀商议，最后由盛宣怀接办汉阳铁厂和大冶铁矿，并进行资源重组，将大冶铁矿、汉阳铁厂、萍乡煤矿三座厂矿合并，成立中国的第一家大型钢铁联合企业——汉冶萍公司。成立汉冶萍公司之后，大冶铁矿还经历了日本人的掠夺开采。

Because of the operation of business entities, the capital turnover problem soon appeared. Zhang discussed with Sheng Xuanhuai who was both a governor and a merchant. At last, Sheng took over Hanyang Iron Plant and Daye Iron Mine, and combined these two enterprises with Pingxiang Coal Mine to form China's first joint enterprise of iron and steel, Han-Ye-Ping Coal and Iron Co. Ltd.. After the foundation of the company, Daye Iron Mine was once plundered by Japanese.

中华人民共和国成立以后，1958 年“武钢”成立的时候，就把大冶铁矿作为“武钢”的原料供给基地。从此大冶铁矿的开采进度越来越快，直至 2003 年东露天采坑闭坑，并由此形成了现在我们看到的这个采坑。

After the foudation of the People's Republic of China, in 1958, Wuhan Iron and Steel Group Co. LTD. was set up. Daye Iron Mine was taken as its raw material supply base. Then the exploration of Daye Iron Mine increased quickly. In 2003, the East Open Mining Pit was closed.

Finally, the present mining pit took shape.

整个采坑东西长度为2400米，从对面的山体到我们现在所站的位置南北宽度距离为900米，上下垂直高度为444米，共有37级台阶，每一级台阶高12米，台阶平均宽20米左右，坑口的横截面积是108万平方米，相当于150万个标准足球场的面积。

The mining pit is 2,400 meters from the east side to the west side. The distance from the south side to the north side is 900 meters. The vertical height is 444 meters. There are 37 steps in the mining pit. Every 12 meters there is a step. Every step extends 20 meters wide. The cross-sectional area of the mining pit is 1.08 million square meters which is equal to 1.5 million standard football fields.

在矿山公园，天坑的一个掌子面宽度是20米。游客朋友们可以计算好宽度，如果有人能将石子扔出三个掌子面之外，那他的门票我们就当场退还给他，感兴趣的朋友可以试试！

A tunnel face of the mining pit is 20 meters wide. If you can throw a stone over three tunnel faces, we will return the money of the ticket to you. Who would like to have a try?

2003年之后，天坑矿石品位降低，储量逐年减少，矿石分布呈鸡窝状，不是很集中，如果再采用工业开采，投入的成本会很高。所以东露天采坑大面积的机械化开采全部结束。现在看到的一些在坑底运矿石的设备，其实是在进行挂帮矿的开采，也就是少量的零星开采了。过去这里是工业开采矿产资源，如今这里是旅游开发矿冶文化。

Since 2003, the mining pit has encountered a series of problems. The grade of ores is falling down, the ore reserves are decreasing, and the distribution of ores is not concentrated, just like a chicken nest. If mechanized mining is still adopted, the cost will be very high. So the large scale mechanized mining stopped. Now we see some equipment carrying the ores at the bottom of the mining pit. This is only small quantity of mining. In the past, in this area, mineral resources are explored to develop industry. Now mining and metallurgical culture is exploited to promote tourism.

游客朋友们，观礼台这边有一个科普长廊，全长 40 米，有十大板块，分四大部分介绍矿冶文化。黄石国家矿山公园是全国工业旅游示范点、全国 4A 级风景区、全国科普教育基地。这个矿冶文化长廊介绍了矿冶文化科普知识，游客朋友们可以更直观地了解这里的矿冶文化。

Please come to the viewing platform which is a popular science gallery. It is 40 meters long with 10 sections which is divided into four parts to introduce the mining and metallurgical culture. Huangshi National Mine Park is a national industrial tourism demonstration spot which is both a national 4A scenic area and a national popular science education base. The gallery provides the popular science knowledge of mining and metallurgical culture, which offers the tourists a direct understanding.

穿过这个长廊，我们即将来到天坑“宝葫芦”的上半部。相比较而言，我们刚才参观的天坑“宝葫芦”下半部要小一些，而且略显狭长。现在往左边参观，这里有一位“孔方兄”在等候大家呢！我听到有游客朋友说，这是五铢钱。这可说对了！这是矿山的工人利用一些废弃设备上的元素，制作的一个五铢钱的工件雕塑。

Walking through the gallery, we will get to the upper part of the mining pit. By comparison, the lower part of the pit is smaller, longer and narrower. On the left, there is a Kongfangxiong waiting for us. Some tourists know this is wuzhu money which is an artifact sculpture of the money. It is made by the miners with materials from the abandoned equipment.

五铢钱始铸于西汉武帝元狩五年（前 118 年），钱重五铢，上有“五铢”二篆字，故名五铢钱。通常是右“五”左“铢”。它的标准重量为 4 克，直径为 2.5 厘米，厚 0.12 厘米。它继承了秦半两钱的形制，确立了圆形方孔，内外有郭，并发展成为轻重大小适度的铜质钱币。自汉武帝元狩五年至西汉末年，币制不复改变。

Wuzhu money was first cast in 118 B. C. whose weight was wuzhu. Two Chinese characters "五铢（wuzhu）" were carved on it. So it was called wuzhu money. Normally the "五（wu）" was on the right and the "铢（zhu）" was on the left. Its standard weight was four grams, diameter was 2. 5 centimeters, and thickness was 0. 12 centimeters. It inherited the shape of half-liang money of the Qin Dynasty which was round externally and square internally. Slowly, it developed into a copper coin of proper weight and proper size. Until the late years of the Western Han Dynasty, the currency system stayed the same.

东汉光武帝建武十六年（40 年）铸东汉五铢钱。此钱的直径为 2. 5 厘米，重 3. 4~3. 5 克，外郭较窄。灵帝时铸"四出五铢"，即钱背有四道斜纹，由穿孔四角至外郭，其形制、质量与东汉五铢钱相同。三国两晋南北朝时期，蜀汉铸"直百五铢"；魏孝文帝太和十九年（495 年）始铸"太和五铢"，宣武帝永平三年（510 年）铸"永平五铢"，孝庄帝永安二年（529 年）铸"永安五铢"；西魏文帝大统六年（540 年）铸"大统五铢"，形制似"永安五铢"。萧梁初期，曾铸"大样五铢"；北齐文宣帝天保四年（553 年）铸"常平五铢"。

Wuzhu money of the Eastern Han Dynasty was cast in 40A. D. whose diameter was 2. 5 centimeters and weight was from 3. 4 to 3. 5 grams. Its external circle was narrow. Later on, different wuzhu money was cast by different emperors. Emperor Ling cast "sichu wuzhu money" whose shape and weight were the same as the wuzhu money of the Eastern Han Dynasty. During the Three Kingdoms Period, Shu State cast "zhibai wuzhu"; In 495, "taihe wuzhu" was cast; In 510, "yongping wuzhu" was cast; In 529, "yong'an wuzhu" was cast; In 540, "datong wuzhu" was cast; In 553, "changping wuzhu" was cast. There are many other kinds of wuzhu money in different times.

581 年，隋统一后，另铸“开皇五铢”，结束了长达一百余年币制混乱的局面。唐武德四年（621 年）铸“开元通宝”，至此废止五铢钱。五铢钱流通七百余年，是中国历史上铸造数量最多，流通时间最久的钱币。据史书记载，制作隋五铢的原材料就是采自这里的铜和铁。

In 581, the Sui Dynasty united the whole country and cast “kaihuang wuzhu”, which ended the disorder of currency for more than one hundred years. In 621, “kaiyuantongbao” was cast. Then wuzhu money was abolished. Wuzhu money has been circulated for more than 700 years. In Chinese history, its number is the largest and its circulation time is the longest. According to the historical records, the raw materials of wuzhu money of the Sui Dynasty are the copper and iron of Daye Iron Mine.

游客朋友们请随我一起来看这里。我所站的这一片地砖，铺成一个红色的半圆形，四周是呈放射状的白色花岗岩地板，而这里正好处在天坑的东部，使人自然而然就想到了成语——日出东方。这里就是日出东方广场了，为什么把这里设计成如此模样呢？

Please follow me. Some tiles are extended into a red semicircle. Around the semicircle, there are tiles made of white granite. It is just in the east of the mining pit. So it reminds us of the idiom “The sun comes out in the east.” Here is the Sunrise Oriental Square. Why is it designed like that?

这寓意着三个美好的愿望。第一个美好的愿望是希望毛主席老人家的光芒与日同辉，永远照耀着矿山。第二个美好的愿望是希望毛主席能把温暖和幸福传递给矿山人。第三个美好的愿望是所有矿山人的一个美好祝愿，送给所有来到矿山公园游览的朋友，希望今天所有的游客朋友们能够感受毛主席的温暖，并祝愿游客朋友们在以后的岁月里，家庭幸福，生活和美，工作顺利，步步高升。

The design of the Square contains three good wishes. The first one is that the light of Chairman Mao will shine on the mine forever. The second one is that Chairman Mao will deliver the warmness and happiness to the miners. The third one is that all the miners wish the tourists a happy life and a successful career.

游客朋友们从这里往远处看，就会看到东露天采坑一级一级的台阶。中国有一句俗语“芝麻开花节节高”，这也是日出东方广场的美好寓意。

From this direction, we can see the steps of the mining pit. There is a Chinese saying：“Rise joint by joint like sesame flowers on the stem.” This is also the nice connotation of the Sunrise Oriental Square.

游客朋友们请看毛主席像的两边，有十四组铜浮雕。这十四组铜浮雕都是采用大冶铁矿的精铜，也就是优质铜制作的。感兴趣的朋友可以敲敲看，铜的声音是很清脆的。现在我给大家介绍第一组铜浮雕，首先介绍铁的历史，铁的历史也可以说是世界工业文明的发展史。

On both sides of the portrait of Chairman Mao, there are 14 sets of copper reliefs which are made of refined copper of high quality from Daye Iron Mine. If you are interested, you can knock at it and listen. The voice is very crisp. Now let's begin with the first set of copper reliefs. At first, I will introduce the history of iron which is also the history of the world's industrial civilization.

顺着这个时间脉络，我们从这里了解到，世界上最早掌握炼铁技术的是小亚细亚的赫梯人。古时候，由于受医疗条件和环境的影响，任何一个国家存在的时间都不超过五十年。而赫梯王国存在了一百年，为什么这个国家存在的时间这么长呢？这说明当时他们的军事力量是非常强大的，那为什么是这样子的呢？

Along the time sequence, we learn the history of iron. In the world, the Hittites of Asia Minor are the first masters of iron smelting technology. In ancient times, influenced by the medical conditions and environment, the existence of any country did not last more than fifty years. But Hittite existed for a hundred years. The reason why it existed longer is that their military forces are very powerful. Why is it so?

因为当时的赫梯人掌握了炼铁技术，垄断了炼铁技术，而且保密了炼铁技术，而别的国家使用的是青铜器。铜的熔点比较低，铜的韧性没有铁强。我们可以细想一下，赫梯人与其他国家作战，他们使用的铁质兵器就比铜质兵器有优势多了！但为什么他们又只存在了一百年呢？因为随着岁月的流逝，炼铁的技术最终还是普及开来。从此赫梯王国就逐步走向衰退，直至瓦解。

The Hittites mastered iron smelting technology and kept it as a secret. At that time, other countries still used bronze wares. Because of a relatively low melting point, copper is not as tough as iron. If the Hittites had battles with other countries, their iron weapons would have an obvious advantage over copper ones. But why did it exist only for a hundred years? With the passage of time, iron smelting technology eventually spread to other countries. From then on, Hittite gradually declined and at last collapsed.

我们继续来看第二组铜浮雕，从亚细亚文明来到欧洲爱琴海文明。这组浮雕刻画的是两个外国人的形象，他们手里都拿着武器。人类最初掌握炼铁技术后，主要不是运用于生产或生活，最多的还是运用于战争。那时候人类的文明发展就是弱肉强食，谁厉害谁的地位就会越稳固。

Now let's look at the second set of copper reliefs. Here we come from Asian civilization to European Aegean civilization. On this set of reliefs, there are two foreigners who have weapons in their hands. From this we learn that iron smelting technology is not mainly used in production or life, but mostly in war. At that time, law of the jungle was also the law in development of human civilization. If he is more powerful, his position will be more stable.

再往前走，这组浮雕描绘的是祭祀场景。在最早的西周时期，中国的老百姓信奉神灵。在当时的环境下，科技不发达，医疗条件不发达，生产力水平非常低下，所以西周人的寿命非常短。因此，人们非常信奉神灵，希望得到上苍的庇佑。他们制作大量的铁质祭祀物品，祭祀神灵，同时也运用于战争。

Then let's go forward. This set of copper reliefs describes the scene of the sacrifice. In the Western Zhou Dynasty, Chinese people believed in the gods. At that time, science and technology was underdeveloped. The medical conditions were poor. And the productivity level was very low. So their life span was very short. They deeply believed in the gods, because they hoped to get the gods' blessing. So they made a lot of iron ritual items to sacrifice to the gods. At that time, iron was also used to make weapons.

我们再往前看，这组浮雕描述的是神话传说，讲述的是铁拐李在铁山冶炼铁拐，得道升天，最终把炼铁的技术传授给了铁山的老百姓的故事。从此这里的采炼冶铁之火熊熊燃烧，连绵不断！相传铁拐李炼就的铁拐能降魔除妖，他的宝葫芦里装的是包治百病的灵丹妙药。

Let's look at the front. This set of reliefs tells us myths and legends which are about the story of Tieguai Li. He once smelted his iron crutch in Tieshan. Then he passed on the iron smelting technology to the people here. Since then, the fire of mining and smelting is burning without stop. According to the legend, his iron crutch has the magic to destroy the demon, and his treasure gourd is filled with a panacea.

我们再一起看这组铜浮雕，刚才我们介绍的是神话传说，现在给大家介绍一些有史可考的矿冶文化。中国历史上最早有文字记载的冶铁活动是在三国吴王孙权时期。在孙权统治时期，他把铁山作为一个炼制兵器的原材料基地，大兴炉冶，大肆冶炼，制造大量的兵器，并运用于战争以巩固自己的江山。

Let's come to see this set of copper reliefs. Just now, I talk about myths and legends of Tieshan. Now I'll introduce the records of mining and metallurgical culture. In Chinese history, the earliest written records of iron smelting activities appeared in the Three Kingdoms Period. At that time, Tieshan was ruled by Sun Quan, King of Wu State who took Tieshan as a raw material base of weapon smelting. Prosperous and large-scaled furnace-metallurgy brought out a lot of weapons which were used in wars in order to consolidate the country, which ensured the prosperity of the State.

这里还有一个细节要介绍，这组铜浮雕底部描绘的建筑就是典型的楚文化建筑物。沿着浮雕墙继续往前走，我们就会看到墙上有一个人物浮雕，他是中国最早的铁务机构官员，其职位相当于现在的冶金部部长，他的衣冠冢就葬在铁山。

There is a detail. At the bottom of this set of copper reliefs, there is a typical building of Chu culture. Move forward along the relief wall, we will see the first Chinese official of iron service agency on the wall, who is equal to the current minister of Department of Metallurgy. His cenotaph was buried in Tieshan.

这组铜浮雕介绍的是隋炀帝铸造钱币的场景。因为当时市场上流通的钱币越来越少，后来就出现了通货膨胀的现象。隋炀帝作为一国之君，他认为只有铸造更多的钱币，才能有效地抑制通货膨胀，所以在这里我们看到了一个古人铸造五铢钱的场景。

This set of copper reliefs is about Emperor Yang of the Sui Dynasty. During his reign, there was less and less money in circulation on the market. Later the phenomenon of inflation appeared. Emperor Yang believed that if he cast more money, he could effectively defeat inflation. This is a scene of the ancient people casting wuzhu money.

请大家随我继续往前走，现在看到的这组铜浮雕介绍的是抗金名将岳飞炼剑的故事。岳飞当年来到这里屯兵炼剑，炼制的剑韧性非常好，可以削发如泥，但是特别脆，轻轻一折就容易断。岳飞百思不得其解，非常郁闷。当地的老百姓就告诉他，在铁山的东边，有一座东方山，是佛教圣地，里面供奉的菩萨很灵验，希望菩萨会帮助他。

Please go forward. This set of copper reliefs tells Yue Fei's story of refining sword. He was the famous general fighting against the Jin who once came here to station his troops and refined swords. The swords were so tough that they cut hair very easily. But they were very crisp. When they were gently folded, they broke easily. Yue Fei was really puzzled and very depressed. Then the local people told him a secret. In the east of Tieshan, there was a holy place of Buddhism which was Dongfang Mountain. The Bodhisattva in the mountain was very spiritual. He hoped the Bodhisattva would help him.

于是岳飞就带着人前往东方山祈求菩萨指点。途经栗山，此山因盛产栗树而得名。在栗山有一座栗山寺，仅次于东方山的弘化禅寺。岳飞路过栗山寺时，看到两只小黑鸡，通体黑亮，眼睛也是黑亮黑亮的。他们看见岳飞撒腿就跑，岳飞觉得好奇怪，于是就一路追赶，追至一山洞前，两只小黑鸡钻进了洞中，岳飞也钻进了山洞，进去后却不见两只小黑鸡的踪影。

Then Yue Fei led some soldiers to Dongfang Mountain to pray for Buddha guidance. They passed Li Mountain which was named so because there were a lot of chestnut trees on the mountain. There was a temple named Li Mountain Temple which was smaller than Honghua Temple on Dongfang Mountain. When Yue Fei passed Li Mountain Temple, he saw two black chickens. Their whole bodies were black, and their eyes were black too. They ran away when they saw Yue Fei. Yue felt strange, so he ran after them. When he ran to a cave, the two black chickens got into it. Yue went into the cave after them, but he could't find any trace of the two black chickens.

好一阵纳闷，他正要转身离开时，忽然听见两人在讲话。仔细听说话人的声音，其中一个声音说道："这个岳飞在铁山炼剑，但总炼不出好剑，不知是何原因?"另一个声音说道："哈哈！那是因为他不知道栗山上的栗树是最好的燃料，用栗树做燃料的话，他一定会炼出好剑的。"此时，岳飞才恍然大悟，原来自己所炼制的剑因为火候不够，导致所炼之剑韧性有余，刚性不足。

Yue felt puzzled and was about to turn back. Suddenly he heard two people speaking. When he came closely, he could hear what they were talking about. One of them said, "Yue Fei refines swords in Tieshan, but he can't produce good swords. Do you know the reason?" The other said, "That is because he does not know the chestnut trees of Li Mountain is the best fuel. If he uses the chestnut trees as fuel, he is bound to refine good swords." After hearing that, Yue found out the method to refine good swords. In the past, because the temperature was not high enough, his swords were only tough but not rigid.

能说此话的必定是高人，岳飞四处寻找，也不见踪影，此时方才明白原来是仙人在指点他。于是他急忙带人在栗山砍了许多栗树带回来，从那之后岳飞炼制的剑就刚劲有力，游刃有余。现在科学实验证明，栗树燃烧所产生的热值是非常高的。或许当年岳飞就真的采用了栗树做燃料炼剑。

Yue Fei looked around, and tried to search for the two speakers. But he could't find any clues. Then he realized that they must be the immortals who wanted to help him. He hurried to bring soldiers to cut many chestnut trees from Li Mountain. After that, his swords were both tough and rigid. Now scientific experiments prove that when chestnut trees are burnt, the caloric is very high. Perhaps Yue Fei really uses chestnut trees as fuel to refine swords.

紧接着我们看到的是关于中国近代工业发展历程的介绍。在清末时期，张之洞聘请英国工匠郭师敦，也就是我们现在看到的这组铜浮雕中的外国人，他探得铁山蕴藏丰富的矿产资源，从而拉开了中国近代工业发展的帷幕。张之洞在铁山创建了大冶铁矿。这组浮雕中，张之洞的身后有一条铁路，这条铁路就是前面我们介绍过的张之洞建造的华中第一条铁路。

Later we will see the reliefs about the history of Chinese modern industrial development. In the late Qing Dynasty, Zhang Zhidong hired Gou Shidun, a British craftsman who is the foreigner in this set of copper reliefs. Guo discovered rich mineral resources in Tieshan. Then the curtain of the development of modern industry in China was opened. Zhang constructed Daye Iron Mine in Tieshan. Here in these reliefs we can see a railway behind Zhang which is the first railway in central China constructed by him.

在接下来的铜浮雕当中，我们会看到盛宣怀将大冶铁矿、汉阳铁厂、萍乡煤矿合并成中国第一家大型钢铁联合企业——汉冶萍公司。汉冶萍公司作为中国第一家大型钢铁联合企业有着自己的企业文化。铜浮雕当中的这两把锤子和这一把钳子构成了汉冶萍的厂徽，这是中国最早的企业文化，非常具有代表意义。

The next copper reliefs show us Han-Ye-Ping Company which is China's first large scale iron and steel enterprise. It was set up by Sheng Xuanhuai who merged Daye Iron Mine, Hanyang Iron Plant and Pingxiang Coal Mine. Han-Ye-Ping Company had its own corporate culture. Its factory logo consisted of two hammers and a pair of pliers. This is the earliest corporate culture in China, so it is of representative significance.

顺着浮雕墙，接下来就会看到有关日本掠夺开采大冶铁矿的那一段屈辱历史。据说当时日本人将这些掠夺开采的矿石都储存在日本的近海，以备后需。接下来的几组铜浮雕介绍的是中华人民共和国成立后矿山发生的翻天覆地的变化。在这里可以看到中国第一支女地质队员们建设矿山的飒爽英姿。中华人民共和国成立后矿山人遵循毛主席的指示，发扬“守山吃，伴山眠”的精神，不辞辛劳建设矿山。

Along the relief wall, we will recall a history of humiliation. In the 20th century, Japanese plundered and exploited Daye Iron Mine. They stored the ores in the offshore of Japan for future needs. The next several sets of copper reliefs present the great changes of the Mine after liberation. Here we can see the bright and brave images of China's first female geological team. After liberation, the people of the Mine follow Chairman Mao's instructions. They are hard-working in constructing the Mine.

刚才我们看到的露天采坑是通过牙轮钻填充炸药进行爆破，使矿石崩落来进行采矿的。但在矿山还有一种地下开采，就是游客朋友们现在所看到的这组铜浮雕描绘的场景。六七十年代，矿山工人在井下作业时，采用风钻进行打眼填充炸药，通过爆破开采矿石。随着科技的发展，这个采矿工序得到了改进，现在使用的是美国进口液压式台车，利用它进行钻孔凿岩。

In the open mining pit, explosives are filled through the rock drill. Then the rocks are blasted and the ores are falling down. This is a kind of mining method. Another method is underground mining, which is shown in this set of copper reliefs. In the sixties and seventies of the last century, miners worked underground. They used wind drills to drill holes and filled the holes with explosives. Then the rocks were blasted and the ores were successfully mined. With the development of science and technology, the mining process has been improved. Now hydraulic trolleys are imported from the United States which are used to drill holes.

最后两组铜浮雕介绍的是亚洲第一天坑，以及亚洲第一硬岩复垦基地。亚洲第一天坑与我们刚才所看到的崖画有着异曲同工之妙。

The last two sets of copper reliefs introduce the first mining pit and the first hard rock reclamation base in Asia. The mining pit is similar to the cliff paintings.

游客朋友们，介绍完浮雕墙，我们来到了毛主席手托矿石的石雕像前。这座石雕像是迄今为止中国最高、最大的毛主席手托矿石的个性化雕像，由二十多位工匠师，经过长达半年的时间，采用140吨优质花岗岩精心雕刻制作而成。完成之后的雕像净重58吨，高达9.15米，从中国的雕刻之乡——河北曲阳运回。

Now let's look at the statue of Chairman Mao who is holding the ore in his hand. So far, it's the highest and largest stone statue of Chairman Mao which is 9.15 meters high and 58 tons heavy. Originally, 140 tons of high-quality granite is used in the carving. It takes more than twenty craftsmen half a year to finish the statue. The statue is carried back from Quyang of Hebei, the town of Chinese carving.

据说，这个毛主席雕像在矿山立起来以后，曾经发生了一些异象，雕像背后曾经出现过白色的光环。大冶铁矿尖林山车间的一位退休工人，在一次雨后用手机给毛主席雕像拍照。他在拍出来的照片中，奇异地发现主席身后有五彩光环。于是他就将这件事告诉领导，领导当时也觉得奇怪，于是就安排人用照相机拍摄雕像，但却拍不出主席身后的光环。于是领导就将拍出光环的手机，花了2000元收购珍藏起来，现在这部手机就收藏于大冶铁矿博物馆。

It's said that after the statue is erected in the Mine, some abnormal phenomena appear. A white halo once appeared behind the statue. After a rain, a retired worker from Jianlinshan workshop of Daye Iron Mine took a photo with his mobile. To his surprise, he found a colorful halo behind the statue. He told it to his leaders who also felt strange. So they arranged someone to take pictures with a camera, but they failed to get the halo again. Later they bought the mobile which caught the halo with 2000 yuan. Now the mobile is collected in Daye Iron Mine Museum.

现在继续往前走，在我们的右手边，被白色栅栏围起来的是大冶铁矿东采作业区。随着矿山资源的转型，现在这里还有一些零星的地下开采。我们看到的这个红色井架，就是现在的生产提升主井。听矿山的老矿工们说，这是当年日本人在这里开凿的，当时的主井还没有多深，大概只有 90 米，但开采出来的矿石都是非常优质的磁铁矿。

Let's go forward. On our right, this is the east mining area of Daye Iron Mine which is surrounded by a white fence. Because of the resources transformation of the mine, there is only some sporadic underground mining. A red framework of shaft stands over there which is the main shaft for production and hoisting. The old miners tell us that it was dug by the Japanese. At first, it was not very deep, only about 90 meters. But the ores explored from this shaft were all high-quality magnetite.

中华人民共和国成立之后，矿山迎来了新的曙光。矿山的工人自己当家做主，建设矿山的热情高涨。为了开采到更多的矿石，矿山的工人继续开凿竖井，深达 180 米。现在采坑底部所开采出来的矿石，就是通过这条竖井提升上来的。

After the foundation of the People's Republic of China, the mine takes on a new appearance. The miners become the masters of the Mine. So their enthusiasm of construction is on the rise. In order to explore more ores, the miners continue to dig the shaft to a depth of about 180 meters. Now the ores are explored at the bottom of the mining pit and they are hoisted from this vertical shaft.

在竖井的左边，游客朋友们看到的这个穿山洞，是 20 世纪 20 年代末汉冶萍公司开凿的运输矿石的巷道，由当时的工程设计师盛芷皋设计并指挥开凿的，至今还在使用。

On the left of the shaft, there is a tunnel dug by Han-Ye-Ping Company which was used to transport ores in the late 1920s. It was designed and dug by the engineering designer Sheng Zhigao which is still in use today.

游客朋友们顺着我手指的方向就会看到那边的山顶有一座半山亭。在半山亭不远处有一座日本人入侵大冶铁矿掠夺开采矿石的时候修建的碉堡，仅存 1.5 米高，但上边留下的弹孔和瞭望口，清晰地见证了那段屈辱的历史。

There is a mid-hill pavilion on the top of that mountain. And not far away from the pavilion there is a blockhouse which was built by the Japanese when they began to plunder and exploit Daye Iron Mine. It is only 1.5 meters high, but some bullet holes and loopholes are left on it, which witnesses the history of humiliation.

参观完这边的竖井、运矿巷道、日军碉堡遗址，我将带领游客朋友们去看看中国最早的"防盗门"。游客朋友们，我们现在看到，在一片绿荫中隐藏着一扇厚重的铁门。这就是我刚才所说的中国最早的"防盗门"，这里有三扇这样的"防盗门"。

We have visited the vertical shaft, the tunnel to transport ores and the site of the Japanese blockhouse. Now I'll show you the earliest "security door" in China. There is a thick and heavy iron door hidden among the green trees which is the earliest security door in China. And there are three such doors in this area.

其实，这是汉冶萍公司在清末时期建造的炸药库，用于存放炸药和一些备品备件。这些炸药和备品备件非同小可，所以游客朋友们看到的这些铁门非常厚重，并且门闩不仅用厚厚的小铁板做成，还有两道不同的门闩，所以堪称中国最早的"防盗门"。

Actually, this is the site of explosive warehouse which was constructed by Han-Ye-Ping Coal and Iron Co. Ltd. at the end of the Qing Dynasty. It was used to store explosives and spare parts. For a mine, explosives and spare parts are by no means a trivial matter. That's why these iron doors are so thick and heavy. The bolt is made up of small thick iron plate. There are two different bolts for each door. So they are considered to be the earliest security doors in China.

我们现在就进入洞中参观。刚走进洞中时，游客朋友们需要稍作停留，让我们的眼睛有一个视觉转换的时间，以适应洞中的环境。日本人入侵大冶铁矿掠夺开采矿石的时候，将这里作为存放炸药和一些备品备件的露天仓库。洞中环境基本维持原貌，我们抬头看到洞中的岩层非常坚硬，没有采取任何支护，历经了 90 多年的岁月，这里都没有垮塌，可见大冶铁矿的岩层结构非常紧密。

Now let's enter the cavern. Please stop for a while. Let our eyes have a better adapt to the environment of the cavern. When Japanese plundered and exploited Daye Iron Mine, they also used the cavern as an open warehouse for explosives and spare parts. The cavern maintains its original appearance. Now raise your head, you will see that the rock formation in the cavern is very tough. Though there isn't any support, it doesn't collapse for more than 90 years. It is a good evidence for the compactness of the rock structure of Daye Iron Mine.

游客朋友们随我一起往前走，注意脚下的路。当年存放炸药的时候，地下铺着厚厚的木板，用来防潮。讲到这里，要提醒大家注意安全！注意我们脚下的台阶！防止滑倒！我们继续往前走，走到这里似乎就到了洞室的尽头，其实不然！

Please go forward with me, and watch your step. When the explosives are stored here, the floor is covered with thick planks which is moisture proof. Please be careful. It is very slippery here. Let's move on. It seems that we have arrived at the end of the cavern, but actually it is not true.

在这里我们可以看到“洞吧”两个霓虹灯闪烁的大字，走近之后会发现“洞吧”左侧还有一个洞室，别有一番天地。游客朋友们进入这个“洞中洞”，就会发现其与我们刚才所看到的洞的构造不同，这里是日本人用来存放雷管和一些特殊备品备件的地方。

Here we can see two big characters "Hole Bar" with neon lights. Approaching near, we find another cavern on the left side of the bar which is an entirely different world. If we enter this "hole in hole", we see different structures. This cavern was used to store detonator and some special spare parts by the Japanese.

洞室顶部有专门用于通风的通道，通向室外。洞室的一边还有一扇木门，游客朋友们猜猜，在这里建一扇木门有什么用途呢？现在我将这扇木门打开，游客朋友们就会一目了然。原来木门外是修建的排水沟，所以我们看到洞室里面是非常干燥的。顶部也修缮成非常有规则的拱形，整齐地排列着，这与我们刚才看到的潮湿的洞室有所不同。

On the top, there is a special ventilation channel which extends to the outside. On the other side of the cavern, there is another wooden door. What is the use of that door? When I open the door, you will be clear at a glance. A drainage ditch is built out of the door, so the cavern is very dry. The top of the cavern is designed into regular arch which is arranged in good order. This cavern is different from the one we see just now.

由此可见，洞室修建在这里非常隐蔽，所以存放雷管和一些重要的备品备件就非常安全。参观完汉冶萍公司炸药库遗址之后，我们走出洞外，稍作休息。

The cavern is well hidden here. So it is a safe place for storing detonator and important spare parts. After we visit the site of explosive warehouse of Han-Ye-Ping Company, let's go out of the cavern and have a rest.

刚才我们参观了日本人修建的炸药库遗址，接下来请游客朋友们随我一起，沿着眼前这条蜿蜒的山路，拾径而上，前往日军碉堡遗址参观。沿路上山的时候游客朋友们请注意安全。我们现在来到了一座半山亭，在这里登亭远眺，就会看到矿山的全景。

We've just visited the site of explosive warehouse of the Japanese. Now, please follow me. Let's go along the winding road to visit the blockhouse site of the Japanese army. Please watch your step when we climb the mountain. Now we come to a pavilion in the middle of the mountain where we can have a panoramic view of the mine.

在离半山亭不足20米的地方就是我刚才介绍的日军碉堡遗址，这是当年日本侵略者在矿山掠夺开采时遗留下来的最有利的罪证，上面至今还依稀看得见炮弹扫射过的痕迹。游客们会发现这里有一些不同的瞭望孔，有谁知道这是做什么用的吗？哎！对了，我听到游客说是为了方便不同的机枪扫射。

The blockhouse site of the Japanese army is about 20 meters away from the pavilion, which is the best evidence left by the Japanese invaders that they plundered and exploited the resources of Daye Iron Mine. Today we can still see the traces of projectile's firing and shooting. Here are some different lookout holes. What's the use of them? Yes, they are convenient for different machine guns to shoot.

1938年至1945年期间，日本掠采矿石501万吨，运回日本的就有417万吨，所以我们永远都要铭记那段屈辱的历史。看完碉堡遗址，我将带领大家参观此次行程的最后一站——“井下探幽”。

From 1938 to 1945, Japanese plundered and exploited 5.01 million tons of ores, among which 4.17 million tons were shipped to Japan. So we should remember this history of humiliation forever. Next, I'll show you around the last stop of this trip which is the underground exploration.

现在流行一种说法是：“请朋友吃饭，不如请朋友出汗，送家人礼品，不如送家人健康。”现在我们来到“井下探幽”的入口，我们现在在海平面 84 米处，我们所要到达的井下游览区在海平面负 53 米处，高度差 137 米。

Nowadays there is a popular saying: "It is better to help your friends sweat than to invite them to dinner; it is better to keep your families healthy than to give them gifts." Now we are standing at the entrance of the underground exploration. We are now at 84 meters above the sea level. Next we will go to the underground which is at 53 meters below the sea level. So there is a height difference of 137 meters.

接下来有专职的下井工作人员带领大家下井参观。请游客朋友们详细阅读有关的安全须知，按照下井的安全要求来做，以确保每一位游客的安全！结束了“井下探幽”的参观，请大家随我沿着这边的小路返程，最后所有的游客回到我们第一站参观的主碑集合。

Professional workers of the mine will lead us to the underground. Please read the safety instructions carefully. Do as required to ensure our safety underground. After the underground exploration, please follow me back along the path of the mountain. At last, we will assemble in front of the main stele which is also the first stop of this trip.

游客朋友们，此次矿冶文化之旅即将结束，回望远处，那郁郁葱葱的亚洲最大复垦林就像一段织锦，蜿蜒于矿山之中，而近处工业博览园的运矿机车，就像岁月的刻刀，刻画着矿冶文化这片蓝图！沿着小石桥，穿桥而过，回望矿山公园，这幅美丽的工业画卷怎能让人忘怀！

Now our trip of mining and metallurgical culture is coming to an end. When we look back at the far distance, we see the largest green forest of reclamation in Asia which winds through the mine, just like a line of brocade. In the near distance, we see the transporting locomotives in the Industrial Expo Park which draw a blueprint of the mining and metallurgical culture. Walk along the small stone bridge, and look back at the Mine Park. How can we forget this beautiful industrial landscape?

经过三个小时的矿山公园的参观游览，景点讲解就到这里了。谢谢！

That's all for our three hours' trip of Huangshi National Mine Park. Thanks for your support.

第二章
矿冶文化的翻译学研究

Translation Studies of Mining
and Metallurgical Culture

第一节　矿冶类文本的多元化特点及翻译原则 *

Diversified Features of Mining and Metallurgical Texts and Translation Principle

摘要：文章从文本类型理论入手，首先界定矿冶类文本的范围，结合实例分析该类文本的多元化语体特点，提出了术语与文化兼顾的信息性翻译原则，以期提高矿冶类文本的翻译质量，更好地促进世界矿冶文化的交流。

关键词：矿冶类文本；矿冶文化；翻译原则；信息性原则

随着全球经济的复苏、矿业经济的迅猛发展及矿冶文化的日渐兴起，矿冶领域的国际性交流日渐增多。2005 年 6 月在加拿大召开的矿冶文化研讨会重点探讨了矿业、矿区和矿工文化的历史及再生等问题；2010 年 3 月在新加坡召开的“2010 亚洲矿业大会”为亚洲的采矿公司及矿业投资者提供了一个很好的平台，同时也让世界进一步了解了亚洲矿业群体、矿业并购与融资等情况；2010 年 8 月首届国际矿冶文化旅游节在湖北省黄石市成功举办，宣传和宏扬了黄石深厚的矿冶文化。

国际矿业群体间的交流，中国矿业走向世界，矿冶文化的传播与宏扬

---

* 作者邵春美，原载于《黄石理工学院学报》(人文社会科学版) 第 28 卷第 1 期，2011 年。

等，都依赖于翻译活动的有效开展，但与矿冶相关的翻译，目前并未在翻译界受到应有的重视。本文拟从文本类型理论入手，通过对矿冶类文本的分析，阐述其翻译原则，以便更好地指导矿业领域的翻译实践。

一、文本类型理论及矿冶类文本的界定

（一）文本类型理论

翻译研究与文本类型和语篇分析理论密不可分，翻译的对象就是文本或语篇，对文本类型的划分及语篇进行分析，对翻译研究有着积极的意义。

彼得·纽玛克（Peter Newmark）根据文本的可译性程度，将文本划分为表情型文本、信息型文本及召唤型文本[1]；克里斯蒂安·诺德（Christiane Nord）将文本功能划分为指称功能、表情功能、感染功能以及寒暄功能[2]；卡塔琳娜·莱斯（Katharina Reiss）为便于进行翻译质量评价，将文本划分为信息型文本、表情型文本以及操作型文本[3]。张美芳认为，文本功能理论有助于客观地分析翻译文本的功能和语言特点，有助于译者采取适当的翻译策略[4]。文本类型的划分及文本功能理论对翻译实践的助益作用体现在宏观层面上，翻译策略随着文体的不同而变化，无法关注到文本的微观操作层面，具有一定的局限性。另一方面，随着翻译学科的细化及译者专业化水平的不断提高，对特定领域的翻译要求也越来越高。因此，对翻译原则的探讨，有助于指导特定领域的翻译实践。

（二）矿冶类文本的界定

矿冶类文本既涵盖文学文本类型，又包括应用型文本类型，具体来说，矿冶类文本主要包括：博物馆、展览馆中对矿产资源的介绍及宣传资料；矿业法律法规；矿山公园的景点介绍及宣传手册；矿业国际会议的相关材料；矿冶文化的艺术表现形式；等等。这些矿冶类文本根据其所在语境中的使用功能主要分为两大类，即外宣性文本和法律类文本。外宣性文本

以宣传信息为主，侧重点在文化方面，其他的文本功能如诱导性功能、美感功能等处于次要地位；法律类文本的主要内容是规约性信息，其对相关方有一定的法律约束力。本文主要侧重于外宣性矿冶类文本的多元化语体特点及翻译之讨论。

二、矿冶类文本的多元化特点及翻译原则

翻译原则可以用于更好地指导翻译实践，但其也来源于翻译实践。认清矿冶类文本的语体特点有助于翻译的操作，从而在实践中提炼出翻译原则，并在翻译活动中去考证翻译原则的有效性。

(一) 矿冶类文本的多元化特点

矿冶类文本的多元化特点体现在信息的多样性及文本类型的多元化。矿冶类信息包括：(1) 描述性信息，如对煤矿指标的描述；(2) 文化性信息，如介绍某矿产遗址的历史；(3) 美学性信息，如矿区流传的故事或音乐；(4) 规约性信息，如矿业法律中对采矿、探矿权的规定；等等。同时，矿冶类文本的跨学科性也足以说明其多元化特点，涉及考古学（如矿产挖掘、开采)、历史学（如矿产遗址、年代)、美学（如音乐舞蹈中融入的矿冶文化因素)、经济学（如矿业投资、融资)、法学（如矿业法律法规）等。

同时，矿冶类文本所包含的信息也是与多方面相关联的，如环境、化学、生态、地质、金融等。

该类文本的多元化特点决定了文本中包含的矿冶术语和文化性信息较多。

(二) 矿冶类文本的翻译原则

矿冶类文本涵盖的范围较广，文体特点也各不相同，“在对外宣传翻译中，译者应遵循信息准确无误的效度原则和经济简明原则[5]”。外宣性矿冶类文本旨在宣传矿冶文化，且多用事实性的描述，如：“在中东的西

奈及阿拉伯谷地，考古学家发现了公元前 13 世纪至公元前 11 世纪古埃及法老王朝在提姆纳采冶铜矿的遗址。资料显示，开采的古巷道均未进行支护，竖井直径为 60~70 cm，开采深度最深为 36 m，平均深度在 8~15 m。平巷最宽 1m。采矿工具仅发现了石锤、木槌和铜凿，还发现了一架能够被修复的绞车。此外，还发现了炼炉炉壁、炼渣、石砧、石球等冶炼遗物。”（摘自某市博物馆对古埃及铀矿的开采与冶炼的说明）因此，在具体的翻译实践中，译者应遵循“凸显矿冶文化 ”这一信息性原则，从词汇、句法及语篇三个语言层面着手，有效地发挥其文本功能。

矿冶类法律文本主要是规约性的矿业法律或相关规定，如“今后所有有意在哥斯达黎加进行矿产开发的企业，首先要满足一系列严格的环保要求，其中包括要有完善的环境管理体系、每砍伐一棵树要补种 3 棵、保护矿区的地表和地下水资源不受污染等”。（引自《哥斯达黎加解除开矿禁令》）在翻译该类文本时，应遵循法律效力对等的原则，因为立法性文本的意图是对社会成员行为等方面做出的许可类、禁止类的规定，法律效力为第一要旨，而语言内容上的对等也是服务于法律效力这一最高准则的。

在翻译实践中，针对上述两种矿冶类文本提出的信息性翻译原则，既凸显了描述性的信息，也注重了法律效力。同时，无论是外宣性的文本，还是法律性的文本，均不可忽略文化因素，在翻译转换过程中，文化性的信息应引起译者的特别注意。“广义的矿冶文化包括三种形态：知识、观念和艺术；三个层次：精神、制度和物质。”[6]比如，新闻中对一些矿址的报道，矿山公园对矿产资源的介绍，博物馆对各种矿石的历史回顾，其中无一不包含着文化性的信息。

译者应注意的是，矿冶类文本中会出现很多专业术语，既有矿冶类的词汇，也有相关行业的词汇，如“铁矿石”“溜井”“明井”“钨矿”“铜凿”“净热值”“灰渣”“吸水厚度膨胀率”“带多层挂渣的炉壁残块”“木炭粉”“采冶技术”“矿脉”“矿体”“选矿”“精矿”“品位”等。还有，各朝代的名称、采矿工具、冶炼技术等相关词汇出现也较频繁，这对翻译造成了一定的困难。因此，译者应做好专业术语方面的知识积累和准备。

三、个案研究与讨论

（一）个案研究

凸显矿冶文化、精确使用术语，是对矿冶类文本译者在翻译实践中的基本要求，也是指导翻译过程的主要原则。现结合某博物馆展厅中相关文本以及一份煤的化验报告进行阐释。

例 1 铜绿山春秋时期采矿遗址局部复原。这里复原的是铜绿山 7 号矿体采矿遗址的局部。该遗址于 1979 年至 1980 年由中国社会科学院考古研究所发掘。发掘面积 400 平方米，共清理出 60 余个竖井、盲井，20 余条平巷和斜巷，以及一条排水巷道，随同出土的还有大量用于矿山生产的工具。

译文： Partial Restoration of the Spring and Autumn Period mining sites in Tonglu Mountain.

Here is the partial restoration of the Spring and Autumn Period No. 7 mining sites in Tonglu Mountain. The site was excavated by the Archaeological Institute of Chinese Academy of Social Sciences from 1979 to 1980 with an area of 400 square meters, in which more than 60 vertical shafts, blind wells, and more than 20 Lane and Drift, as well as a drainage tunnel were unearthed along with a large number of instruments used in the mines production.

例 1 的译文并未凸显矿冶文化，没有遵循相应的翻译原则，必将导致译文不能完全传递原文的主旨，不能有效地实现文本功能。首先，对这一小段简介的标题翻译，未充分传递“春秋时期”这一特定历史性文化信息，仅译为“the Spring and Autumn Period”，这会引起目的语读者的误解，但因标题不宜太长，建议在正文中明晰“春秋时期”这一应凸显的文化性信息。其次，标题的译文逻辑不清，有些实义词未大写。正文部分的问题主要是专业词汇翻译不够精确，如“竖井”“盲井”分别译为

“vertical shafts”“blind wells”，殊不知“shaft”一词本身就表示竖井，且“well”多指打水的井或油井。“20余条平巷和斜巷”译为“20 Lane and Drift ”实属对专业术语掌握不清，且存在语法错误及大小写不明的情况。英译文仅由两句组成，第二句过长会对目的语读者造成负担，弱化文化性因素在读者头脑中的印象。建议改译为：

Partial Restoration of Mining Sites in Tonglu Mountain in the Spring and Autumn Period.

Here lies No. 7 ore body of partial restoration of mining sites in Tonglu Mountain in the Spring and Autumn Period（770B. C. —476B. C.). The site was excavated by the Archaeological Institute of Chinese Academy of Social Sciences from 1979 to 1980 with an area of 400 square meters. And over 60 shafts and blind shafts，more than 20 gallaries and inclined drifts，and a drainage lane were available after cleaning. A large number of tools used for mine production were unearthed as well.

例 2 黄石地区，除了发现众多的古代矿冶遗存外，还发现了三座古代城址。这些矿冶遗存大多分布在古城址的周围。研究者认为，这三座古城址应是矿冶生产的管理中心，同时也是铜材的集散地。

译文：In addition to many unearthed mining relics，three ancient city sites have also been discovered in Huangshi area. The mining relics unearthed were mainly located around the area of the ancient city sites. Thus，researchers consider that the three ancient city sites were supposed to be the administration center of mining production and distribution center of copper.

例 2 的主要意图是想表达位于黄石地区的三座古城址的重要性，但译文对原文第一句话的处理明显偏离了信息焦点，且译文的前两句话之间缺乏连贯性。在对原文进行转换时，为凸显矿冶文化，译者应充分理清逻辑关系，如处理不当，则会使文本失去应有的功能。建议改译为：Three ancient city sites were discovered in Huangshi area with lots of ancient mining and metallurgical remains surrounded. Thus, researchers believe that the three ancient city sites were administrative center of mining and metallurgical production and distributing center of copper.

例 3　Basic results as received:

—net calorific value 6200kkal/kg

—TS 0. 8%

—coal 0~50 mm

—total moisture wt. pct 14%

—volatile wt. pct 24% ~37%

—ASH wt. pct 15%

—carbon wt. pct 50

—HGI 45

译文：收到的基本结果：净热值 6200kkal/kg；TS 0. 8%；煤 0~50mm；总湿度 wt. pct 14%；挥发性 wt. pct 24% ~37%；灰 wt. pct 15%；碳 wt. pct 50；HGI 45。

例 3 是煤的检验报告的一部分，对比原文，译文可谓简洁明了，对于业内人士来说，具有一定的可读性，但对于非专业人士来说，译文中未译的英文部分会对其阅读造成一定的障碍。原文中涉及的都是煤的各项指标，专门术语的专业性很强，译者应本着对读者负责的态度，仔细查阅相关术语的准确译法，方能凸显描述性信息。建议改译为：

收到的基本检验结果：

—净热值为 6200kkal/kg

—吸水厚度膨胀率为 0. 8%

—煤为 0~50mm

—总湿度重量-压力-容量-温度 14%

—挥发性重量-压力-容量-温度 24% ~37%

—灰渣重量-压力-容量-温度 15%

—碳重量-压力-容量-温度 50

—可磨性指数为 45

（二）讨论

近几年，对应用翻译的研究呈多元化的态势，有“翻译研究的语用学转向”的观点[7]，即“对翻译研究语言学转向与文化转向的超越”[7]；有基于体裁分析的翻译模式，其主要理念是对比源语文本和平行文本[8]；有将“信、达、雅”与“目的论”整合提出“独立成篇”的翻译理念[9]；等等。“一部人类文明发展史，也可以看成一部矿冶发展史。”[6]无论是经济领域还是文化艺术领域，矿冶元素都以其特殊性而渗透其中，因此，对矿冶类文本翻译的研究无疑具有重要的意义。各种翻译理念在矿冶类文本翻译中的有效性仍有待进一步研究，本文仅抛砖引玉地期待译界重视矿冶类文本的翻译研究，并依据其语体特点相应地提出其翻译原则：术语与文化兼顾的信息性原则。术语与文化密不可分，译者在翻译时应尽最大努力兼顾，对术语的正确分析有助于人们更好地认识与研究矿冶文化，矿冶文化的有效传播与发展有利于人们深入了解矿冶信息，准确理解术语的含义。但本文侧重于讨论外宣性的矿冶类文本，甚少涉及具有法律效力的法律类文本，笔者期望对矿冶类文本的分类与译论有更深入的探讨。

四、结语

本文关注的焦点是外宣性矿冶类文本，其中包含了大量专业术语，文化信息性强，在翻译实践中，译者只有遵循凸显矿冶文化这一原则，才能使文本真正地发挥其功能，才能有效传递矿冶文化信息。另一方面，目前矿冶类文本的译者大多缺乏矿冶业的相关知识，在翻译过程中遇到生僻词汇也在所难免，译者应积极查阅相关资料、不断学习，这样才能在国际交流中成为合格的矿冶文化传播者。

◎ 参考文献

[1] Newmark Peter. Approaches to Translation [M]. Hemel Hempstead: Prentice Hall, 1981.

[2] Nord C. Translating as a Purposeful Activity—Functionalist Approaches Explained [M]. Manchester: Jerome Publishing, 1997.
[3] Reiss K. Translating Criticism: The Potentials and Limitations: Categories and Criteria for Translation Quality Assessment [M]. Translated by Erroll, F. R. Manchester: St. Jerome Publishing, 1971/2000.
[4] 张美芳. 文本类型理论及其对翻译研究的启示 [J]. 中国翻译, 2009 (5): 15.
[5] 曾利沙. 对《2002 年中国的国防》(白皮书) 英译文评析——兼论对外宣传翻译的“经济简明”原则 [J]. 广东外语外贸大学学报, 2005 (4): 5.
[6] 石璋铭, 项锐. 矿冶文化内涵的探寻 [J]. 黄石理工学院学报 (人文社会科学版), 2008 (1): 21.
[7] 李菁. 翻译研究的语用学转向 [M]. 上海: 上海译文出版社, 2009.
[8] 谢家成, 刘洪泉. 基于体裁分析的专门用途语篇翻译模式及运用 [J]. 上海翻译, 2010 (2): 30.
[9] 刘季春. 独立成篇: 超越“忠实”的忠实 [J]. 上海翻译, 2010 (1): 10.

第二节　矿冶类文本的信息类型及翻译*

Information Type and Translation of Mining and Metallurgical Texts

摘要：近年随着矿业的迅猛发展及矿冶文化在不同国家之间的交流，与矿冶类相关文件的翻译渐渐增多。本文首先对矿冶类文本的定义和特点进行阐述，依照文本类型理论对矿冶类文本中包含的信息进行划分，并分析该类文本中的信息特点，从而分析此类文本的翻译策略，以期能够对矿冶类文本的译者在翻译实践中有所助益。

关键词：信息类型；矿冶类文本；翻译策略；翻译；策略

随着经济全球化的发展，矿业经济更是蒸蒸日上，国际性交流与合作不断增加，2008 年 11 月，第十届中国国际矿业大会在北京举行；2009 年蒙古国与加拿大矿产业圆桌会议在多伦多举行；第八届阿根廷国际矿业博览会于 2011 年 5 月在布宜诺斯艾利斯成功举办。这些均体现了矿业在世界范围内的重要地位。2012 年将有更多的矿业交流登上国际舞台，如第 80 届加拿大勘探开发者协会年会将于 3 月在多伦多举办，四年一次的美国拉斯维加斯矿业展将于 9 月 24 日在拉斯维加斯举行。中国的矿冶产业走向国际舞台，国际矿冶企业之间的交流，以及矿冶文化的宣传都与翻译息息相

* 作者姜逸云、邵春美，原载于《海外英语》，第 16 期，2012 年。

关，矿冶类文本翻译质量的提高也必然有利于矿业进一步的发展。

矿冶类文本主要是指文本内容与矿冶方面密切相关的文本，如矿区故事、矿冶历史的宣传资料、矿业法律等。

一、矿冶类文本中的信息类型

矿冶类文本涉及的体裁较多，其“多元化特点体现在信息的多样性及文本类型的多元化”。(邵春美，2011：64) 因此在翻译时应首先明确文本中所包含的信息类型，进而采取相应的翻译策略。矿冶类文本中的信息类型主要包括以下几类：

(一) 外宣性信息

外宣性信息常见于宣传资料手册、广告牌中，旨在有力地吸引读者，激发读者潜在的感情达到相应的宣传目的，

例 1　黄石蕴藏着丰富的矿产资源，历史悠久的矿冶文化，其规模之大、持续生产时间之长、采冶技术之先进，在国内外都十分罕见。在黄石这块土地上，矿冶之火绵延数千年不灭，是黄石历史进程中最本质的特征。

例 1 节选自《黄石矿冶文化展简介》，文化展的简介旨在达到宣传的目的，因而其中包含大量的外宣性信息。

(二) 事实性信息

事实性信息旨在让读者了解相应的事实。

例 2　采矿工具仅发现了石锤、木槌和铜凿。还发现了一架能够被修复的绞车。

本例是《古埃及铜矿的开采与冶炼》中的一段文字，目的是传递客观的史实，让读者对所描述的事物有更深刻的认识，内容具体，属于典型的事实性信息。

（三）描述性信息

描述性信息主观色彩较强，对事物的描述主要是从原文作者的角度进行。

例 3　据《大冶县志》记载："铜绿山'山顶高平，巨石对峙，每骤雨过时，有铜绿如雪花小豆，点缀土石之上，故名'。"

此类信息中带有主观性的言辞，对事物的描述主要是从原作者的角度进行。

（四）文化性信息

文化性信息内涵丰富，文本涉及的文化内容也千差万别。例如矿区流行的故事和民谣均是对矿区风俗和生活习惯的一种艺术表达形式。

（五）美学性信息

美学性信息经常以歌曲、文学作品和舞蹈等方式出现，有较强的美学色彩。

例 4　人在山中，山在江中，江在城中，城在湖中。

该例选自黄石国际矿冶文化节的主题曲《心中炉火正通红》，歌词具有浓厚的艺术美感，朗朗上口，语言优美，富有韵律。

（六）规约性信息

规约性信息主要指涉及条约或章程的信息，常见于矿业法律和矿业合同中。

二、矿冶类文本的翻译

矿冶类文本中包含的信息主要有外宣性信息、事实性信息、描述性信息、文化性信息、美学性信息、规约性信息等。在翻译该类文本时首先应对不同的信息进行区分，进而采取相应的翻译策略。矿冶类文本繁多，该文主要以事实性、文化性和描述性信息为例来探讨其翻译。

例 5　单孔石铲：新石器时期，上宽 11. 5cm，下宽 13cm，中间长 12. 5cm，孔径 1. 4cm，鲶鱼墩遗址出土。

译文：Haplopore Stone Shovel：Neolithic Period；UpperWidth：11. 5cm；Under Width：13cm；Middle Length：12. 5cm；Pore Diameter：1. 4cm；Unearthed from Nianyudun Archaeological Site.

通过分析，原文中包含的全部为事实性信息，翻译时应注意专业词汇的选择，避免出现让读者误解的内容，同时应在专业性高、不易理解的地方进行注释。在翻译实践中，译者应充分思考如何使所译出的信息符合事实性信息的特点。本例中“单孔”应翻译为 haplopore，“haplo-”表示“单的”，而不能用“mono-”或“single”，“pore”指细孔、微孔、气孔或者毛孔等细小的孔，而不能译为“hole”，因为“hole”主要是指较明显的实体的洞。“鲶鱼墩”作为一个特定的专有名词，翻译的时候也应格外注意其翻译策略，通名应视作专名的组成部分，先音译，并与专名连写，后重复意译。如“鲶鱼墩”不可以直接根据“鲶鱼”的意思翻译为“catfish site”或“bullhead site”，这样容易误导读者，尤其容易误导没有相关文化背景的外国读者，因此正确的译法是“Nianyudun Archaeological Site”。

例 6　在中东的西奈及阿拉伯谷地，考古学家发现了公元前十三世纪至公元前十一世纪古埃及法老王朝在提姆纳采冶铜矿的遗址。

译文：In Sinai and Arab Valley in mid-eastern districts，archaeologists discovered copper mining and smelting relics in Timana during the reign of Egyptian Paraho which lasted from B. C. 13th，century to B. C. 11th century.

通过分析，文本中出现了与文化相关的信息，如“中东的西奈及阿拉伯谷地”“古埃及法老王朝”“提姆纳采冶铜矿的遗址”等。翻译时应当传递出文化内涵，注意读者的不同文化背景，适当地予以注释。以上信息内容要根据其意义内涵分别翻译为“located in Sinai and Arab Valley in mid-eastern districts”“during the reign of Egyptian Paraho which lasted from 13th century B. C. to 11th Century B. C.” “copper mining and smelting relics in Timana”。其中需要注意的是，翻译古埃及法老王朝时可以将其后面的时间年份作为定语紧随其后，既避免了重复翻译的冗杂又恰如其分地对它进行了解释说明。此类文化性信息面体现着丰富的历史性，在译文中同样要体现原文中的历史、地理等因素。

翻译描述性信息时应着重注意形容词的翻译，重点放在描述性较强的文字上。

例 7　据《大冶县志》记载：“铜绿山‘山顶高平，巨石对峙，每骤雨过时，有铜绿如雪花小豆，点缀土石之上，故名’。”铜绿山盛产孔雀石，孔雀石是种氧化铜矿，有时会出露地表，成为矿体露头。其色彩亮丽，尤其是当雨水冲洗后，点缀在土石之上，十分醒目，成为古代寻找铜矿的指示物。

译文：According to the records of Daye County Annals, the name of Tonglu (green color copper) Mountain derived from the fact that the summit was high and flat with large rocks surrounded face to face and after storms there appeared copper decorating soil and rocks in green color and in the shape of snowflake beans. Tonglu Mountain is rich in Malachite which falls into the category of oxidized copper ore which either outcrops ground surface or becomes outcrops of ore body. Also, Malachite has bright color especially after rains and becomes decorations of soil and rocks. Thus, in ancient times Malachite became the indicator for ancient people looking for copper ore.

上述文本中包含的描述信息主要有“高平、巨石，如雪花小豆、色彩亮丽、十分醒目”等，翻译这段文字时应准确传递描述性信息，即从符合原文作者描述的角度来翻译。

三、结束语

随着矿冶文化与矿业经济的不断发展，矿冶文本的翻译在国际交流中变得越来越重要，高质量的译文能够及时且高效地传播矿冶文化，因此矿冶文本的翻译应该受到更多的重视。在翻译矿冶类文本的实践中，译者应该首先分析其中所包含的信息类型，进而采用相应的翻译策略使译文符合原文的信息特点。

◎ 参考文献

[1] 吴玉霞．文本类型理论对翻译实践的指导［J］．东京文学，2009（5）．

[2] 张美芳．文本类型理论及其对翻译研究的启示［J］．中国翻译，2009（5）：53-60．

[3] 张美芳．翻译研究的功能途径［M］．上海：上海外语教育出版社，2005．

[4] 邵春美．矿冶类文本的多元化特点及翻译原则［J］．黄石理工学院学报：人文社会科学版，2011（1）．

[5] 贾文波．应用翻译功能论［M］．北京：中国对外翻译出版公司，2004．

[6] Peter Newmark. Approachs to Translation［M］. Hemel Hempstead：Prentice Hall，1981.

[7] Reiss K. Translation Criticism—The Potentials & Limitations［M］. Shanghai：Shanghai Foreign Language Education Press，2004.

第三节 博物馆矿冶类文本的翻译原则*

——以黄石博物馆为例

Translation Principles of Mining and Metallurgical Texts in Museums —A Case Study of Huangshi Museum

摘要：以黄石博物馆矿冶类文本的现有英译为研究对象，探讨了该类型文本翻译时应遵循的基本原则及策略，并将其运用到对博物馆解说文字的误译对应分析，以期引起译者对外宣文本英译规范性与学术性的关注，努力保持相对统一的外宣表述形式，以译出更符合国际文化传播规范要求的译文。

关键词：黄石博物馆；矿冶类文本翻译原则；规范性

博物馆是征集、典藏、陈列自然和人类文化遗产的重要场所，其作为非盈利性机构对公众开放，并发挥着为公众提供学习、教育、娱乐、交流等服务的重要功能，是实现跨文化交际与地域文化传播的重要媒介。为更好地介绍中国的历史和地域文化，博物馆外宣文本的翻译十分重要。博物馆介绍的翻译是典型的应用文体的翻译，而应用文体的翻译注重信息传递的效果和受众者的反应，提供真实信息和传递文化是这类文本的主要作用。博物馆简介的目的在于让普通游客读懂、看懂，从而获取相关的文、

* 作者曹芸，原载于《开封教育学院学报》第34卷第2期，2014年。

史、地及习俗方面的知识。英文简介面向国外游客与考察者，是向国际友人宣传中国传统文化、提供博物馆馆藏鉴赏知识及学术信息的直接途径。

由于中西方文化表达方式的差异，以及博物馆文本本身的特殊性，国内许多博物馆介绍的英译文存在许多译文信息传递失误的问题，特别是一些极具地域文化特色的博物馆文本的翻译，更是有待研究。

一、博物馆文本翻译的国内外研究现状

国内外许多专家学者都从不同角度对博物馆文本翻译进行过一系列研究，并提出在翻译过程中应遵循的一般原则和应采用的翻译策略。英国当代著名翻译理论家纽马克认为，不同文体的文本翻译应遵循不同的翻译原则和翻译策略。对于以目的语文化为归属的信息型文本，如博物馆宣传手册，应注重读者的理解和反应，在表达方式、格式措辞等方面应尽可能符合该文本在译入语中的习惯。在国内，李道胜也认为博物馆解说词属于指示功能和信息功能文本，所以在翻译时应突出信息传递功能，适当增加文化信息或删除低值文化信息。师新民指出博物馆文本翻译要遵循四个原则：民族性原则、简洁性原则、信息性原则、回译性原则。这些前人的研究都指出博物馆文本翻译应遵循的一般性原则，即在翻译时应做到语言精练、用词准确，最大限度传递原文的信息。

但是，在具体的博物馆介绍翻译中，还鲜有学者对特定区域文化范畴下的博物馆文本，如“湖北黄石博物馆矿冶文化类文本”的翻译进行研究，并分析其文本特点。笔者在此提出博物馆简介的具体翻译策略，仅以黄石博物馆为例，总结出博物馆简介的翻译原则：准确性、信息性、简洁性。

二、博物馆简介的翻译原则

准确性、信息性、简洁性原则具体是指在翻译中用最贴近而又最准确的方式再现源语所要传递的文化信息。译文要求最大限度地呈现源语的形式、意义、风格和文化内涵等，而且更加关注读者对译文信息的领悟和反

应。该翻译原则能更准确地结合文化内涵，将源语传达给目的语的读者。

博物馆是一个国家对外宣传本国文化的重要窗口，也是对外文化交流的重要资源，所以博物馆中的解说词是有效传递本国文化信息的重要载体。这种解说词大体上属于公示语，是科技英语的分支，在翻译时也应遵循以下几个原则。

（一）准确性原则

准确性原则，即翻译中的“信”，指忠实原文。译者必须准确地把原文的内容及思想表达出来，不可擅自增删内容或改变意思。译者要绝对尊重原作者的思想、观点、立场及个人感情，不可凭自己的好恶去肆意歪曲。任何文本的翻译都必须遵守这一原则。所以，博物馆解说词这种应用性文本在翻译时也必须遵守准确性这一首要原则。译者在将原文语言内容转换到译文语言内容的过程中，要做到选词、概念表达、物与名所指准确。如果译文失真，不仅难以正确、有效地传递原文的信息，而且容易被被受众曲解，起不到传播文化的作用。

（二）信息性原则

博物馆解说词都承载着一定的信息，具有直接或间接的说明作用。这样的解说词能使人见名明义，实用性很强。但是由于文化背景的不同，不同的民族对同一事物的理解也存在极大差异。如中国人了如指掌的知识点在中文材料中只字不提，外国游客会因为缺乏相应的知识而影响对该材料的理解。对此，译者需要在译文中利用增补法来增添相关的信息。而有时，汉语中用的一些词本身没实际意义，却被直接译成了英文，使外国游客不能理解，导致跨文化交际的失败。这时，译者就须使用减译法。

（三）简洁性原则

博物馆解说词的翻译应言简意赅，特别是文物译名，其用词、造句、行文要简洁明了、精练通顺。译者应在尽可能用最少的文字准确传达最多的信息的同时，让受众在最短的时间内获取最流畅的信息量。同时，译者还应考虑外国读者的接受能力，在简洁的前提下使译名具有自释性。

三、黄石博物馆英译实例分析

黄石作为矿冶之都、青铜文化发展的摇篮，其博物馆里使用的大多是矿冶类文本。凸显矿冶文化、准确使用术语，是对矿冶类文本译者在翻译实践中的基本要求，也是指导翻译过程的重要原则。可惜的是，馆内解说词和展品的英译存在很多问题。现将这些错误分类择要评点，重译如下。

（一）语言失误

黄石博物馆外宣文本英译中存在的最明显的问题就是语言失误，其中包括拼写错误、语法错误、用词不当等。

1. 标题首字母大写

如“A brief introduction of Huangshi mining and metallurgical culture”（《黄石矿冶文化展简介》）应为“A Brief Introduction of Huangshi Mining and Metallurgical culture”；再如“Mining and smelting culture in the prehistoric age”（史前时期的矿冶文化）应为“Mining and Smelting Culture in the Prehistoric Age”。在《黄石矿冶文化展简介》的文本英译中，很多地方都出现了这样的问题。

2. 语法错误

如“Han-Ye-ping iron and coal mines Limited corporation, founded in the late Qing Dynasty established the pioneer status of Huangshi in the development of China's modern industry.”（清末汉冶萍煤铁厂矿有限公司的创办，确定了黄石在中国近代工业发展中的先驱地位），其中“established”前应加“,”；再如“Huangshi mining and metallurgical culture is not only one of the most important elements in China's Bronze culture, but also contribute a great deal to the human civilization and social development.”（黄石矿冶文化不仅是中华青铜文化的一个重要组成

部分，而且也为人类文明和社会发展做出了卓越贡献），其中“contribute”应为“contributes”。

3. 用词不当

例如“竖井”，被翻译为了“vertical shafts”，其实“shafts”本身就表示“竖井”，所以“竖井”应该译为“shafts”。“盲井”被译为“blinds wells”，而“well”是指打水的井或出油的井，所以“盲井”应该译为“blind shafts”。

以上三种错误违背了翻译的准确性原则，使得目的语的读者不能准确地了解中国的矿冶文化。

（二）文化信息处理不恰当

黄石博物馆外宣文本的英译中，普遍存在文化缺省的问题——特别是对年代交代不清。比如“商周时期的采矿方法分为……”被译为“In the Shang and Zhou dynasties”。外国读者对中国的“商周时期”不甚熟悉，所以译者在翻译时最好能补充一些原文中没有的背景信息，如“商周时期”所处的具体年代。这样就给了读者更多的相关信息，帮助其更好地理解。所以笔者将“商周时期”译为“In the Shang and Zhou Dynasties（1600B. C. —256B. C.）”。这样就能使西方读者了解这一时代具体是什么时候，甚至可以将中国的这一时代与其生活的国家的这一时代进行对比，从而更好地理解中国文化。这样译文就符合信息性原则。

（三）译文过于复杂

黄石博物馆的外宣文本中，大多都有配套图片，在翻译的过程中应尽量做到简洁，但是有些译文过于复杂。例如“The use of a continuous length of rope is demonstrated and the method of timber lining in Greek and Roman mining contrasts with the hoisting approach in mining of China's warring states period.”（在古希腊、罗马等地，矿井提升采用垂直提升，与中国战国时期采矿业中的提升方法形成对比）这句话在翻译时

就显得过于复杂，而且用词不当（“对比”此处是比较相同之处，不宜用contrast）。因此，笔者将其简化为“Mining hoisting features vertical hoisting in ancient Greek and Roman which is in line with that of the warring states period in China.”另外，其他地方也存在翻译不符合简洁性原则的现象，有待简化。

四、结语

随着时代的发展，博物馆外宣文本的英译在跨文化交流与传播中发挥着愈来愈重要的作用。笔者从应用型文本翻译所遵循的准确性、信息性和简洁性翻译原则出发，以黄石博物馆的矿冶类外宣文本译文为例，探讨了如何有效地进行博物馆文本翻译，并指出现有译文中存在着不少有待改进的地方，期待更多的学者和研究人员不断提高博物馆外宣文本英译的质量，让读者更好地了解和认同中国历史和地域文化。

◎ 参考文献

[1] 丽卜青，胡雪英．博物馆文物展品英译研究——以浙江省博物馆为例［J］．中国科技翻译，2011（3）：47.

[2] 师新民．考古文物名词英译初探［J］．中国科技翻译，2007（8）：61-63.

[3] 邵春美．矿冶类文本的多元化特点及翻译原则［J］．黄石理工学院学报，2011（1）：64-65.

[4] 豆红丽．中国博物馆文本英译模式初探［J］．郑州航空工业管理学院学报，2011（2）：165-168.

[5] 郑佳．从翻译目的论看博物馆解说词的英译——以中国文字博物馆为例［J］．华中师范大学研究生学报，2011（1）：88.

第四节　公知性矿冶外宣文本英译质量研究*

Study on the Quality of English Translation of Mining and Metallurgical Publicity Texts

摘要：本文首先对公知性矿冶外宣文本进行界定，并从词汇、句法及语篇三方面探讨翻译该类文本的难点及翻译原则。外宣翻译文本的质量保证需要译者在把握上述要素的前提下，积累相关的专业语汇，并能灵活运用翻译策略与技巧；另一方面，须由相关职能部门牵头组建地方性译者网络同盟，构建地方性外宣信息共享资源库，以提高地方性外宣文本翻译的整体质量。

关键词：外宣文本；矿冶文化；翻译策略；翻译质量

一、引言

2010年中国译协首次将翻译工作冠名为“语言服务业”并对其服务范围予以了界定，更彰显了翻译的应用性。它不仅是跨文化交流互动最直接的手段，更是促进当前不同文化之间政治、经济、文化等领域广泛沟通与合作的桥梁。然而，相比主流文化外宣翻译文本的多级质量监控与有效管

---

* 作者方晓梅、邵春美，原载于《湖北师范学院学报》（哲学社会科学版）第34卷第4期，2014年。

理，地方文化的外宣文本因其包罗万象又缺乏相对一致的评价标准和校审体系，导致同区域、同行业、同系列产品的译名缺乏统一性和规范性，失去翻译应达成的跨文化宣介目的。[1][2]本文作者以引导应用型人才社会实践研究为契机，以地方特色文化对外宣传信息翻译文本质量为调研对象，组织英语专业高年级学生采集了所在地区现有的矿冶文化宣传网站、场馆简介、企业外宣介绍等英语翻译资源信息（含文档、音视频资源）近7万字，以功能语言学和跨文化交际理论为文本分析的理论依据，对采集的外宣素材分类归纳与分析，探讨运用文化差异补缺、文体风格顺应，以及合理利用文献资源、建立地方特色文化翻译语料库等方法推动外宣翻译质量的提高。

二、矿冶类外宣文本的界定

不同质态和多元化特色的地方文化构成了“中国文化”这一宽泛的定义。黄石（大冶）是中国青铜文化的发源地之一，这里有“世界文化遗产瑰宝”美誉的铜绿山古铜矿遗址，有昭示中国近代工业文明发端的汉冶萍钢铁厂，有海内外熟知的华新水泥厂等工矿企业，以及由它们共同创造的矿冶文化。传播矿冶文化的目的“不仅是记录和展示矿冶文明，更重要的是记录社会化、工业化时期的社会文明变迁”。[3]2011年和2013年由黄石市举办的首届与第二届国际矿冶文化旅游节，推动了矿冶文化走向国际舞台，也为业界产品与技术交流与合作、跨文化矿冶史学研究、矿冶文化保护与生态环境修复研究提供了平台。翻译是跨文化交流不可或缺的工具，开展矿冶类外宣文本的翻译研究，是实施让中国“文化走出去”战略、加强地方特色文化的对外传播，并使之成为人类共有的文明财富的重要举措。

诺德（Nord）将翻译文本功能分为：指称功能（referential function）、表情功能（expressive function）、感染功能（appellative function）和寒暄功能（phatic function）四种。[4]但与矿冶文化外宣相关的文本既包含了矿冶文学文本所具有的表情功能，又包含了矿山公园导游文本所具有的感染功能，还包含了古矿冶遗址简介为代表的指称功能文本。统计近五年间本地区矿冶类外宣文本资料情况，按企业宣介、网站新闻、场馆简介、旅游景点指南、文化产品与工业产品说明书等栏目对所采集的外宣文本予以分类界定。(表 1)

表 1 **矿冶类外宣资料分类**

<table>
<tr><td rowspan="16">矿冶类外宣文本</td><td rowspan="3">企业及产品宣传</td><td>矿冶类生产或加工企业简介</td></tr>
<tr><td>招商引资公告、项目投资指南</td></tr>
<tr><td>设备安装与操作指南、生产技术手册</td></tr>
<tr><td rowspan="4">矿业网站信息</td><td>工矿企业网站信息</td></tr>
<tr><td>地方政府网站中矿冶企业新闻信息</td></tr>
<tr><td>矿冶文化研究机构网站信息</td></tr>
<tr><td>地方传媒网站或其他公开信息源（如档案馆）中相关信息</td></tr>
<tr><td rowspan="3">场馆介绍</td><td>展品名称及简介</td></tr>
<tr><td>博物馆、展览馆的宣传手册</td></tr>
<tr><td>矿冶文化场馆与展品解说词</td></tr>
<tr><td rowspan="4">旅游与文化宣传</td><td>古矿冶遗址的说明等</td></tr>
<tr><td>矿山文化公园的简介、景区与景点导游词</td></tr>
<tr><td>工矿城市文明与公用设施外宣用语</td></tr>
<tr><td>矿工文学与矿冶题材的艺术作品</td></tr>
<tr><td>其他资料</td><td>文物保护法规、矿区或展馆管理条例</td></tr>
</table>

除本表中归纳的类型外，矿冶文化对外传播亦包括其他的翻译文本或非文本形式，如与矿冶文化传承有密切关联的矿冶文学、矿区传说、矿工歌谣、矿区习俗、采矿谚语或俚语等语言文化艺术，以及规约性矿业法律文本和操作规程等。但文学文本翻译对意义与意境的侧重与表 1 中所列文本以事实为重的翻译要求不同，矿业法律文本的措辞严谨性与外宣文本的写实性也决定了翻译策略上的差异，因此上述两类文本未列入本文讨论范畴。

三、矿冶类外宣文本英译的难点与翻译策略

基于上述对矿冶类外宣文本研究范围的界定，在考虑地方文化虽具有显著性局域特征或跨文化差异性的基础上，将以“读者为中心”确定为这类应用性文本质量评价的主要依据。[1]从外宣文本关注的译语读者、语言间的文化差异、译者处理文本的策略与技巧角度三个维度，分别对现行矿冶类外宣文本中来自词汇、句法、篇章等不同层面的翻译问题与难点予以分析，是为这类文本的翻译实践和经验积累寻找策略借鉴。

1. 词汇难点与翻译策略

矿冶类外宣文本多含地矿、冶炼、成型、化工等领域的专业术语，如矿物名称、遗址或遗物名称、冶炼工具与采冶技术类词汇等，这往往是翻译的第一大障碍。[5]除专业术语外，词汇层面的难点还包括对文本中涉及的时间、地名等的处理，需要一定的翻译策略。如表 2 所示：

表 2　**词汇翻译的难点与策略**

难点	翻译策略	翻译实例	
时间	现代时间直译为阿拉伯数字	1973 年	in 1973 或译为 in the year of 1973
	古代时间须补全信息	春秋时期	the Spring and Autumn Period (770B. C. —476B. C.)
地名	大地名直译处理	湖北省	Hubei Province
	地名预设信息不足须补全	大冶	Daye County, located in Huangshi City, Hubei Province
书籍名称	采用已有的规范表达，译文斜体 无规范表达时借鉴译入语平行文本	《管子地数》 《大冶县志》	*Dishu Methods for Exploiting the Earth by Guanzi* *Daye County Annals*

续表

难点	翻译策略	翻译实例	
数字单位	与原语罗马数字或阿拉伯数字保持一致	XI 号矿体	No. XI Ore Body
	中英文数字单位不一致时须补全信息	10 座炼炉	ten smelting furnaces
颜色词	目的语中有对等词时须直译	铜绿	patina in color
	目的语中无对等词，应做注解		

2. 句法难点与翻译策略：指代词、无主句、古代文献的正确诠释

本文引用了大量源自本地区外宣文本的译句，这些译句反映了翻译过程中的句法处理、古代文献释译、同文不同译等方面存在的问题。

例 1　1965 年以来，铜绿山矿在生产建设中，不断发现古代采矿遗迹和冶炼古炉渣。

译文： Since year 1965 among the production and construction about Tonglu Mountain Mine we continuously find ancient mining site and ancient slag.

例 2　1976 年 5 月，在调查冶炼遗址时，发现柯锡太村周围堆积着大量古炉渣。

译文： In May of 1976 when investigating the smelting sites they found it accumulated lots of ancient slag around Kexitai Village.

上例节选自《铜绿山古矿冶遗址简介》，属汉语中典型的无主句，原译文分别采用“we”和“they”作主语，存在指代不清的问题。除此之外，对术语“古炉渣”的翻译，在语法上存在歧义，给译入语读者带来理解上的困难。此类无主句的英译应尽量采用被动语态（除非主语已在上下

文中明示）。上述两例改译为：

Since 1965, ancient mining sites and smelting slag deposits have been unearthed in the process of the establishment and development of Tonglu Mountain Mine.

A lot of ancient slag deposits were found around Kexitai Village in May 1976 when smelting sites were investigated.

历史文献在外宣类文本中多被援引以佐证观点或说明事实，其古体化的语言给译者翻译带来困难，译者充分明晰文献翻译在语境中引用的目的并深入挖掘其含义，根据文献信息与语境的关联度采取相应的翻译策略，使译入语读者能借助译文获取准确信息，是外宣翻译成功的关键要素之一。[6][7]如果文献的引用旨在增添汉语的描述性而无益于译入语读者的理解，则应采用删减性翻译策略。

例 3 据《大冶县志》记载：“铜绿山山顶高平，巨石对峙，每骤雨过时，有铜绿如雪花小豆点缀土石之上，故名。”

译文 A：According to the record of *Daye County Town Records*, the peak of Tonglu Mountain is high and flat, megalith facing each other, when the pour passes there is patina like snow peas sprinkling above the soil and stones, so get the name.（摘自《铜绿山古矿冶遗址说明》“前言”。）

译文 B：According to the records of Daye County Annals, the name of Tonglu Mountain derived from the fact that the summit was high and flat with large rocks surrounded and after storms there appeared copper decorating soil and rocks in patina and in the shape of beans like snowflakes.（摘自《黄石矿冶文化展简介》）

例 3 所示的译文差异系根据不同语境要求采用了不同的翻译策略。译文 A 为直接引证方式翻译，因原文的目的是引用典故说明其历史，虽然译文错误较多但运用的翻译策略是正确的；译文 B 采用了解释性翻译策略，因为此处的语境并不要求凸显史实，旨在说明其名称的由来，所以，对历史文献的英译应充分符合引用的目的，进而采取恰当的翻译策略达成引用的目的。但译者应充分注意，同文不同译虽然是由翻译目的所决定的，但如果此句原文出现在矿冶文学作品中应保持相同的译法。

3. 语篇难点与翻译策略：标题的翻译、分项列举时结构的一致以及信息的推进

在博物馆展品的介绍中或古矿冶遗址的说明中通常都配有真实的图片、器物或遗物，单个的介绍或说明往往配有标题用以概述。标题应用语准确且精炼，使译入语读者能够快速地理解说明性文字。

例 4　古代矿井提升

译文： Rising of Ancient Mining Well（摘自《柯锡太冶炼遗址说明》。）

译文除术语表达不准确、单复数误用外，还存在理解歧义问题。标题作为语篇的核心应力求语言准确精练，应译为：Hoisting of Mining Wells in Ancient Times。

例 5　采用浅井和重砂分析技术

自成体系开采技术

采用鼓风竖炉炼钢技术

译文： Adopt analysis technique by shallow well and heavy sand

Natural system about exploiting technique

Adopt smelting technique by blast shaft furnace（摘自《采冶技术成就》。）

例句中译文动宾结构与名词短语混用，导致译文存在语法结构、术语表达和语法规范等多项翻译问题，应译为：

Analytical technique in shallow wells and heavy concentrate

Systematized mining technology

Steel-making technique based on mast furnaces

诸如此类的错译不仅严重影响文本质量，更使外宣的效果大打折扣。采用规范化译语与译名能使说明性文字发挥出应有的功效；同样，采用分项列举的方式能使文本条理清晰。由于矿冶类文本类型较为固定，且同类文本的信息构成及逻辑推进方式大体一致，因此译者须首先从语篇的宏观层次上把握文本结构、分析信息的构成及推进方式、找出信息焦点，才能在翻译中凸显重点信息，实现提高外宣文本翻译质量的目的。

四、提高外宣文本翻译质量的措施与建议

应用型翻译在当今全球化进程加速的过程中始终是各领域信息交流的主要内容。地方文化的对外传播有赖于优质足量的翻译文本做推手。[8]矿冶类外宣文本的英译是区域文明走向世界共享最直接、最经济的方式。优化黄石矿冶文化外宣文本的翻译质量更是提升城市知名度、增强文化软实力的辐射作用、扩大矿冶文化品牌效应、推动文明的保护与传承的有效途径。

然而，本项目研究也说明当前矿冶类外宣文本的翻译现状令人堪忧：译本不仅存在时效性大大滞后的问题（信息陈旧），而且许多译文如同学术著作，其间充斥着过多的专业术语，对外宣信息传播应具有的通俗性和大众化考虑不足；一些译者对原文内容不熟悉，望文硬译，或未考虑跨文化差异，翻译中缺少对汉语概括性语言的必要注解或阐释，易致英文读者如坠云雾之中。分析此类问题产生的根源，一方面是相关企业或机构缺少专职翻译人员，或现有翻译人员水平有限；另一方面是外宣翻译始终处于各自为政的散乱状态，缺乏一个整合信息资源的中心和相对稳定的译者群体。另外，缺少既有工程或矿冶学科知识又具备良好的文字诠释能力的译者。这些是造成译文质量问题的根本原因。

外宣文本的诠释与译者水平能力紧密关联，译者的语汇与矿冶知识积累、译者翻译策略与技巧的灵活运用，均对文本的最终质量起着决定性影响。[9]因此，提高本地区矿冶类外宣文本翻译质量，需要多方支持和联手

行动。首先，政府文化管理部门提供政策引导并能给予实际扶助。通过建立译员信息库和译者群的网络联动，培养一支素质与业务能力俱佳的外宣翻译队伍。第二，在外事与旅游管理机构的协调之下，建立和完善本地区公示语、特色文化与产品的翻译语料库，实现区域性资源共享。在保护语言文化多样性基础上，加强外宣译语的统一性与规范性。第三，以政策鼓励地方高校培养应用型人才，强化面向业界的服务意识。倡导校企合作共建英文网站（页），同时，高校翻译专业应以合作课题形式承接企事业单位与团体机构合法的外宣翻译内容。

由于外宣文本来源广泛、覆盖多行业多领域，具有多样性等显著特点，地方政府应创造有效的激励机制，吸引有兴趣、有能力的译者投注精力，不断开展翻译实践，培养一批对区域经济与发展、特色文化有充分了解的应用型译者，从而为区域内长效性翻译人才队伍建设奠定坚实的基础。

◎ 参考文献

[1] 陈小蔚．对外翻译中的文化自觉与受众意识 [J]．中国翻译，2013，(2)：95-100.

[2] 郭晓勇．中国语言服务业的机遇与挑战 [J]．中国翻译，2014 (1)：9-11.

[3] 陈继林，钟丽萍，杨泽喜．黄石——矿冶文明之都 [M]．武汉：湖北人民出版社，2009.

[4] Nord C. Translating as a Purposeful Activity: Functional Approaches Explained [M]. Manchester: St. Jerome Publishing, 1997.

[5] 邵春美．矿冶类文本的多元化特点及翻译原则 [J]．黄石理工学院学报，2011 (1)：63-67.

[6] 袁晓宁．外宣英译中的改写现象探究——以“南京湖泊宣言”翻译为

例［J］. 中国翻译，2012（3）：123-125.
［7］张传彪．外宣文本与翻译变通［J］. 江南大学学报（人文社会科学版），2010（5）：106.
［8］胡六月．地方文化的对外翻译与传播——以绍兴地方特色词汇的翻译为例［J］. 东方翻译，2011（1）：82-85.
［9］张美芳．文本类型理论及其对翻译研究的启示［J］. 中国翻译，2009（5）：53-55.

第五节 矿冶古都黄石对外旅游宣传资料英译现状调查及对策研究*

Investigation and Countermeasures of English Translation of Tourism Publicity Materials of Huangshi

摘要：旅游信息的宣传不仅是一种旅游活动，也是一种文化交流。翻译实践是跨国界、跨文化、跨不同社会、跨时间和空间的心理沟通活动。为了更好地促进旅游业的发展，旅游宣传材料的翻译显得尤为重要。本文在功能翻译理论的基础上，通过对黄石一些对外旅游资料翻译现状的分析，提出了四种翻译策略。

关键词：旅游宣传资料；英译现状；对策研究

一、引言

素有“江南聚宝盆”之称的黄石是以大冶铁矿天坑、铜绿山古铜矿遗址为代表的矿冶文化和华夏青铜文化的发祥地。它依山傍水，拥有众多集人文历史于一体的风景名胜，被誉为“山水宜居城市”，洋溢着现代城市的新鲜气息。如今，黄石正面临着城市转型和产业结构调整，低碳、绿色的旅游业自然被看作区域发展的新方向之一。虽然近几年来到我市观光旅

---

* 作者陈维维，原载于《华章》第 15 期，2014 年。

游的外国游客在逐年增加，但是城市旅游外宣品资料的翻译水平却没有跟上现实发展的步伐，旅游景点宣传文本翻译质量不尽如人意，存在翻译不规范等诸多问题。译文翻译质量不高，可读性差与实现推介和宣传城市的良好对外形象，开拓地方旅游市场的目标是相悖的，对于我市旅游业的健康发展也是极其不利的。因此，笔者认为旅游资料的译介工作应当引起重视。那么，当前如何在功能翻译理论的指导下，准确地介绍当地的旅游资源及民俗文化等信息，以树立良好的对外形象，促进双边文化交流，推动地区旅游业的发展应是翻译工作者的研究重点。

二、外宣材料英译现状

自 2012 年以来，笔者就开始着手调查黄石市旅游外宣材料的英译现状，旨在提出相应的对策措施，希望能为相关部门提供该方面的启示和建议，建立较完善的翻译组织，使译者有章可循，有例可鉴，从而为促进我市旅游业的发展，为振兴我市经济发展贡献力量。

三、旅游文本的特点及功能

旅游文本是一种应用型文体，其语言特征较独特，其文本类型涉及旅游宣传册、景区景点介绍、旅游宣传广告、旅游指示牌、民俗风情画册等。旅游文本的功能主要有以下两点：一是指称功能。各民族地区因生活习惯方式、自然条件气候、社会历史结构等方面的差异，也就形成了各民族特有的思维方式和审美情趣。因此，旅游文本中人们使用语言的形式和风格也各不相同。为有效传递自然地理、文化风俗等方面的信息，译者必须用读者所能接受的语言和形式来表达，以吸引游客，达到预期效果。二是召唤功能。招揽游客，“召唤”潜在的游客实现其旅游行为。

四、“动态对等”理论及其可行性

奈达的“动态对等”翻译概念是指“在接受语中用最相近的自然对等语再现源语的信息，首先是语义，其次是风格”。在动态对等翻译中，译者应着眼于译文读者的反应，翻译时不受制于原文的语言结构（即不拘泥于形式对应），而专注于原文的意义和精神；从语言功能角度看，城市旅游宣传资料必须提供足够的信息，具有信息功能；城市旅游宣传资料的对外介绍是经过润色的优美语言，语言越生动、越形象，就越能上口，人们就更容易感知和掌握，因而具有表达功能；城市旅游宣传资料主要是通过对城市的介绍宣传，扩大人们的知识视野，激发人们来该城市旅游、参观、投资的兴趣，从而具有呼唤功能。[1] 功能对等翻译涉及两个国家的语言和文化，好的译文应让读者感觉就像是在读用自己的母语编写的有关他国的外宣资料，而不是感觉在读译文，动态对等要求在翻译时应该采用译入语的语法与习惯。因此，作者认为运用动态对等（功能对等）理论来指导城市旅游宣传资料的英译是适用的。

五、外宣材料翻译的现状调查及定量分析

1. 研究内容及问卷设计。为掌握第一手信息，笔者对课题的最初设计方案进行了认真研究，并与其他英语专业教师和学生收集材料，努力达到预期的研究目的。该方案按照世界旅游组织对旅游者基本需求的分类，将收集到的黄石市旅游产品对外宣传材料及公示语翻译的研究内容大致分为三个类别，152 份样本的基本分布情况如下表所示：

研究内容	功能领域类别	份数	百分比
旅游景点中英文解说词	游	60	39.5%
旅游产品中英文说明书、中英文广告和企事业单位简介	购	53	34.9%
历史文化、民俗风情等中英文介绍（中英文纪录片、画报、报纸、杂志）	文化传播	24	15.8%
其他	其他	15	9.9%

从上表可以看出，黄石对外开放程度在不断扩大。鉴于中国的对外开

放程度日益加强，越来越多的资金和游客涌入我国各城市。在这一大好形势下，黄石市应进一步加强旅游宣传翻译工作，除了继续关注短期外国游客的食物、住宿、娱乐、购物、交通、旅游外，还应加强黄石市整体国际语言环境、人文环境建设，以满足在我市定居工作的外籍人士的长期需求。调查问卷所涉及的内容涵盖黄石市的主要旅游景点对外宣传材料及公示语翻译材料。从国际交往人员对旅游公示信息的需求及旅游商务的角度出发，笔者将对外宣传材料及公示语分为以下五大类（如下图所示），采取当面发放，当场限时测试的方式。

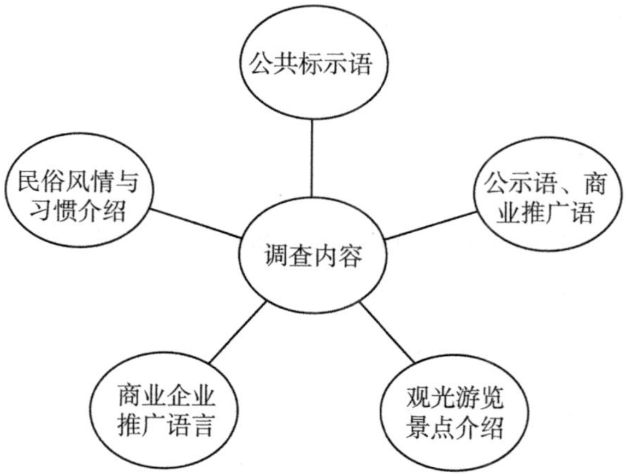

2. 调查对象。调查对象拟定为湖北理工学院外国语学院三四年级在校学生 40 名，外国语学院专业任课教师 20 名和外籍教师 5 名。

3. 研究工具。该项调查主要运用 SPSS 统计分析软件对研究结果进行分析。课题组成员统计并分析了收回的有效问卷，将样本反映出的错误现象分为：中式英语、语言累赘、拼写错误、语法错误、表述错误、漏译、乱译等。调查发现，“乱译”“表述”和“拼写”错误出现的频率居高。

问卷调查结果表明，目前我市对外旅游宣传资料的翻译较注重单纯的语言转换，而忽视了中西文化差异的协调，这可能是译者面临的一个棘手的问题。作为一种跨文化、跨地域甚至跨国界的文化交流活动，旅游材料的翻译需要兼顾双重文化背景，以求达到译文的准确和完美。

六、旅游文本汉英翻译策略探析

旅游外宣资料的英译属于应用翻译的范畴，其初衷是希望外国游客能够了解中国文化，提升游客的精神感受，激发其游览兴趣，乐意亲临实地。遵循功能翻译目的论中对等原则以及相关语用等效的说法，笔者提出了以下几点建议：

1. 以词语的语用内涵为导向，“让译语受众更快、更清楚地理解汉语表达的内涵，避免误读、误解，减少双方在语言交流方面的障碍，以便快速迅捷地沟通交流”。[2] 在旅游景点的公示语、标识语的翻译过程中，译者不能按照中文习惯表达来逐字翻译，更没必要加入过多的修饰成分，只须借鉴相对应的等效表达，将信息传达出即可。

例 1　不得乱扔烟蒂，护林防火人人有责。

译文：Don’t throw your cigarette ends everywhere. It’s everybody’s responsibility to prevent forest fire.

该告示牌的目的在于提醒游客要将烟蒂扔进垃圾桶，避免引起火灾。原来的译文虽然没有语法错误，但显得生硬，缺乏灵活性。试译为：Be careful with your cigarette ends。

2. 以译入语的语篇规范和表达方式为导向，达到译文在目的语中的语篇规范和交际功能的目的。英汉两种语言在旅游宣传品的表达方式和习惯上存在很大差异，翻译过程中要实现理想的交际状态，就必须充分考虑译文的语用功能。因此，在处理旅游外宣资料英译时，要根据目的语语言表达方式和习惯，适当调整或删减源语宣传材料中的冗余、渲染、夸张等信息，保留主要信息，使译文符合英语外宣资料的语篇规范。下例译文尽管在语言形式、结构、内容上做到了完全对等，但是忽略了英文的表达方式和习惯。

例 2　爱护花木，切勿攀摘！

译文：Stay away from flowers and trees.

上述译文能简洁地传达原文信息，但不符合英文表达方式。试译为：Take care of flowers and trees. Do not pick and harm them。

3. 协调中西文化差异。中国和西方国家由于宗教信仰、价值观、思维方式、传统习惯等差异而造成了文化差异。张美芳在第一届国家旅游暨文化创意产业（多语种）翻译研讨会上曾经说过，“译者处理文化问题，是为了跨文化交际，也是为了文化遗产的传承。然而传承并不等于一成不变地传递，它意味着在文化的传承中要有创新”。[3] 翻译不仅是两种语言之间的转换，更是一种跨文化交流和融合。文化差异是不可避免的，所以在处理文化内涵深厚的旅游文本翻译时，译者必须学会克服与生俱来的语言表达习惯和思维上的定势，要充分考虑中西方文化的差异，使原文和译文之间的出入最小化，使得译文通顺、准确、合理，为读者所接受。

例 3 绿色生态旅游

译文：The Green Excursion

“绿色”在中西文化中的内涵截然不同，在中国文化中象征“活力，年轻及和平”，而在西方文化中，常和“嫉妒，缺乏经验，知识浅薄”等联系在一起。因此，此译文会在西方游客心中产生不好的联想。试译为：Eco-Tour，能准确传达原语的文化内涵。

4. 以译文读者为翻译导向。根据功能翻译理论的基本原理，译文能否被受众所接受，接受程度的多少是衡量旅游宣传资料英译质量高低的唯一标准。因此，旅游外宣资料的翻译要充分考虑译文读者的价值观念、生活习惯、思维方式、兴趣爱好等主客观因素，尽量减少文化信息交流中所出现的障碍，扬长避短，灵活运用各种翻译方法，在准确传达原文本信息内容的前提下，有效发挥译文的优势，增强感染力，最终达到吸引游客来此一游的目的。

七、结束语

毫无疑问，旅游资料翻译质量的好坏会直接影响到旅游业乃至该地区经济的发展。功能翻译理论对旅游宣传资料的翻译活动有着很深的借鉴和指导意义。为更好地促进旅游及文化外宣事业的发展，达到功能翻译的目的，我们应对旅游资料的翻译活动予以足够的重视。译者应具有传播中国优良文化的责任感和职业责任感，努力提高自身修养与业务能力，采用灵活的翻译策略和方法处理旅游宣传文本的翻译；另外，本文试图呼吁相关部门高度重视对旅游资源的翻译，尽快制定相应的翻译标准，真正实现外宣目的，为黄石旅游业的发展做出自己应有的贡献。

◎ 参考文献

[1] 赖文斌．浅谈“动态对等”理论下的城市外宣资料英译［J］．太原城市职业技术学院学报，2009（12）．

[2] 周弘．旅游外宣品汉英翻译语用功能对等及翻译策略探析［J］．新余学院学报，2012（4）．

[3] 姚宝荣，韩琪．旅游资料英译浅译［J］．中国翻译，1998（5）．

第六节　西方现代修辞学视角下矿冶文化的外宣翻译*

Publicity Translation of Mining and Metallurgical Culture from the Perspective of Western Modern Rhetoric

摘要：数十年来延续传承的矿冶文化是黄石地区最具代表性的主流文化，为宣传黄石地区特色文化，使其能真正达到影响、感召、吸引国外受众的效果，外宣翻译是最重要的手段之一。外宣翻译的译文能否被国外受众接受及认同，最关键的在于外宣翻译译文的内容与形式是否能达到相应的交流效果。因此，本文针对黄石矿冶文化的英译现状，在西方现代修辞学理论的指导下，研究矿冶文化的翻译策略，旨在提高外宣译者的修辞意识，使黄石矿冶文化真正“走出去”。

关键词：矿冶文化；外宣翻译；西方现代修辞学；翻译策略

一、引言

作为中国古代矿冶文化的主要发祥地，黄石有着“青铜之都”“钢铁摇篮”“水泥故里”及“有色王国”之美称。随着黄石矿业经济不断发展，矿冶文化的国际性交流日渐增多。2012 年 11 月 17 日，“黄石矿冶工业遗产”（包括铜绿山古铜矿遗址、汉冶萍煤矿厂旧址、华新水泥厂旧址和大

---

* 作者倪京、邵春美，原载于《海外英语》第 23 期，2014 年。

冶铁矿露天采场）入选《中国世界文化遗产预备名单》。为了使黄石矿冶文化更好地走出国门，融入世界，研究黄石矿冶文化的英译现状，有着十分重要的意义。目前，在外宣翻译中关于如何对外宣传黄石矿冶文化还很少有学者提及，各种对外宣传的文本翻译也存在诸多问题，使得翻译质量不容乐观。基于此，本文试图通过比较外宣翻译与西方现代修辞学的特点与联系，并结合黄石矿冶文化对外翻译的真实译例来探索和分析外宣翻译原则及策略，旨在使黄石矿冶文化更好地被国外受众接受，达到有效交流之目的。

二、外宣翻译与西方现代修辞理论

关于受众的探讨和研究，西方现代修辞学一直予以高度重视，在修辞学上有很大造诣的亚里士多德将受众看作修辞术三大要义之一。比利时学者佩雷尔曼和奥布来茨-泰特卡指出："任何性质的话语都必须以受众为转移。"在某种情况下得体合适的论辩内容和形式，在其他场合可能会显得滑稽古怪；现代修辞学更加凸显了受众的重要性。20 世纪以来，新修辞学更加注重对受众的研究，并将研究的对象从演说者和作者渐渐向听者和读者转移。

无论是从实现外宣翻译的目标来看，还是借鉴西方现代修辞学的理论观点，赢得受众是最关键的因素之一。因此，作为外宣译者，首先要具备充分的受众意识。基于外宣翻译的这种特点，黄友义（2004：27）较早提出了以受众为依归的"外宣三贴近"原则，即贴近中国发展的实际，贴近国外受众对中国信息的需要，贴近国外受众的思维习惯。为了更好地提高受众意识，外宣译者应充分了解并把握国外受众的语言和思维习惯。陈小慰（2007）指出，"外宣翻译的受众是外国人，他们所处的历史文化环境与我国完全不同，思维方式、行为习惯和价值准则也相差甚远"。为此，外宣译者应在充分了解和熟悉本地区传统文化及译文内容的基础上，在翻译过程中充分把握国外受众的期望，采用国外受众习惯的思维方式和接受方式进行表达。

通过分析外宣翻译与西方现代修辞学的观点，可以看出，在翻译过程中，译者不应仅仅考虑单词拼写、语法等方面的错误，而忽略国外受众在语言、文化上的障碍。我们应借鉴西方现代修辞学理论观点，以受众为中心，充分融入国外受众的语言文化中去，将外宣译文作为对话交流的方式与他们沟通，“使翻译真正成为‘桥梁’，而不是隐形的‘障碍’”。

提高受众意识，是外宣译者进行外宣翻译的一个前提。相对于受众意识而言，建立起“认同”观念则是进行外宣翻译时进一步所要达到的目标。外宣翻译是以西方受众为前提的一项跨语言、跨文化的翻译实践活动，是否能达到预期的目的，主要看外宣翻译的手段是否合适及其翻译内容能否为西方受众所认同及接受。“认同”观念是由美国当代著名修辞学家肯尼斯·伯克（Kenneth Burke）提出的，他认为“说服是认同的结果”（Burke，1969），并将修辞重新定义为“认同艺术”。陈小慰通过分析古今中外关于“认同”说的理论，认为“修辞是表达和接受双向互动的交际活动，受众是不可缺少和必须考虑的因素。说服的成功取决于受众对说服者言谈方式的认同。因此，为了实现对外宣传的目的，外宣译者应充分借鉴西方现代修辞学的观点，在提高受众意识的前提下，以国外受众易于接受的方式进行外宣译文的翻译，与他们沟通和交流，从而建立起“认同”观念。

在西方现代修辞学理论中，修辞主要是指通过象征手法来影响人们的思想、态度、行为等的一种手段。袁卓喜（2013：1）指出“外宣翻译所追求的宣传效果是成功的说服”，“西方有十分悠久的雄辩传统，要与西方受众进行成功的交流，需要遵循西方的劝说机制”。外宣翻译要求外宣译者应具备受众意识，建立“认同”观念，其最终目的是进行对外宣传，对国外受众进行劝说和交流。因此，为了达到外宣翻译劝说与交流的目的，外宣译者应该通过外宣译文对国外受众进行有效的说服，从而更好地交往和传播文化。基于这种特点，外宣译者须借鉴西方现代劝说机制进行外宣译文的翻译。

三、西方现代修辞学对矿冶文化外宣翻译的启示

（一）增强译者的修辞意识，提高译者的修辞艺术

作为外宣译者，要想使地方文化真正“走出去”，与国外受众进行沟通和交流，就必须有较好的修辞意识。袁卓喜（2013：1）认为“人一旦运用语言进行有目的的交流，就不可避免地进入了修辞语境。外宣翻译是一种特殊的话语构建活动，有着明确的交际目的，其修辞环境是显而易见的”。可以说，修辞情境是外宣译者增强修辞意识、提高修辞艺术所要考虑的首要因素。西方现代修辞学研究中把修辞情境作为重要课题研究的修辞理论大家比彻尔（Lloyd Bitzer，1968）将修辞情境分成紧急状态（exigence）、受众（audience）和制约因素（constraints），并且指出修辞活动一旦出现，就必定存在某种修辞情境。矿冶文化作为黄石地区特色文化，处于矿冶行业这个独特的领域中，外宣译者要想将黄石矿冶文化传播给国外受众，达到沟通及交流的效果，就必须意识到如何将黄石地区与国外地区矿冶文化这两个独特的修辞情境连接起来，建立起“桥梁”，使这两种文化相互交融，找到共鸣。因此，为了提高外宣译文的翻译质量，达到交往与传播的预期目的，外宣译者必须提高自身的修辞意识，不断升华修辞艺术，将自身融入这种特殊的修辞语境中进行译文的翻译，以国外受众的身份与国外受众进行沟通交流。

（二）修辞情境下的矿冶文化翻译策略

为了在国际上传播黄石地区特色文化，增进外部世界对黄石矿冶文化的认识和了解，外宣译者应该弄清楚国外这种修辞语境的差异，并做出必要的调整，采用西方受众可接受的方式进行外宣译文的翻译。

例 1　在古希腊、罗马等地，矿井提升采用垂直提升，与中国战国时期采矿业中的提升方法形成对比。

原译： Vertical hoisting method was adopted in mining hoist-lug in ancient Greece and Rome contrasting with hoisting method adopted during the Warring States Period in China.

在原译文中出现了“战国时期”一词，这是中国古代的纪年方式，这相对于国内受众来说，比较容易理解和认识，但相对于身处异域的国外受众而言，无疑是生涩难懂的。因此，译者应该提高受众意识，增添公元纪年法作为补充和解释，建议改译为：

Vertical hoisting method was adopted in mining hoisting in ancient Greece and Rome contrasting with hoisting method adopted during the Warring States Period（403 B. C. —221 B. C. ）in China.

例 2 S01 陶甗（Yin），西周生活遗物，高 31. 5cm，口径 22cm（铜绿山 11 号矿体古矿井地表出土）

S03 陶鬲（Li），西周生活遗物，高 12cm，口径 14. 5cm（铜绿山 11 号矿体古矿井地表出土）

原译：S01 Tao Yin，Western Zhou Dynasty（1129 B. C. —771 B. C. ）Living Legacy，Height：31. 5cm，Calillre：22cm（Unearthed from the surface of 11th Ore Body，Ancient Mine in Tonglu Mountain）

S03 Tao Li ，Western Zhou Dynasty（1129 B. C. —771 B. C. ）Living Legacy，Height：12cm，Calibre：14. 5cm（Unearthed from surface of 11th Ore Body，Ancient Mine in Tulu Mountain）

例文中的“陶甗”和“陶鬲”都中国古代陶制炊器，这两种炊器对于国内许多受众来说都少有耳闻，对于国外受众来说，如果不加以注释，知道这两件陶制炊器的人更是寥寥无几。因此，译文内容很难与国外受众建立起“认同”观念，从而难以达到交流与沟通的效果。为了建立起“认同”观念，译者可将这两种炊器加以注释，不仅能使国外受众更形象地了解铜绿山古矿井所出土的这两种器具，而且也能达到与国外受众交往的预期目的。可改译为：

S01 Tao Yin（Pottery Yin，an ancient cooking pottery），Western Zhou Dynasty（1046 B. C. —771 B. C. ）Living Legacy，Height：31. 5cm，

Calihre：22cm（Unearthed from surface of 11th Ore Body，Ancient Mine in Tulu Mountain）

S03 Tao Li（Pottery Li，an ancient cooking pottery），Western Zhou Dynasty（1129 B. C.—771 B. C.）Living Legacy，Height：12cm，Calibre：14. 5cm（Unearthed from surface of 11th Ore Body，Ancient Mine in Tulu Mountain）

例 3　炉火照天地，红星乱紫烟。

原译：The furnace glitters the heaven and earth，the sparkles mix the purple smoke.

这是中国诗句中很常见的五言诗，译者想译好这两句，必须得先弄懂其深层意思。原译中的“天地”并不实指“天”和“地”，因此不宜翻译成“heaven and earth”，可直接翻译成“universe”即可。“紫烟”也并不是指紫色的烟雾，而是指炼炉时散发的带有水汽的烟雾。“smoke”指浓的带有固体物质的烟雾，显然不合原文，应改为“mists”较为合适。同时，考虑到原文与译文的对称性，原译文可改译为：The furnace glitters the universe，the sparkles mix the mists。

例 4　黄石地区，除了发现众多的古代矿冶遗存外，还发现了三座古代城址，这些矿冶遗存大多分布在古城址的周围。研究者认为，这三座古城址应是矿冶生产的管理中心，同时也是铜材的集散地。

原译：Three ancient city sites have also been discovered in Huangshi area except for many unearthed mining relics among which the mining relics unearthed were mainly located around the area of the ancient city sites. Researchers consider that the three ancient city sites were supposed to be the administration center of mining production and distribution center of copper.

通过比较原文和译文可以发现，若像原译文那样直译，则显得译文冗长难懂，且容易产生误解，不利于被国外受众所接受。同时，原文最后一句话是对前面的总结，译者应按照国外受众的思维方式和行文方式，在原译文当中添加相应的逻辑连接词“thus”，建议改译为：

In addition to many unearthed mining relies, three ancient city sites have also been discovered in Huangshi area. The mining relics unearthed were mainly located around the area of the ancient city sites. Thus, researchers consider that the three ancient city sites were supposed to be the administration center of mining production and distribution center of copper.

通过对黄石矿冶文化外宣译文的分析，可以得出：译者在面对国外受众的情境下，应采用必要的翻译方法如增添、释义及改变句法形式等，并始终要具备受众意识，以建立“认同”观念为目标，最终达到劝说与交流的预期目的，实现交往与传播的目标。

四、结束语

在西方现代修辞学理论的指导下，本文从修辞的角度以“受众意识”、“认同”及“劝说与交流机制”为导向来分析矿冶文本外宣翻译的特点及其原则和策略。外宣翻译以追求译文的交际效果为目的，是特殊的翻译实践活动之一。鉴于外宣翻译的这一特点，外宣译者身兼两大重任，一是对于源语信息的完整表达，二是通过对源语文本的翻译达到跨文化交际的实际效果。因此，为实现矿冶文本外宣翻译的预期效果，译者不仅要增强个人的修辞意识，还应当借鉴西方现代修辞学中“受众意识”“认同”及“劝说与交流机制”等理论，充分发挥修辞语言的力量，提升黄石矿冶文化外宣文本翻译的质量，从而更好地宣传和弘扬黄石矿冶文化。

◎ 参考文献

[1] Perelman, Chaim, Olbrechts-Tyteca. The New Rhetoric: A Treatise on Argumentation [M]. Notre Dame: University of Notre Dame Press, 1969.

[2] 黄友义. 坚持“外宣三贴近”原则，处理好外宣翻译中的难点问题

[J]. 中国翻译, 2004 (6): 27-28, 31.
[3] 陈小慰. 对外宣传翻译中的文化自觉和受众意识 [J]. 中国翻译, 2013 (2): 95-100.
[4] 陈小慰. 论译文话语的修辞力量 [J]. 中国外语, 2011 (3): 95-104.
[5] Burke K. A Rhetoric of Motives [M]. Berkeley: University of California Press, 1969.
[6] 陈小慰. 外宣翻译中 "认同" 的建立 [J]. 中国翻译, 2007 (1): 60-65.
[7] 袁卓喜. 现代修辞视角下的外宣翻译——基于西方劝说机制理论的思考 [J]. 解放军外国语学院学报, 2013 (1).
[8] Bitzer L . The Rhetorical Situation [J]. Phylosophy and Rhetoric, 1968 (1): 1-14.

第七节　语域理论视角下矿冶文化的翻译策略探析*

On the Translation Strategies of Mining and Metallurgical Culture from the Perspective of Register Theory

摘要： 黄石市矿冶文化的对外宣传是黄石发展地方特色文化的重要组成部分。文章以语域理论为指导，针对黄石矿冶文化对外宣传文本的英译现状，结合具体译例，探讨地方特色文化对外翻译中出现的问题，并提出应对策略，使黄石矿冶特色文化的翻译更好地服务于对外交流。

关键词： 对外宣传；语域理论；翻译策略

黄石以浓厚的矿冶文化而闻名，是华夏青铜文化的发祥地之一。矿业经济的迅猛发展及矿冶文化的日渐兴起，矿冶领域的国际性交流日渐增多，这也使得研究黄石地方文化的英译具有重要的现实意义。目前，如何对外宣传这些具有特色的地方文化还鲜有学者提及，各类矿冶文化对外宣传文本的翻译也仍存在许多问题，如拼写错误、语法错误、搭配错误、中式英语、文化信息丢失及语用失误等。因而，研究相关翻译策略可有效地指导翻译实践。本文以黄石矿冶文化为例，分析地方特色文化在翻译时存在的问题，提出解决问题的思路，以期为宣传和弘扬矿冶文化以及地方特

* 作者郑馨念、邵春美，原载于《湖北理工学院学报》（人文社会科学版）第31卷第2期，2014年。

色文化的英译工作起到抛砖引玉的作用。

一、语域理论与地方特色文化的对外翻译

语言交际总是以语篇的形式出现，由于不同的交际需要，语篇便出现了许多变体，这种变体所形成的范畴，便被称为语域。韩礼德提出“语域由三个主要的变量来衡量，即语场、语旨和语式”[1]。人们根据交际目的、交际对象和交际方式的差异选择使用的语言，这三方面因素体现在语域的三项参数中，即语场、语旨和语式。语场是指语篇涉及的主要内容；语旨是指语篇中所涉及的参与者之间的关系和其交际意图；语式是指语言在语篇中的交际形式。三项参数中任何一项的改变都会引起交际意义的变化，从而引起语言的变异，产生不同类型的语域。这就从客观上要求人们在使用语言时，不仅要注意它的准确性，更要根据语域三项参数的变化做出相应改变。地方特色文化的对外翻译就是一种与语域相关而产生的语言变异。每一领域的语言都有其各自的语言规则和语用规律，地方特色文化的对外翻译也不例外。以语域理论指导翻译过程，可以提高矿冶文化文本类型的翻译质量。译者在翻译过程中可根据语域的变化及自己对所述主题和特色文化术语的掌握情况，对信息传递方式、修辞手法、语体的切换等进行分析，从而更好地完成对地方特色文化文本的翻译。

二、黄石矿冶文化对外翻译实例分析与翻译策略探究

（一）语场与地方特色文化的对外翻译策略

“语篇范围，又称语场，指语言发生的环境。”[2]语场对于译者翻译地方特色文化文本的启示作用在于突出其文本的主题。

第一，矿冶文化的对外翻译要突出主题特色。

从对外宣传角度看，外国读者的文化差异、不同接受心理和特殊信息需求，决定了地方特色文化的翻译不能对源语文字直译，需要进行必要的改译。矿冶文化的对外翻译必须以突出主题信息或特色信息为原则，以便

使读者充分认识到所读内容的主旨。如果译文中失去了这种信息，就会造成语场错位，影响译文功能的发挥。

例 1 目前，公园内有世界第一高陡边坡、亚洲最大露天采坑、亚洲最大硬岩复垦基地等 8 个珍稀级矿业地质，矿业生产和矿业活动遗迹、遗址均得到有效保护并持续利用。

译文：At present, the park boasts of 8 precious remains for mining geologies, mining production and mining activities, including the highest steep slope across the whole globe, the largest open-pit mining as well as the largest reclaiming in hard rocks base in Asia, which all have received effective protection and sustainable utilization. （摘自《黄石国家矿山公园简介》）

原文的主题在译文中没有得到有效彰显，其本意是想表达公园具有“世界第一高陡边坡、亚洲最大露天采坑、亚洲最大硬岩复垦基地”的独特性，但该译文的处理明显偏离了信息焦点，因此，应打破原文的句子排列，进行语篇结构重组，使得重点信息突出，吸引读者。可改译为：

At present, the park has the highest steep slope across the whole globe, the largest open-pit mining as well as the largest reclaiming in hard rocks base in Asia. All these 8 precious remains for mining geologies, mining production and mining activities have received effective protection and sustainable utilization.

第二，矿冶文化的对外翻译要注意相关术语的译名。

地方特色文化术语有很强的专业性，甚至很冷僻，不是身处其地的译者容易忽略或产生错误理解。黄石矿冶文化中涉及的大量事实性、描述性的矿冶文本需要译者在翻译该类文本时对原文语言准确把握，使译文中专业术语的使用符合本语篇的语场。

例 2 该遗址于 1979 年至 1980 年由中国社会科学院考古研究所发掘。发掘面积 400 平方米，共清理出 60 余个竖井、盲井，20 余条平巷和斜巷，以及一条排水巷道，随同出土的还有大量用于矿山生产的工具。

译文： The site was excavated by the Archaeological Institute of Chinese Academy of Social Sciences from 1979 to 1980 with an area of 400 square meters, in which more than 60 vertical shafts, blind wells, and more than 20 Lane and Drift, as well as a drainage tunnel were unearthed along with a large number of instruments used in the mines production.
（摘自黄石市博物馆中关于“铜绿山春秋时期采矿遗址局部复原”的说明）

译文存在的问题是专业词汇翻译不够精确，如，“竖井”“盲井”分别译为“vertical shafts”“blind wells”，而“shaft”一词本身就表示竖井，且“well”多指打水的井或油井；“20余条平巷和斜巷”译为“20 Lane and Drift”也属于对专业术语掌握不清，且不论语法错误及大小写不明的情况。建议改译为：

The site was excavated by the Archaeological Institute of Chinese Academy of Social Sciences from 1979 to 1980 with an area of 400 square meters. And over 60 shafts and blind shafts, more than 20 galleries and inclined drifts, and a drainage lane were available after cleaning. A large number of tools used for mine production were unearthed as well.

（二）语旨与地方特色文化的对外翻译策略

“语旨，是指参与者之间的关系，包括参与者的社会地位以及他们之间的角色关系。”[3]地方特色文化的源语发出者为当地政府机构，译入语接受者为来中国参观的外国游客，二者文化背景差异较大，为达到对外宣传这一目的，译者必须在翻译文本中补充必要的语境信息，使译文更加清晰明了，有利于译入语读者对关键信息的理解。

第一，矿冶文化的对外翻译要结合信息内容进行适当增补，以表达出其中蕴含的特有文化信息。

例3　据史料记载和考古发现，公元226年（三国，吴，黄武五年）这里就有了开采活动，迄今已有1780年的历史。中国古代冶金工业文明在此薪火相传，如铜草花一样盛开。

译文：According to historical records and archaeology findings, in 226 A. D. ,（Three Kingdoms, Wu, Huangwu fifth year）there were mining activities with a history of 1780 years. The culture of Chinese ancient metallurgy industry is passed on from generation to generation, and blooms like the copper primrose.（摘自《黄石国家矿山公园简介》）

"铜草花"在原文中不仅仅是字面上的理解，它更是黄石大冶所独有的一种能够比较准确地显示铜矿藏地的特色植物，翻译时应凸显出这种特有的文化信息，使译入语读者易于理解。建议改译为：

According to historical records and archaeology findings, in 226 A. D,（Three Kingdoms, Wu, Huangwu fifth year）there were mining activities with a history of 1780 years. Here, the culture of Chinese ancient metallurgy industry is passed on from generation to generation, and blooms like the copper primrose, which is a kind of unique flora growing in Daye to indicate the underground copper deposits.

例 4 为了在大冶铁矿掠夺更多的铁矿石并将其运回日本炼成钢铁，制成武器，屠杀中国人民及亚洲各国人民，"日铁"在矿山采取劫夺式开采方式进行开采。

译文：In order to rob more iron ores at Daye Iron Ore and to send them back to Japan for making steel, manufacturing weapons, which would be used to slaughter Chinese people as well people allover Asia, "Ri Tie " employed plundering manner in extracting iron ores.（摘自《黄石国家矿山公园简介》关于"'日铁'开凿竖井"的说明）

"日铁"这个词为"日本日铁矿业公司"的简称，外国游客并不知道其意义和隐含的历史文化信息，翻译时若补充"the Nittetsu Mining Co. , Ltd. founded by the Japanese "，外国游客便可知道这是一家由日本人创办的矿业公司。建议改译为：

In order to rob more iron ores at Daye Iron Ore and to send them back to Japan for making steel, manufacturing weapons, which would be used to slaughter Chinese people as well as people all over Asia, "Ri Tie", the Nittetsu Mining Co., Ltd. founded by the Japanese, employed plundering manner in extracting iron ores.

第二，矿冶文化的对外翻译要注意信息内容的类比。为使译入语的读者能更好地理解源语，译者可以把源语资料里的有关内容转化为译入语读者熟悉的内容。这种类比的方法，常常可以帮助外国读者结合本国的历史文化理解他国文化。

例 5　黄石历史悠久的矿冶文化，萌芽于史前时期，鼎盛于商周至秦汉，延续至明清，“孙权筑炉炼兵器，岳飞锻铁铸刀剑”，其规模之大、持续生产时间之长、采冶技术之先进，在国内外都十分罕见。

译文：The profound history of mining and metallurgical culture in Huangshi began in prehistoric times and developed to prosperity from the Shang and Western Zhou Dynasties to the Qin and Han Dynastlies till the Ming and Qing Dynasties. "Sun Quan built the furnace to make weapons, Yue Fei forged iron to make swords," it was very rare at home and abroad for its scale and long history of production as well as the adoption of the advanced technology.（摘自《黄石矿冶文化展简介》）

原文中的孙权和岳飞为中国古代两大有名的军事家，为了便于外国读者理解，可对他们作进一步的解释，以帮助西方人了解我们的地方特色文化，建议改译为：

The profound history of mining and metallurgical culture in Huangshi began in prehistoric times and developed to prosperity from the Shang and Western Zhou Dynasties to the Qin and Han Dynasties till the Ming and Qing Dynasties. "Sun Quan built the furnace to make weapons, Yue Fei forged iron to make swords," both of them are two famous militarists in the history. It was very rare at home and abroad for its scale and long history of production as well as the adoption of the advanced technology.

（三）语式与矿冶文化的对外翻译策略

“语式是指语言交际形式，是一种带有评注、说教、描述等概念的渠道或媒介，分为书面语和口语。”[4]在地方特色文化的对外翻译上，要表现出语言在场景中所起的作用关键在于对其描述性的修辞以及文体的不同选择。

第一，矿冶文化的对外翻译要注意描述性修辞的改译。由于西方民族的审美习惯与中国截然不同，“西方传统哲学强调分析型抽象性思维，在主观与客观物象关系上，更多地强调模仿和再现，这也使西方的语言客观理性，结构严谨，而中国强调语言的言辞华美，虚实统一”[5]。

例 6 黄石国家矿山公园位于湖北省黄石市铁山区，东临长江滚滚波涛，西依雉山蒙蒙烟雨。园区面积 23 平方公里，园内树茂草丰，泉清石奇，鸟语花香，景色优美宜人。

译文：Huangshi National Mine Park situated in Tieshan District, Huangshi City, Hubei Province, neighbors the Yangtze River on the east, and borders the Mountain Zhi on the west. The land area of the park is 23 square kilometers. There are abundant trees and grasses, streams and rocks, twittering of birds and fragrance of flowers. It's really a beautiful place.

第二，矿冶文化的对外翻译要注意书面语与口语的选择，要表现出语言在场景中所起的作用，译者必须注意语体的选择。

例 7 断层从顶部标高 +276 米延伸至坑底 -168 米，垂直高度达 444 米，沿边坡长达 600 米。断面与边坡呈 30 °角，光滑面清晰可见，经历张扭和压扭二期地质活动；断层上窄下宽，破碎带沿边坡宽 5～30 米，常见压碎岩、透镜体、糜棱岩以及角砾岩。

译文：The fault extends from the top elevation +276 meters to the −168 meters and the vertical level is 444 meters, the length of the slope is more than 600 meters long along the slope. The section and the slope is 30 degree angle, the smooth surface is clearly visible and it has experienced twist and second phase pressure of geological activity; the fault has narrow top and wide bottom, and the width of the fracture zone along the slope is 5 ~ 30meters, crush rocks, the lens body, mylonite and breccia can all be seen on the slope.

译文生硬晦涩，没有表现出语言在场景中所起的作用。若译入语读者为相关专业人士，那么译者应选择理论性和专业性较强的书面语作为文体形式，把握翻译的准确性和客观性。建议改译为：

The fault extends from + 276 meters above the sea level to the pit bottle -168 meters below the sea level, hence, the vertical height is 444 meters. The fault is 600 plus meter long along the side slope. The fault is at 30 degree angle to the side slope, with the smooth side completely visible. The fault undergoes the second-phase geologic activities of strain wrench and stress wrench. The fault is narrow at the top and wide at the bottom; the broken belt is 5 ~ 30 meters wide along the side slope abundant with crushed rocks, lenticular ore body, sedimentary rock and breccia.

若译入语读者为一般外国游客，以书面语形式直译会使译入语读者感到理解困难从而失去阅读兴趣，使语言发挥不了应有的交际作用。建议改为更加口语化、通俗易懂的非正式文本：

The vertical height of the fault is over 400 meters, and after undergoing the geologic activities, the fault is narrow at the top and wide at the bottom and is at 30 degree angle to the side slope, on which there are many crushed rocks can be seen.

三、结语

在地方特色文化的对外翻译中，对语域的分析是必要前提之一。语场的作用体现在突出主题特色、准确把握地方特色文化术语，“对术语的正确分析有助于人们更好地认识与研究矿冶文化”[6]；语旨的作用体现在参与者角色关系可通过对信息内容的增补和类比使译文便于译入语读者理解接受；语式的作用表现在对语体的不同选择上。语域的三项参数并不是孤立的，它们相互联系，共同构成了语域的整体。地方特色文化的对外翻译过程，就是在译语中寻找尽可能起相似作用的语篇的过程，译者必须将这三项参数进行系统分析，评估源语与译语的匹配程度，使译文传递的信息为读者所接受，最终促进地方特色文化的对外宣传，使悠久灿烂的地方文化顺畅地走向世界。

◎ 参考文献

[1] Halliday M A K, Hasan R. Language, Context and Text: Aspects of Language in a Social-semiotic Perspective [M]. Geelong, Vic.: Deakin University Press, 1985.

[2] 谭英．语域理论指导下的科技英语翻译 [J]．科技信息，2011 (24): 139-140.

[3] 汪少华．语域理论新探 [J]．山东外语教学，2000 (2): 6-7.

[4] 李有华．语域视角下的旅游文本翻译 [J]．外国问题研究，2009 (4): 44-46.

[5] 孙媛媛．语域理论与翻译 [J]．课外阅读，2011 (4): 221-223.

[6] 邵春美．矿冶类文本的多元化特点及翻译原则 [J]．黄石理工学院学报（人文社会科学版），2011 (4): 63-67.

第八节　矿冶类外宣文本的翻译研究*

——以文化操纵派为视角

Translation Study on the Publicity Texts of Mining and Metallurgical Culture from the Perspective of Cultural Manipulators

摘要：随着矿业经济的迅速发展和矿冶文化的不断兴起，矿冶领域的国际交流也日益频繁，矿冶文化的传承特别是对外传播具有十分重要的意义。翻译是矿冶文化对外传播最直接和最有效的途径。本文从文化操纵派的视角研究矿冶领域外宣文本的翻译，注重翻译过程中的文化自觉和文化自信原则，以满足西方受众阅读的需要，从而对矿冶文化的对外传播起到积极的推动作用。

关键词：矿冶文化；外宣文本；文化操纵派；文化自觉；文化自信

随着文化全球化的趋势，外宣翻译彰显了其重要的作用和地位。翻译作为对外文化传播最直接的手段，促进了国与国之间政治、经济、文化等领域的广泛交流。笔者所在地是中国千年的矿冶古城，近些年，政府大力发展矿业经济，对内对外宣传矿冶文化，矿冶类外宣文本的英译就是使矿冶文化顺畅地走向世界最直接可靠的保证。本文基于文化操纵派的视角，

---

* 作者曹芸，原载于《郑州航空工业管理学院学报》（社会科学版）第34卷第5期，2015年。

以文化自觉和文化自愿为原则，浅析矿冶类外宣文本的翻译研究。

一、矿冶类外宣文本翻译的国内、国外研究现状

目前国内外专家学者对矿冶类外宣文本翻译进行研究的还比较少，而矿冶文化的研究也是近些年才提出的。石璋铭等（2008）在研究矿冶文化的内涵与外延的基础上分析了矿冶文化如何实现从传统到现代的过渡；孙淑云（2010）对如何传承和传播中国古代矿冶文化提出了具体的建议和措施；舒韶雄（2011）对矿冶文化旅游的开发进行了系统研究，指出旅游形象的提升、矿冶文化节的推广及电子商务等都对矿冶文化的对外传播起着积极作用；沈光华（2011）提出宣传矿冶文化及申报黄石为国家历史文化名城是宣传文化部门的主要任务。然而对矿冶类外宣文本进行翻译研究的只有寥寥几人。邵春美（2011）对矿冶类外宣性文本进行了界定，并在其多元化语体特点的基础上提出了矿冶类文本英译时应采用术语与文化兼顾的信息性翻译原则。因此，本文以翻译的文化操纵派为视角，从文化自觉和文化自信角度探讨矿冶类外宣文本的翻译，以期从这一崭新的视角拓宽外宣翻译的研究角度，同时对矿冶文化的对外传播起到助推作用。

二、矿冶类外宣文本的翻译原则

要想让他国了解中国矿冶文化，除了亲身体会外，还需依靠阅读译文来了解，所以矿冶类外宣文本的翻译在对外传播中起着重要的作用。功能学派翻译理论与文化学派翻译理论是西方翻译学的两大分支，两者的共同之处就在于“在翻译过程中译者对文本的介入、操控”。文化翻译论者认为，文本并不是一个语言静止不动的标本，而是译者在充分理解作者意图后，将这些意图创造性地再现于另一种文化的语言表现，因此，翻译不仅仅是复制和模仿，而是对文化的协调和操控。

“文化自信”是一个国家、一个民族、一个政党对自身文化价值的充分肯定，对自身文化生命力的坚定信念。只有对自己的文化有坚定的信心，才能鼓起奋发进取的勇气，焕发创新创造的活力。中华民族素有文化

自信的气度，正是有了对自己民族文化的自信心和自豪感，才能在漫长的历史长河中保持自己、吸纳外来，形成独具特色、辉煌灿烂的中华文明。所以，当人们在提及兵马俑，畅谈丝绸之路，甚至谈到不被人熟知的缶时，都怀有坚持对自己历史文化的自信。

巴斯奈特说过，翻译研究中应注重文化观以及将文化作为翻译的单位，不同文化的功能等值是手段，文化的转换才是翻译的目的。在翻译过程中，译者应该尽量在译语文化中找到原语文化的对等功能，即翻译的文化自觉原则，在翻译时应根据目的语的语用和受众的接受习惯做适当调整。目的语受众对信息的接收和领会受到所在国语言文化环境和观念的深刻影响，相同文化团体成员之间的“认同感”形成了属于该团体成员自己对事对物的共同标准和期待。因此为了实现对外宣传的目的，确保信息本身的可信度，译者“不能仅仅把词句翻译出来，而必须把这些词句化为目的语受众的心理语言”。他必须同时考虑源语文化和受众文化，能够设身处地站在目的语受众的位置上观察问题，根据受众的语言习惯，做出适当的调适，以获得他们的认同，达到预期的宣传效果。因此，在能找到与受众语文化相似或接近的对等翻译时，译者应尽量遵循文化自觉原则进行处理。

英国著名语言学家莱昂兹认为，语言系统受到两个结构的制约，一是“底层结构”，即人类共同的生理特征和世界的原有结构，必定会使人类语言趋向于具有相同之处，亦能找到不同民族之间的文化的相似或相同之处；另一种是“上层结构”，即各个民族不同的文化结构，必定会导致各民族的语言在表现形式上呈现各种各样的差异。这种差异必然会带来英汉翻译中的文化冲突。这种冲突是由于人们赋予语言不同的文化内涵而造成的，在翻译的过程中容易形成文化障碍，译者难以在译语中找到与源语文化意义相对应的、具有承载同样文化信息的表达方式。此时，应该遵循文化自信原则进行翻译。特别是矿冶类外宣文本的翻译，因其中很多涉及源语民族特有的历史文化，如果不作解释而直译，受众必然不能理解。而有些词根本就是宣传的一部分，承载着许多文化内涵，如果舍弃它们，或者用译语中类似的词汇替代它们，反而可能造成译文功能缺失，没办法让世界真正了解中国矿冶文化，使得文化传播出现障碍。

三、矿冶类外宣文本英译实例分析

作为矿冶之都、青铜文化发展的摇篮，政府对宣传矿冶文化做出了积极的举措，因此，彰显矿冶文化，精确使用译文，是对矿冶类文本译者在翻译实践中的基本要求。在翻译过程中，译者应以“文化操纵理论”作指导，在自觉地“忠实”于各方的基础上，使译文功能在译语语言和文化环境中得以充分发挥，坚持以文化自觉和文化自信为原则，做好矿冶类外宣文本的翻译。

1. 文化自觉原则是指为了实现对外宣传的目的，确保信息本身的可信度，也为了让目的语受众更好地理解和接受译文，译者在翻译时应尽量在译语文化中找到与源语文化对等功能的翻译。

例1　走进国家矿山公园，感受中国秀美黄石。

这是湖北黄石国家矿山公园入口处的宣传标语。标语是整齐的八字并列结构，朗朗上口。但是如果译为并列结构，则不符合英语语言习惯，译文会显得非常别扭，很难获得目的语受众的认同。因此，译者可以从具体语境和英语习惯模式出发，将其改译为：

Welcome to Huangshi National Mine Park.

这样既符合英语语言习惯，简洁明了，也能让受众欣然接受。因此，在矿冶类外宣文本的翻译中，只要能找到译语文化中的对等翻译，都应尽量采用文化自觉原则，使矿冶文化的传播更加顺畅。

2. 当找不到译语的对等翻译时，我们应遵从文化自信原则。

（1）年代。

无论是矿冶博物馆、矿山公园的外宣文本，还是矿冶文学都出现了较多的以朝代来纪年的方式，这是中国特有的记录时间的方法，而译语里是没有对等翻译的，因此译者在翻译时，应以文化自信为原则，作适当补充。

例 2 约商代小乙时期……

译文： the Xiaoyi period in the Shang Dynasty（3260 years ago…）

翻译时补充一些原文中没有的背景信息，补充具体年代，使目的语受众了解这一年代具体是什么时候，还可以将中国这一时代与其生活的时代进行横向比较，回忆自己民族的历史，从而更好地理解中国文化。

例 3 战国时期，我国已经进入铁器时代……

译文： The Warring States Period（475 B. C. —221 B. C.）…

（2）货币。

矿冶博物馆展览了许多先秦时期的古代货币——铜钱，包括圆钱、刀币、布币等，这些也是具有中国特色的文物，在译语中没有对等翻译，所以译者在翻译时应尽量忠实于中国文化，翻译出特色。

例 4 刀币

译文： knife-shaped copper coin（used as money in feudal China）

例 5 布币

译文： spade-shaped copper coin（used as money in feudal China）

在直译后面加入背景信息，可以帮助受众了解不同于他们的文化氛围和社会环境，从而让受众了解文物本身的文化信息。

（3）劳动工具。

还有些展品是中国独有的，在译语中无法找到对应的表达，译者应创造出新的表达方式来传达其文化内涵。

例 6 编钟

译文： Bian Zhong（bell-chime）

例 7 铜镢

译文： bronze Jue（big hoe，a kind of farm tool）

这种半音译加注释或全音译加注释方式，就是人们通常所说的 Chinglish（中国式英语），它完全可以承载中国传统文化的内涵与意义，在跨文化交际中发挥重要的作用，同时也彰显出汉语言的魅力，让受众有继续了解汉民族语言的兴趣。

四、结语

翻译是把一种语言转化成另一种语言，是把一种语言所承载的信息毫无遗漏地用另一种语言表达出来。而外宣文本的翻译是一种门面工作，是一个地方、一个民族对外交往水平和人文环境质量的具体体现，也是文化软实力的具体体现。湖北黄石以“矿冶文化”为名片，着力打造矿冶文化古都，为黄石的发展迎来了前所未有的机遇。笔者基于文化操纵派视角，以文化自觉和文化自信为原则，对黄石矿冶类外宣文本的翻译问题进行研究，希望能推动矿冶类外宣翻译研究，提高黄石对外宣传和对外交流水平，为树立黄石国际形象尽一份绵力。

◎ 参考文献

[1] 费孝通. 论人类学与文化自觉 [M]. 北京：华夏出版社，2004.

[2] 张国新. 英汉翻译中的文化冲突、文化融合与文化变形 [J]. 湛江师范学院学报，2000 (3)：87.

[3] 陈小慰. 试论“译文功能理论”在应用文类翻译中的指导作用 [J]. 上海科技翻译，1996 (3)：9-10.

[4] 李开荣. 试论文物名称英译文化信息的处理 [J]. 中国科技翻译，2001 (4)：11-13.

[5] 郦青，胡雪英. 博物馆展品英译研究——以浙江省博物馆为例 [J]. 中国科技翻译，2011 (3)：47-49.

第九节　黄石矿冶文化外宣翻译问题探析*

——以“铜绿山古铜矿遗址”为例

On Problems in C-E Translation of Huangshi Mining and Metallurgy Culture—A Case Study of Tonglushan Ancient Copper Mine Relics

摘要：矿冶文化是黄石城市文化的主体文化，传承与弘扬矿冶文化对黄石城市转型与经济社会发展至关重要。黄石矿冶文化外宣翻译质量不高，这严重影响着黄石矿冶文化外宣效果。文章以黄石矿冶文化最有影响力的代表——铜绿山古铜矿遗址为例介绍英译文本，分析、总结黄石矿冶文化外宣翻译中存在的突出问题，提出提高黄石矿冶文化外宣翻译质量的建议。

关键词：黄石；矿冶文化；外宣翻译；问题；建议

2007 年 1 月，中共黄石市第十一届委员会全体会议明确提出“矿冶文化是黄石城市文化的主体文化”[1]。为对外宣传黄石矿冶文化，黄石博物馆、铜绿山古铜矿遗址、国家矿山公园等场馆都采用了中英文对照的介绍，然而，笔者实地调查发现，黄石矿冶文化宣介材料的英译质量不高，不仅没有达到预期的对外宣传效果，反而有损黄石历史文化名城的形象。

---

* 作者郭淑英，原载于《湖北理工学院学报》（人文社会科学版）第 33 卷第 3 期，2016 年。

目前，黄石矿冶文化外宣翻译质量问题引起了人们的重视，已发表的有关黄石矿冶文化外宣翻译学术论文有 7 篇，主要对矿冶类文本特点和翻译原则[2]、翻译质量[3]、翻译策略[4]等进行了研究。鉴于矿冶文化在黄石城市转型与经济社会发展中的重要地位，对黄石矿冶文化外宣资料翻译质量的研究显得格外重要。因此，笔者对黄石矿冶文化外宣翻译存在的突出问题进行研究，提出提高黄石矿冶文化外宣质量的建议，助推黄石矿冶文化走出国门，走向世界。

一、黄石矿冶文化外宣翻译存在的突出问题

广义的矿冶文化是人类在长期的矿冶开发实践中所形成同时又反作用于人类矿冶开发实践活动的知识、观念和艺术，以及与之相适应的矿冶开发实践活动的组织形态、制度安排和行为准则，是由此实践活动所产生的物质财富和精神财富的总和[5]。由于黄石矿冶文化外宣远远落后于内宣，矿冶文化资料英译文本较少，因此，笔者选取历史最悠久的铜绿山古铜矿遗址作为代表，对黄石矿冶文化外宣资料英译问题进行研究。

（一）缺乏对译文受众信息需求研究，译文的信息性和可接受性差

目前黄石矿冶文化外宣翻译最大的问题是直接照搬对内宣传的内容，生怕漏词漏句、改词篡义。对译文受众的背景知识、思维方式、认知能力、阅读习惯等缺乏了解，在翻译时没有合理地取舍原文信息。

外宣要取得预期的效果，首先要让目标读者愿意看，并能看得懂[6]。外宣翻译的一个原则是“贴近国外受众对中国信息的需求”[7]。在翻译过程中，为了使译文更好地被目标读者接受，译者需要考虑读者的背景知识和阅读习惯，从而把译文中的信息性维持在一个合理的程度[8]。如铜绿山古铜矿遗址 11 号矿体地层堆积及出土遗物的介绍及翻译：

例 1　第三层：黑灰土夹炼渣，厚 5~35 厘米，出有瓷碗残片、“开元通宝”钱币等，为隋唐层。

原译：The third layer：black dust mixed with slag，with thickness of 5～35 cm，unearthed with bowl fragments，“Kai Yuan Tong Bao” money and so on，is the Sui and Tang layer.

原译采用“音译+类词”翻译“开元通宝”，这是一般的常用译法，由于没有增补对该货币的解释，译文读者还是无法理解该译文。将“隋唐层”逐字翻译成“the Sui and Tang layer”，如果译文读者缺乏相关的背景知识，就会不知道此处“隋唐”指“中国的隋朝和唐朝”。译文中没有增补相关信息，也没有揭示原文中的关键信息——第三层是在隋唐年间形成的。译文太晦涩，容易让目标读者丧失兴趣而停止阅读。

但由于文化差异，原文作者与原文读者之间的默契通常不存在于原文作者与译文读者之间，译文读者很难产生原文读者所产生的联想，从而对译文的理解和欣赏效果都会大打折扣，除非译者给予相应的文化信息补偿[9]。斯坦纳将这种补偿解释为“恢复译文和原文之间的平衡”，并认为“凡未对译文进行补偿并使其恢复基本平衡的译文均为不合格的译文”[10]。

针对译文受众缺乏的文化背景知识，在翻译“开元通宝”时，应采用音译加注法，增补相关知识：“开元通宝”——唐代货币，用铜、金、银、铅等制作的硬币。对于“隋唐层”，要透彻理解原文内涵，提供实质信息。此例翻译还可运用编译技巧，采用过去分词短语代替完整的句子，调整词序，整合、增补信息，改变段落信息的排版，揭示原文的实质内涵，采用译文受众习惯的行文方式，使重点信息一目了然，增强译文的外宣效果。建议将例 1 改译为：

The third layer：5～35 cm black dust mixed with slag；formed in the Sui and Tang Dynasties（581A. D.—907A. D.）；Unearthed cultural relics：porcelain bowl fragments，“Kaiyuan Tongbao ”（currency of the Tang Dynasty；coins made of copper，gold，silver，lead，etc.）

例 2 铜绿山古铜矿采掘始于商代晚期，经西周、春秋战国延续至汉代（约公元前 12 世纪至公元 1 世纪），时间长达千余年。

原译：Copper mining began in the ancient Tonglushan the late Shang

Dynasty, by the Western Zhou Dynasty, the Warring States continue to the Han Dynasty (12th century B. C. to 1st century), as long as over a thousand years.

在外宣英译中，当涉及过于繁复的社会文化背景知识时，译文受众因其文化的差异和社会背景的不同，常会遇到理解上的困难，这时我们应该调整信息，增加相应的解释，或根据具体情况仅择其主旨意义译出[11]。例2中，原文对于遗址的年代做了详细说明，突出了古铜矿开采和冶炼经历的朝代之多，时间之久，主题突出，符合汉语读者的阅读习惯。而多数外国读者对中国历史朝代缺乏了解，原译文基本按照原文顺序逐字逐句翻译，条理不清，逻辑混乱，复杂的社会文化背景知识和佶屈聱牙的译文只会令他们丧失阅读兴趣。

原文中的实质内容是介绍铜绿山古铜矿悠久的历史，采掘历时之久，因此，只要译出主要信息“铜绿山古铜矿采掘始于商代晚期，延续至汉代（约公元前 12 世纪至公元 1 世纪）”即可，可改译为：

Tonglushan Ancient Copper Mine Relic is a site for copper mining and smelting from the late Shang Dynasty to the Han Dynasty (12th century B. C. to 1st century A. D.).

甚至原文还可简化为“铜绿山古铜矿采掘时间：约公元前 12 世纪至公元 1 世纪”。因此译文为：

Copper mining and smelting in Tonglushan Ancient Copper Mine: About 12th century B. C. to 1st century A. D.

由此，译文提供了所经历朝代的起止时间，外国读者对遗址的悠久历史有了大概了解。由于此处目的不是进行中国历史知识普及宣传，而是突出铜绿山古铜矿悠久的历史，至于哪个朝代无关紧要，删除朝代信息，反而能让主要信息更加突出，起到更好的宣传效果。

（二）译文错误百出，可读性差

翻译理论中最基本的一条是再现原文的思想内容。但由于认识上或语言水平上的偏差或缺陷，译者在语言转换中往往不能尽善，以致产生诸如句子结构残缺、逻辑矛盾、词语不匹配、缺乏连贯性、繁琐冗长等问题[12]。

例 3 摘自遗址展厅中的《铜绿山古铜矿遗址简介》第一段，译文质量可以用“触目惊心”来形容。完全是根据原文逐字胡译、乱译，存在用词不当、语法错误、条理不清、逻辑矛盾、啰嗦等问题。如果不对照原文看，恐怕也没有几个精通英文的中国人能看懂译文，这样的译文外宣效果可想而知。

例 3　（1）铜绿山古铜矿遗址是 1973 年大冶有色金属公司铜绿山矿在生产过程中发现的。（2）自 1974 年起，考古工作者对这处遗址进行了长达十余年的考古发掘。（3）铜绿山古铜矿采掘始于商代晚期，经西周、春秋战国延续至汉代（约公元前 12 世纪至公元 1 世纪），时间长达千余年。（4）其年代之久远，采掘时间之长，规模之大，保存之完好，科学研究之完整是迄今为止所罕见的。（5）在采矿方面，最大开采深度达 60 米，采用了竖井、平巷、盲井、斜井联合开拓技术，成功地解决了井下通风、排水、提升、照明和井巷支护等一系列复杂技术。（6）在冶炼方面，创先使用鼓风竖炉炼铜，并掌握了配渣及高温技术，冶炼的粗铜纯度达 94%，渣含铜仅为 0.7%，成为人类一处非常有价值的历史遗存。

改译：（1）Tonglushan ancient coppper mine relic was found in the production by Tonglushan mine, Daye Nonferrous Metals Company in 1973.（2）Since 1974, more than 10 years' excavation by archaeologists finds that Tonglushan Ancient Copper Mine Relic is a site for copper mining and smelting from the late Shang Dynasty to the Han Dynasty (12th century B. C. to 1st century A. D.).（3）Tonglushan Ancient Copper Mine Relic is rare for its long history and duration of production, large scale, good state of preservation, and comprehensive scientific research.（4）With shaft, horizontal tunnel, blind shaft and inclined shaft jointly applied and a series of complex problems including but not limited to ventilation, drainage, mineral lifting, lighting, shaft and tunnel supporting tackled, the depth of mining reaches 60 meters underground. (5) The achievements of copper smelting include the first use of blast shaft furnace and mastery of slag and high temperature technology. As a result, the purity of the blister copper reaches 94 % and the average copper content in the slag is only 0.7%.

依据英、汉语不同的词语、句法、篇章特点，在理解原文所要传递的信息的基础上，从词语选择，句子的时态、语态、主谓一致，词序，信息增减等方面着手，采用增译、省译、词性转换、语态转换、句序调整、合译等技巧，按照英语的行文习惯，再现原文的思想内容。对原文 6 个句子的翻译进行分析，具体如下：

第一句：句子逻辑关系明晰化处理，采用语态转换技巧，用被动语态揭示“遗址是被发现的”。

第二、三句：根据英、汉语句子结构差异，汉语常用多分句铺排句式，分析汉语多个分句逻辑内涵，找出各分句在逻辑语义上的主次关系，再用英语相应的词汇、语法手段在译文中按逻辑主次分门别类进行“空间搭架”式的有机组合[13]。第三句的内容是第二句中的行为产生的结果，因此应将两句合译成一句。第三句采用了省译法，在例 2 中已讨论。

第四句：体现了汉语的句式特点，运用结构匀称、节奏鲜明的 5 个排比句突出遗址的历史价值，句子信息重心在前，头重脚轻。根据英文的习惯，为了避免头重脚轻，应调整句序。此句的主干“铜绿山古铜矿遗址是罕见的”，前面的 5 个排比句的内容是得出这一论断的理由，通过增加连接词“for”，明示句子的逻辑关系。

第五、六句：属于汉语典型的无主句，按照汉语句序直译就会造成逻辑矛盾。应在分析句子逻辑关系的基础上，增加连接词“with” “As a result”以明示句子的逻辑关系。第六句中最后一个小句“成为人类一处非常有价值的历史遗存”，此句属于中国式的自吹自擂，第四句中也已有评价“是迄今为止所罕见的”，因此可采用省译删减这些无实质内容的信息。如果要译，可采用分译技巧，单独成句。为了与上文衔接，需增补一些内容，如“鉴于以上原因”“铜绿山古铜矿遗址成为人类……”。

例3的遗址简介包含采矿、冶炼技术介绍，第五句中的专业术语翻译也是难点之一。原译中“平巷”“斜井”“提升”分别译为“lane”“shaft”“upgraded”，但不准确。笔者根据几个专业术语的内涵采用明晰化处理，将其分别译为“horizontal tunnel”、“inclined shaft”和“mineral lifting”。关于专业术语的翻译，译者需查阅相关专业书籍、专业汉英词典或网络，尽量找到已有的术语英文表达，并将查到的英文表达输入网络再次查找，看该表达是否符合英语国家的用语习惯，从而找到更接近英语表达习惯的术语。如果找不到英文表达，也可通过理解术语的内涵，采用意译的方法，揭示术语的实质含义。文化外宣资料不是专业讲座，用通俗易懂的语言对外宣介中国文化就达到了翻译的预期目的。此外，翻译时应结合原文上下文语境，找出原文在具体语境中的实际含义，选用相应的译文形式予以表达。译文选词时也要注意英、汉语之间词句的逻辑搭配关系。

二、提高黄石矿冶文化外宣翻译质量的建议

提高黄石矿冶文化外宣翻译质量，需要外宣部门、矿冶文化博物馆、展览馆、矿冶企业和译者的共同努力。外宣部门等主要从提高矿冶文化外宣翻译质量的重要性、紧迫性和可采取的措施方面努力。译者是翻译主体，对于提高黄石矿冶文化外宣翻译质量至关重要。为此，笔者仅从译者的角度，对提高黄石矿冶文化外宣翻译质量提出以下建议。

（一）凸显黄石矿冶文明的价值

矿冶文化作为一个文化概念，其提出始于湖北省黄石市。矿冶文化被黄石市定位为文化之根、城市之魂[14]。黄石矿冶文化外宣翻译应突出其“唯一”“独特”“先进”三大历史价值与文化特色，译者在翻译过程中始终应围绕凸显黄石矿冶文明的价值和特色这一要旨，用译文传递出这种信息。

（二）遵循“信息适中”原则

黄石矿冶文化外宣翻译必须遵循“信息适中”原则。正如奈达所说：如果译者不向预期读者调整信息负荷量，接收者就可能失去信息中的一些关键因素，或觉得译文太难懂而停止阅读[15]。外宣翻译应贴近国外受众对中国信息的需求[7]。外宣性文本以宣传信息为主，为达到最佳宣传效果，译者需要考虑译文读者对中国文化背景知识的了解，并以此来决定原文信息的取舍。为了避免因缺乏相关文化背景知识而造成译文读者理解困难，翻译时应适当增添相关文化背景知识，如本文例 1 中对“开元通宝”的补充解释——“唐朝货币，铜、金、银、铅等制作的硬币”，以及对中国朝代起止年份的增添。这些均有助于译文读者理解主要信息。

（三）结合使用归化和异化翻译策略

外宣翻译要贴近国外受众的思维和语言习惯[7]，黄石矿冶文化外宣翻译要顾及译文读者的欣赏习惯和心理感受，在译文中尽量使用他们熟悉的语言表达形式，因此，宜采用归化策略。然而，为了能使黄石矿冶文化走向世界，对于带有浓厚中国或黄石特色的文化信息，宜采用异化翻译策略。

在语言形式上使用归化策略，如例 3 中第二、三句的合译，通过利用词汇、语法等衔接手段明示句子逻辑关系，从而实现译文的连贯性。对特色文化因素进行异化处理，有助于将中国特色文化“移植”到译语文化中去。如翻译“古代工匠总结出矿物共生找矿法和指示植物找矿法，《管子》《山海经》记载的矿物共生理论包含了铜绿山古铜矿所创造的技术、经验与成就”这一段话时，由于《管子》一书是先秦时期各学派的言论汇编，是中国特有的文化信息，可异化处理直接音译成“Guan Zi”。考虑到译文读者缺乏文化背景知识，利用加注对《管子》一书作简单解释“Guan Zi”—Compilation of Thoughts and Deeds of great thinkers, philosophers, politicians in the period before the Qin Dynasty (before

221 B. C.)。对于中国朝代、历史人物、经典著作也通常采用异化处理。因此，在黄石矿冶文化外宣翻译中，应以有利于提高外宣效应为出发点，结合使用归化和异化翻译策略。

(四) 灵活运用各种翻译方法和技巧

黄石矿冶文化外宣翻译中应灵活运用直译、意译、音译、音译加注等翻译方法。综合运用各种翻译技巧，如增译、省译、词类转换、语态转换、词序调整、分译、合译、节译、编译等，在译文表达上顺从译文读者的语言和思维习惯，突出读者效应。大多数翻译技巧在前面三个实例中已综合运用，因此，下面仅对涉及段落、篇章层次的节译（或称选译）、编译技巧进行分析。

从应用性文体的翻译来看，全译不是主要的翻译方式，就社会要求或从读者的认知需要来看，并不都须全译[13]。节译是黄石矿冶文化外宣翻译可使用的一种技巧。节译，即有选择地翻译全文的一部分，可根据译文读者的背景知识和认知能力，选译全文的主要信息，也可选译读者感兴趣的信息而删去枝节。编译是在不改变原文信息的前提下，译者所作的文字处理，包括为使译稿顺畅而增加一些连接词，为突出重点而作语序或段落的调整等[13]。

◎ 参考文献

[1] 郭远东. 在第三届中国（黄石）矿冶文化论坛上的讲话 [J]. 湖北理工学院学报（人文社会科学版），2014，31（6）：3.

[2] 邵春美. 矿冶类文本的多元化特点及翻译原则 [J]. 黄石理工学院学报（人文社会科学版），2011，28（1）：63-67.

[3] 方晓梅，邵春美. 公知性矿冶外宣文本英译质量研究 [J]. 湖北师范学院学报（哲学社会科学版），2014，34（4）.

[4] 郑馨念，邵春美. 语域理论视角下矿冶文化的翻译策略探析 [J]. 湖北理工学院学报（人文社会科学版），2014，31（2）：82-86.

[5] 石璋铭，项锐．矿冶文化内涵的探寻［J］．黄石理工学院学报（人文社会科学版），2008，25（1）：79.
[6] 徐明强．外宣翻译的苦恼［J］．中国翻译，2014，35（3）：11.
[7] 黄友义．坚持“外宣三贴近”原则，处理好外宣翻译中的难点问题［J］．中国翻译，2004，25（6）：24.
[8] 张美芳，陈曦．巧传信息　适应读者——以故宫博物院网站材料翻译为例［J］．中国翻译，2013，34（4）：100.
[9] 曹明伦．谈翻译中的文化移植和信息补偿——兼答“自学之友”栏目读者的相关问题［J］．中国翻译，2012，33（4）：119-121.
[10] Steiner George. After Babel：Aspects of Language and Translation［M］. Shanghai：Shanghai Foreign Language Education Press，2001.
[11] 袁晓宁．外宣英译中的改写现象探究——以“南京湖泊宣言翻译”为例［J］．中国翻译，2012，33（3）：125.
[12] 方梦之．翻译伦理与翻译实践——谈我国部分英文版专业期刊的编辑和翻译质量［J］．中国翻译，2012，33（2）：92.
[13] 方梦之，毛忠明．英汉—汉英应用翻译综合教程［M］．上海：上海外语教育出版社，2008：36，238，42.
[14] 谭元敏，李社教．黄石矿冶文化研究述评［J］．湖北理工学院学报（人文社会科学版），2014，31（4）：10.
[15] 谭载喜．奈达论翻译［M］．北京：中国对外翻译出版公司，1987.

第三章
矿冶文学的语言学研究

Linguistic Studies on Mining and Metallurgical Literature

第一节　矿冶小说中隐喻的语篇功能研究 *

——以《窗外的灯光》为例

Study on the Textual Function of Metaphor in Mining Novel *Window Light*

摘要：2000 多年以来，隐喻一直受到许多领域的关注。自 20 世纪 70 年代认知语言学出现后，人们开始从认知的角度研究隐喻，开辟了新的隐喻研究路径。近年来，隐喻的研究逐渐从字词句层面转向语篇层面，进一步拓展了隐喻的研究空间。本文对矿冶小说《窗外的灯光》中隐喻的语篇功能展开研究，既能丰富隐喻的认知研究，也可帮助读者更好地理解和欣赏文学作品。

关键词：隐喻；语篇功能；矿冶小说；《窗外的灯光》

一、引言

作为一种语言现象，许多学者从不同角度对隐喻进行了大量的研究，涉及语言学、心理学、哲学以及文学等领域。自 20 世纪 70 年代认知语言学兴起以来，隐喻的本质和作用获得了重新认识。传统修辞学认为隐喻是

* 作者赵小红、陈维维、李雅颖，原载于《湖北理工学院学报》（人文社会科学版）第 32 卷第 1 期，2015 年。

一种修辞格，认知语言学把隐喻当作一种认知工具，认为隐喻在语言、思维和行动的建构方面起着非常重要的作用。1980 年 Lakoff 和 Johnson 在他们的著作中提出概念隐喻理论[1]。他们认为隐喻“在日常生活中随处可见，不仅出现在语言中，也出现在思想和行动中，人们用以思考与行动的概念体系在本质上是隐喻的”。由于思维和行动中的隐喻是无形的，看得见的语言隐喻就成为人们研究认知隐喻的重要媒介。Lakoff 和 Johnson 的概念隐喻理论突破了传统隐喻研究的藩篱，把隐喻研究带入全新的认知时代。

尽管隐喻研究的历史悠久，但大多数主要集中在字词句的层面，很少有人研究它的语篇功能。21 世纪以来，有关隐喻语篇功能的研究逐渐增多，越来越多的学者逐渐认识到其重要性。国外的学者，如 Kittay[2]，Cameron[3]，Brown[4]，Semino[5]等认为，隐喻不仅存在于孤立的句子中，而且和语境紧密相连，因此必须重视隐喻的语篇研究。一些国内的学者也开始把隐喻研究的重心转向语篇层面。如廖美珍探讨了汉语隐喻的语篇功能[6]，及隐喻的语篇变化与语篇组织程度的关系问题[7]；苗兴伟等认为隐喻是一种语篇策略[8]；张玉蓉从认知角度对隐喻的语篇衔接和连贯功能进行研究[9]；胡金水运用概念隐喻理论分析隐喻在语篇建构中的三大主要功能（衔接、连贯与组篇）[10]；冯志国从语言学和修辞学角度分析隐喻语篇功能研究的理据及其意义[11]。

通过梳理前期国内外关于隐喻的语篇研究发现，文学作品中隐喻的语篇研究非常少，矿冶文学作品中隐喻的语篇研究更少。作家马景源的短篇小说《窗外的灯光》描写了 20 世纪七八十年代黄石地区矿山工人的故事[12]。小说大量使用隐喻表达“我”的思想变化，本文以这些隐喻实例为研究对象，探讨隐喻如何实现构建和组织语篇的功能，以充实该领域的隐喻研究。

二、《窗外的灯光》中的隐喻及其语篇功能

（一）隐喻的分布

《窗外的灯光》中的“我”和秦琪代表着成千上万的矿山建设者，映照着中华人民共和国成立后30多年间中国社会主义建设者们伟大而崇高的品质。出身低微的矿山工人秦琪以自己的勤学肯干、积极创新精神影响着“我”的人生选择。在秦琪的影响下，利用父辈职权取得优越生活条件的“我”，主动要求放弃当前的工作环境，下车间接受生活的挑战。小说的篇幅不长，但“灯”或“光”在文中以不同的形式出现了28次，主要使用“那盏灯 ”的形式，与标题“窗外的灯光”相互照应。具体分布情况如表1所示。

表1　　**隐喻的分布情况统计表**

形式	“光”	“那盏灯”	“灯光”	“灯”	“光晕”	合计
次数	4	12	5	6	1	28

（二）隐喻的语篇功能

根据小说故事发展的顺序和文中“我”对秦琪的态度变化，全文可分成七个部分。文中“我”对秦琪的态度主要反映在“我”对“灯光”的态度上，这基本构成了小说的线索，使全文紧密衔接在一起。

小说的第一部分有几处提到了“我”对“那盏灯”的不满情绪。

“我刚刚合上眼皮，只觉得满屋光灿灿，亮闪闪。真气人，窗外那盏灯又亮了。”

小说的第一段开门见山，直接说出了“我”对“那盏灯”的态度。“光灿灿，亮闪闪”说明灯光严重影响了我睡觉，“又”道出了“我”对那盏灯的极度反感。

“矿山新近修了一幢宿舍大楼，我家搬进来好几天了，窗外那盏灯天天都是到深夜才灭，而天未破亮，那盏灯又先亮啦。”

副词“天天都是”和“又”同样说明了“我”对“那盏灯”的不耐烦和厌恶。

“自从搬进了新居，那窗外刺眼的、令人头晕目眩的灯光，使我没睡过一夜安稳觉，有时脑袋涨得接近爆炸的程度。”

这里修饰“灯光”的形容词“刺眼的”和“令人头晕目眩的”带有明显的贬义，把“我”对“灯光”的反感表达得清楚明了。

“我拉开粉红色的窗帘一看，那盏灯还在亮着……”

从“我”晚上开始睡觉到早上醒来都会看到“那盏灯”，它好像从没熄过，让人难以忍受。到这里为止，“我”还只看到灯光，并未看到人。直到第一部分的结尾处，“我”才看清灯下的人是采矿车间井口推车工秦琪。在“我”看来，他是个穿着讲究、喜欢花草的花花公子，让人看着不顺眼。这一部分与“灯”有关的词基本上是暗指秦琪，属于以物喻人。

第二部分“我”回忆起几个月前秦琪找“我爸爸”的事，对其更加反感，认为他是个追求享受、想入非非的人。加上现在他的灯光让“我”无法睡觉，更加深了“我”对他的厌恶之情，也可以说是灯光让“我”想起更多与秦琪有关的不快。

第三部分“我”对秦琪的反感达到了顶点，同时也使“我”产生了研究他的兴趣。

“下班以后，我找了几张纸，赌气地贴在窗户的玻璃上，不让那炫目耀眼的灯光再打扰我。”

“我”阻挡灯光的行动也阻断了“我”和秦琪的关系，看起来两人似乎再无瓜葛了。

“不知为什么，我竟跑到窗口，下意识地把窗门推开一条小缝儿，悄悄地往外瞧，只见那盏灯上朝楼房的这一面挂上了一块黑布……”

秦琪在灯上挂黑布是对“我”在窗户贴纸的反击，这样反而激发了

“我”了解他的兴趣，为小说的进一步发展埋下伏笔。这一部分基本上还是以物喻人，通过“我”对“灯光”的态度暗指“我”对秦琪的态度。

第四部分是个重要的转折点，由于秦琪对“我爸爸”不文明行为的宽宏大度，完全改变了“我”对他的看法，现在“我”认为他是个胸怀宽阔、有气量的男子汉。至此，“我”对秦琪的反感情绪全消了。

第五部分“我”和秦琪的关系达到了高潮，非常融洽。“看着那盏灯，我非常喜欢。灯一亮，我屋子里立刻被涂抹上一层银灰色，显得格外温柔、恬静……”“我”的窗户已经完全向秦琪敞开了，看到灯光“我”就很喜欢和愉快，甚至感到幸福和陶醉。

“到九点钟，我渴望的那盏灯还没亮，不觉神思恍惚，心里像掉了件什么东西似的。”

“此后，我见窗外的灯光一亮，就去找他讲解晶体管电路基本知识……我只好带着野花的浓郁芳香，恋恋不舍地离开那盏明亮的灯。”

这几句话说明“我”已经离不开“那盏灯”了，道出了“我”想见到秦琪的急迫心情和离开时的依依不舍，“那盏灯”成了“我”每天的期待，“我”希望天天都能看到秦琪，和他一起学习进步。

第六部分又是一个转折点，“我”和秦琪的相处遇到了外来的阻力，家人极力反对我们来往，想让我回到原来的生活道路，按照他们的安排去生活，并以把“我”派去市团委学习收场。

第七部分是小说的结尾部分，这里“灯”的隐喻义从秦琪这个具体的人物转向了抽象的含义。

“老远我就看到了一盏明亮的灯，灯光给旧房添了许多迷人的色彩，也照亮了我向前的路途，我不费任何周折就找到了秦琪的家。”

“离开了秦琪的家，我不断地回过头去，凝望着那盏明亮的灯。”

“我”已经把“那盏灯”看成了前进的方向，它给了“我”信心和力量，指引着“我”开始新的生活。

（三）小结

从以上分析可以看出，主人公“我”对“灯光”的态度在不断变化，由开始的反感厌恶转向后来的慢慢接受和欣赏，到最后的向往追寻。小说从头到尾紧扣“灯光”这个隐喻，与标题“窗外的灯光”的隐喻保持一致。但“灯光”在全文的隐喻义并不是一成不变的，从开始的具体隐喻义，喻指秦琪这个人，慢慢地转向抽象隐喻义，喻指秦琪所代表的生活方式和他不断进取、改革创新的精神。无论是“我”对“灯光”的态度变化，还是“灯光”的隐喻义从具体到抽象的变化，过渡都很自然、连贯，没有任何突兀的感觉，这也是小说故事情节发展推进的两条线索。可以说，“灯光”这个隐喻在小说中起到了衔接全文、连贯组篇的功能，也就是本文所说的语篇功能。小说中隐喻的语篇功能如图 1 所示。

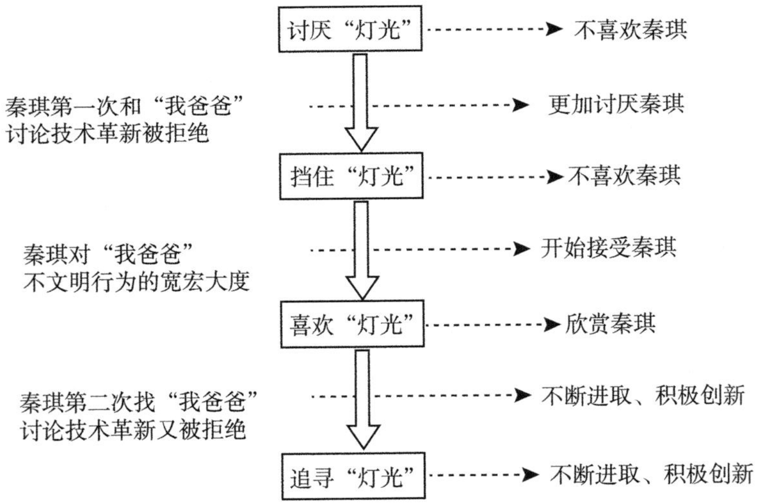

图 1 隐喻的语篇功能图

三、结论

小说《窗外的灯光》从标题到正文都紧紧围绕“灯光”这个隐喻，逐步展开故事情节，全文逻辑严谨，结构紧凑。隐喻的衔接、连贯和组篇功能在该小说中得到了充分的体现，为我们全面深刻地理解该小说提供了帮助。由此可见，矿冶小说中隐喻的语篇功能研究，为矿冶文学的欣赏和解读提供了新的途径，同时也丰富和拓展了对隐喻的研究和对语篇分析的研究。自从人们开始从认知语言学角度研究隐喻以来，隐喻就表现出强大的生命力和解释力，如果从更多的领域和更多的角度对隐喻展开研究，将大大提高我们对隐喻的认识，同时拓宽相关领域的研究空间。

◎ 参考文献

[1] Lakoff G, Johnson M. Metaphors We Live By [M]. Chicago and London: The University of Chicago Press, 2003.

[2] Kittay E F. Metaphor: Its Cognitive Force and Linguistic Structure [M]. Oxford: Clarendon Press, 1987.

[3] Cameron L. Discourse Context and the Development of Metaphor in Children [J]. Current Issues in Language and Society, 1996 (3): 49-64.

[4] Brown T L. Making Truth: Metaphor in Science [M]. Urbana: University of Illinois Press, 2003.

[5] Semino E. Metaphor in Discourse [M]. Cambridge: Cambridge University Press, 2008.

[6] 廖美珍. 隐喻语篇组织功能研究——标题与正文之间的组织关系 [J]. 外语教学与研究, 2007 (5): 177-183.

[7] 廖美珍, 周晓萍. 我们赖以建构和组织语篇的隐喻-隐喻变化与语篇组织程度 [J]. 外国语文, 2010 (4): 51-56.

[8] 苗兴伟, 廖美珍. 隐喻的语篇功能研究 [J]. 外语学刊, 2007 (6): 51-56.

[9] 张玉蓉. 隐喻的衔接与连贯功能研究 [D]. 合肥: 合肥工业大学, 2009.

［10］胡金水．隐喻的语篇建构功能研究［D］．南京：南京师范大学，2011.
［11］冯志国．隐喻语篇功能研究的理据及意义［J］．厦门理工学院学报，2012（3）：108-112.
［12］李社教．黄石矿冶文学作品选［M］．武汉：湖北人民出版社，2010.

第二节　篇章修辞学视角下《红煤》的文本解读*

Text Interpretation of *Red Coal* from the Perspective of Textual Rhetoric

摘要：《红煤》是刘庆邦的一部反映当代煤矿生活现实的里程碑式的作品。它深刻地揭露了农民矿工们在社会大变革中的人性变化与中国煤矿基层机构中掌权者们的群体性病态：腐败。本文以篇章修辞学为理论框架，通过分析矿冶小说《红煤》的布局结构特色和语言修辞特点，深化阐释小说主题，旨在为矿冶文学的研究提供一种新的方法。

关键词：《红煤》；矿冶文学；篇章修辞学；修辞格

一、引言

刘庆邦被誉为当代“短篇小说之王”“中国煤矿文学的旗手”，是中国当代少见的直面当下社会、当下现实的作家，曾经荣获鲁迅文学奖和老舍文学奖。其长篇代表作《红煤》[1]是一部煤矿生活题材的小说，号称是中国煤矿版的《红与黑》，也被认为是一部最具震撼力的关于中国小煤窑黑幕和一个煤老板的奋斗与堕落史的小说，并荣获北京市文学艺术奖。小说讲述了20世纪80年代中期，国有煤矿的农民轮换工宋长玉，不择手段当

---

* 作者胡一娟、李金妹，原载于《现代企业教育》第14期，2014年。

上了村办小煤窑的矿主，随着滚滚而来的金钱，宋长玉的欲望急剧膨胀，作恶多端，最终因井下透水事件逃之夭夭的故事。小说以社会转型时期矿工进城务工为背景展开叙事，具有深刻的时代意义。目前，对刘庆邦矿冶小说《红煤》的研究，国内学者多从主题解读、人与自然视角、社会视角以及《红煤》与其他作品的对比研究等方面入手。[2-6]国内外对篇章修辞学的研究主要集中于理论研究，较少被运用于小说文本。到目前为止，仅有袁晓[7]将篇章修辞学运用于小说文本解读中。本文试图从篇章修辞学的角度，以矿冶小说《红煤》为语料，将篇章修辞学与小说文本相结合，为矿冶文学作品研究提供一个新的研究视野。

二、《红煤》的篇章结构特点

篇章修辞学作为语言学一门独立的分支学科是随着西方及俄罗斯 20 世纪 60 年代篇章语言学的兴起而诞生的[8]。索尔加尼克[9]指出，“篇章修辞学是篇章语言学的一个分支，研究篇章的不同类型、篇章的修辞特征、篇章的展开方式、不同功能语体中的言语规范、言语类型及个人风格”。

篇章的总体布局结构一般包含引言、正文、结论三个部分，而小说文艺篇章的总体布局结构则细分为标题部分、开头部分、主体部分和结尾部分。刘庆邦在创作《红煤》时采用了具有明确的开端和结局、首尾呼应、自成一体的封闭式情节模式。作者平淡的情节布局，为读者展现了一幅矿区生活的图景以及主人公宋长玉的奋斗与堕落史，映射出作品深刻的时代主题。

（一）《红煤》的标题特色

“红煤”本是行话，刘庆邦将其作为作品名，具有深刻的象征意义。一方面，“红煤”本义指一种和铁矿伴生，煤块上面有铁锈，里面也有红筋，被称为红煤的煤。煤本身是黑的，但燃烧后便会变红，并化为灰烬。小说讲述了农民轮换工宋长玉由一个原本质朴、本色的农村青年渐渐变成一个刻薄、势利的不法商人，在人生追求中，人性变质由“红”变“黑”

的故事。小说标题巧妙地运用隐喻，形象地暗示了在社会转型期一些农村青年心理的不健全与不平衡以及农民进城打工的实际生活状态。

另一方面，“红煤”不仅象征着农民工身体上的痛楚，更象征着农民工心灵上的痛苦。煤里，有矿工的血、泪和汗水。小说中，农民出身的矿老板宋长玉因矿井透水事件而逃走；小煤窑矿长唐洪涛得知井下瓦斯爆炸，想尽办法隐瞒矿难。这一出出矿难的背后所折射的是矿老板人性的扭曲以及对矿工生命的漠视；这些沉睡在地下上万年的黑色神木里，也因此融入了矿工的鲜血与生命，成为“红煤”。小说表达了作者对矿工弱势群体生存状态的深切同情，批判了小煤窑主的贪婪、基层官员的腐败和渎职。

（二）《红煤》的开头和结尾特色

《红煤》以一幅煤矿工井下工作图拉开作品的序幕：

> 宋长玉上的是夜班，人们睡觉时，他正在井下用火药和铁器采伐煤炭。他不是夸父，却追着太阳，跟太阳走的是同一条路线。傍晚，当太阳落入地下，他便披挂整齐，下井去了。清晨，太阳刚从东边的山梁冒出来，他也乘坐灌笼从井口升了上来。

作品以开门见山式，直接交代了主人公宋长玉特殊的矿井生活。另外，巧用比喻将宋长玉的夜班采煤工作比作太阳东升西落的运行轨迹，寥寥几笔勾勒出矿工特殊而艰苦的工作环境。他们不仅要在地下进行劳作，还要和大自然进行顽强的抗争，要穿越很厚的地层，穿越黑暗，甚至穿越死亡才能采到煤。在此，作品流露出的是作者对社会底层民众，尤其是对矿工这一特殊生态群体的关注。由此开篇，也奠定了作品的感情基调。

小说最后，刘庆邦将宋长玉为躲避矿井透水事件而仓皇出逃作为小说结尾：

宋长玉没敢开自己的轿车，他让弟弟长山开出一辆货车，连夜把他送到省会的火车站，又连夜搭上一列开往南方的火车，向沿海某大城市逃去……宋长玉如在梦中。

结尾虽出人意料，但又在情理之中。读者也许会思索，“宋长玉结果如何？其家人怎么样了？”然而，小说在此戛然而止，令读者充满想象。在矿难面前，滚滚大水不仅带走了17条鲜活的生命，同时也带走了宋长玉不择手段、处心积虑所追求的财富、名誉、奢华的生活以及幸福的家庭。人性的缺失必将导致毁灭。作品揭示了在城乡对立的二元化社会大背景下，外来务工人员身上固有的小农意识，如短视、势利等，展现了以宋长玉为代表的外来务工人员在追求成为城里人的过程中逐渐人性扭曲、灵魂变异的命运悲剧，从而深化了主题。

（三）《红煤》的特殊情节组合

小说的情节设计，体现着作者对作品架构和语言材料所做的布局和安排。作者对《红煤》的情节进行了特殊或创造性的组合，深刻地揭示出小说主题所具有的鲜明时代感。小说以主人公宋长玉的命运为主线，详尽地展示了主人公宋长玉攀附、奋斗、复仇、堕落的过程，围绕这一情节主线，作者运用多种布局技巧以彰显小说的主题思想。

（1）渲染法。在某个细节上浓墨重彩，夸大突出，改变平常的比例，以引起读者对那些因无意识接受而被忽略的东西。例如在小说第一章矿工洗澡一节，作者将宋长玉洗澡的过程用了6000多字精细地加以描绘，通过矿工们洗澡这一日常生活中的简单事情，表现了矿工们卫生状况的糟糕，展示了矿工们生存环境的恶劣以及生存的艰辛。再如：宋长玉精心设计，给唐丽华写信的情节，作者用了将近5000字加以叙述。由此可以看出他心思之缜密、城府之深。处于社会最底层，无权无势又渴望摆脱农民身份的宋长玉试图攀附矿长女儿唐丽华，通过婚姻往上爬，揭示出底层民众转变身份的无奈。

(2) 插叙法。在围绕主人公宋长玉命运这条主线的发展过程中，作品穿插了一些故事情节，如第一章中给工人送伞的情节。宋长玉回忆起老家的母亲找堂婶子借伞遭轻视的情景。“看来还是有工作好啊！要是还在老家，别说下雨，就是下冰雹，下刀子，谁会给老百姓发伞呢！就冲这一点，他也要在矿上留下来，再也不能回老家去了。”这一心理活动影射出当时农村生活的落后，也交代了宋长玉绞尽脑汁想留在矿上的原因和渴望改变现状的愿望。

(3) 设置悬念。在作品第一章开头部分，作者将宋长玉变得注重洗澡设为悬念，为下文故事情节埋下伏笔。“现在宋长玉变了，洗澡洗得相当仔细”，“跟半年前刚来煤矿时的他也不一样。那时候他洗澡也很潦草”。究其原因，是因为：“小说主人公宋长玉为追求矿上医务室的护士、矿长的女儿唐丽华，想通过洗澡来洗净身上的煤尘，洗去煤矿工人身上的黑色烙印，洗去内心深刻的自卑感，宋长玉的洁癖反映了他内心深处涌动的摆脱农民身份的愿望。”[10]。第五章中，宋长玉借红煤厂煤炭之事怂恿岳父明守福给唐洪涛送个小绞车。在唐洪涛收受贿赂，收下小绞车之后，宋长玉写信举报唐洪涛受贿，这时证据才再一次浮出水面。这就是他处心积虑制造证据的原因，宋长玉为报复唐洪涛，不惜制造证据，突出了其人性的逐渐扭曲与灵魂的变异。

三、《红煤》的修辞手法

在小说《红煤》中，刘庆邦主要运用了对比、暗喻、象征等修辞手法，这极大地提高了语言的表现力与修辞潜能，也对主题的阐释起到了一定的促进作用。

乔集矿矿长唐洪涛对矿工前后不同的态度形成鲜明对比，这也展现了基础掌权者的渎职与腐败。在小说开始，为了体现自己的亲民度，唐矿长公开承诺，“如果有姑娘愿意嫁给矿工，矿上将热烈欢迎，并给予较高的待遇”。后来，发现宋长玉追求其女儿，唐矿长对他发出严正警告，最后甚至借故开除他且永不录用。唐洪涛说一套做一套、嫌贫爱富、虚伪至极的品行表露无遗。作品展现了在城市化进城这一社会背景下，城乡二元社会的对立与矛盾，唐洪涛一类的权利阶层代表着城市对农民的不接纳，而宋长玉则代表着进城务工的农民身份不被认同的尴尬。

老乡孟东辉对宋长玉前后截然不同的态度，体现了他趋炎附势的小农意识。当得知宋长玉和唐丽华在谈恋爱的时候，孟东辉特意讨好，溜须拍马，执意要送木箱子给宋长玉，“他不由分说，把箱子推到宋长玉床下去了”。当宋长玉被乔集矿开除后，又直言不讳地要回了箱子。孟东辉对宋长玉的不同态度和见风使舵的行为，深刻地揭示出农民出身的他身上固有的劣性根：狭隘、势力与鄙俗等。

此外，伴随着宋长玉波澜起伏的个人命运的是红煤厂村自然生态被严重破坏造成的恶果。昔日的旅游胜地红煤厂村山清水秀、水鸟成群，因为煤矿的无节制开采，如今却变得鸟类绝迹，树木死亡，连村民生活用水都发生了困难。与此同时，宋长玉也由一个有理想的农村青年变为一个贪婪、冷血的矿老板。红煤厂村生态环境的逐渐恶化，映射出主人公宋长玉一步一步走向堕落与毁灭的悲惨结局，揭示了社会转型期农民矿工的悲剧命运。

四、总结

就主题而言，《红煤》不仅流露出作者对中国社会转型时期煤矿单位基层机构中掌权者们麻木与腐败的揭露和批判，同时，小说通过宋长玉身份转变前后的所作所为，展现出一幅转型社会农民阶层的生活图景，再现了农民矿工们在社会大变革中不断扭曲的人性变化，揭示了由城乡二元社会结构所衍生的城乡差别、贫富分化、身份差异和文化歧视等矛盾。作品传达出作者对城市化进程中农民工悲惨遭遇的同情和怜悯，以及对社会转型期城乡差异的深刻忧虑。

◎ 参考文献

[1] 刘庆邦．红煤 [M]．北京：北京十月文艺出版社，2009.

[2] 张震，谷显明．变化的时代 不变的奋斗——《红煤》与《红与黑》中主人公奋斗历程比较［J］．湖南科技学院学报，2007.
[3] 张鹏．人与自然——《红煤》的双重视角［J］．名作欣赏，2007 (12).
[4] 张凤梅．社会视角中的文本解读——评刘庆邦新作《红煤》［J］．作家杂志，2010.
[5] 张凤梅．守望在“城乡交叉地带”——刘庆邦矿区小说论［D］．上海：上海师范大学，2008 (4)：21.
[6] 张丽梅．论刘庆邦小说中的“矿井”世界［D］．天津：天津师范大学，2010 (4).
[7] 袁晓．篇章修辞学视野下《贵族之家》的作品分析［D］．长春：吉林大学，2012 (10).
[8] 王凤英．篇章修辞学［M］．哈尔滨：黑龙江出版社，2007.
[9] 索尔加尼克．俄语句法修辞学（复杂的句法整体）［M］．上海：上海外语教育出版社，1989.
[10] 王德颂．为了人类诗意的栖息——评刘庆邦长篇小说新作《红煤》［N］．深圳特区报，2008.

第三节　矿冶小说《洞火》中的隐喻与语篇连贯的建构*

On the Discourse Coherent Functions of Metaphors in Mining Novel *The Hole Fire*

摘要：从小说这一宏观角度，从认知诗学的视角，以隐喻理论作为理论框架，以黄石本土矿冶小说《洞火》作为研究语料，试从一个比喻贯穿语篇始终（黑暗的古矿道中蜡烛代表着人性，并由蜡烛的三种状态引发关于人性的三个方面的隐喻）和由一个中心意象引申出若干相关的次要意象（中心意象“蜡烛”引发其他三个次要意象“烛火”“眼睛”“黑乎乎的洞”）的两个层面，探究隐喻如何起到语篇连贯的作用，旨在拓宽语篇研究的领域，丰富对隐喻的理解的同时提高我们对中国本土作品的解读能力和审美情趣，也为黄石矿冶文学的研究注入新的活力。

关键词：隐喻；认知；语篇连贯；矿冶小说

一、引言

隐喻是人类极其重要的思维方式，世界通过隐喻和象征向人类经验和理解开放。人们在语言和事物、经验与超验、有限与无限、个别与普通、

* 作者李金妹、吕青青，原载于《电子科技大学学报》（社科版）第16卷第1期，2014年。

现实与历史、事物与事物中建立了一种暗示性的隐蔽关联。认知语言学认为，隐喻不仅是一种语言修辞手段，还是一种基本的认知方式，更是一种文学语篇建构的重要手段。1980 年，Lakoff 和 Johnson 出版的《我们赖以生存的隐喻》（*Metaphors We Live By*）[1]标志着隐喻研究从开始的修辞学层面上升到认知层面。

隐喻可以在语言组织的各个层次上体现，例如单词、词组、句子，语篇。经过几十年的发展与探索，隐喻的研究重心已逐步由词汇句法层面向篇章和话语层面转移[2]。魏在江认为语篇是理解隐喻的重要载体，是隐喻意义的体现形式[3]。从语篇的层面去研究隐喻不但可以解释隐喻的功能，还可以阐释语篇信息的发展、语篇的组织机制和语篇的衔接及连贯性。本文从小说语篇这一宏观角度，以矿冶文学小说《洞火》为例，探讨隐喻的衔接与连贯功能，旨在拓宽语篇研究的领域，丰富对隐喻的理解，同时提高我们对中国本土作品的解读能力和审美情趣，也为中国矿冶文学的研究注入新的活力。

二、《洞火》简介及隐喻的语篇功能阐述

矿冶文学是指以矿产资源的认知、探寻、采掘、冶炼、使用与贸易和矿冶人的生产、生活、工作、学习和创作活动等方面为题材的文学作品或文学活动。《洞火》是黄石本土作家、著名编剧胡燕怀的一篇以矿冶为题材的短篇小说。小说以 20 世纪 80 年代国家对黄石大冶铜绿山地区孔雀石矿石资源的大力开采利用，该地区附近的农民受利益的驱使疯狂地盗取公家矿石为背景，以第一人称“我”，一个回乡“窝”了两年的高中毕业生为叙述者讲述了“活物”和“头儿”两个人的寻宝故事，以及“活物”为果儿报仇的故事。小说中，矿区农民“头儿”为利益和金钱所驱使，以自己的妻子果儿为挟持，迫使果儿当年的情人“活物”为向导盗取古矿井中的孔雀石，最终走向了不归路。

作者将第二个故事巧妙地穿插在第一个故事之中，其独特的叙事结构是该小说的亮点之一。作品着眼于人性之善恶美丑的探索，用沉郁的语言

色调描写了人对物质的贪欲，通过对“头儿”“活物”及“果儿”的人生悲剧的描写，表现了作者对爱情的思考，对生命的关怀，同时交织着作者对道德与历史的评判。

这篇小说以独特的叙述视角、细腻的心理描写、优美的语言文字、典型化的故事情节、深刻的主题，成为矿冶文学作品中不可多得的一部佳作，并引起了矿冶文学研究者的广泛关注和好评。如周进珍等从鲜明的地域色彩和特殊的题材等方面探寻《洞火》的艺术、文化与史料价值[4]；陈新瑶从小说寻宝传奇的叙事结构和个体生存体验的叙事视角分析了作者关于人性复杂而含混的表现与思考[5]。

隐喻对语篇的组织和发展起着不可忽视的作用。隐喻的语篇功能，尤其是语篇的衔接与连贯功能受到越来越多的学者的关注。国外方面，Lakoff & Johnson，Hoey，Weinrich 等论述了隐喻的语篇组织功能和连贯功能[6]。在国内，束定芳比较全面地论述了隐喻的修辞功能、语言学功能、诗歌功能、认知功能、文字游戏功能等[7]。张沛论述了隐喻的诗篇衔接功能[8]。廖美珍论述了英语比喻的语篇黏合作用，认为比喻的确立往往支配语篇的格局和模式，支配着语篇词语和术语的选择[9]。方小青、张锦峰以具体的英语诗歌为实例，分析了隐喻对诗歌语篇连贯的建构[10-11]；刘艳春从语篇功能的角度入手探讨隐喻对马丁·路德·金的演讲稿《我有一个梦想》的语篇发展所起到的作用[12]。从已有的研究来看，学者们更倾向于在词汇、句子以及诗歌、散文、演说词等层面上进行隐喻的语篇功能分析，而鲜有对小说层面上的研究。

主题是一个动态的语篇范畴，也是语篇组织的一个重要的意义概念，而语篇的中心主题在很大程度上都是隐喻性的。作者选定一个隐喻，以这个隐喻作语篇主题以此支配整个语篇的脉络，语篇按照隐喻主题这一线索发展下去，从而决定了整个语篇的模式并形成语篇的信息流。以一个比喻贯穿语篇始终，形成一个核心隐喻，支配若干引申比喻或者由一个中心意象引申出若干相关的次要意象[9]。下面本文将详细剖析隐喻；对小说《洞火》的语篇连贯的建构机制。

三、《洞火》中的隐喻与语篇连贯建构

意象主义代表庞德认为，好诗要形成意象，须避免抽象，努力使抽象与具体结合起来，注意运用自然事物作适当的象征[13]。文学语言的重要特点之一就是大量运用隐喻性语言，形成意象。小说也同样如此，如能用合适的自然事物精确地象征所要表达的思想感情，就能形成好的小说意象；而且要象征得自然，不露人工斧凿的痕迹。

在小说《洞火》中，作者用了大量的隐喻。本文将从认知诗学的视角出发，沿用廖美珍的观点，对这些隐喻在语篇中的建构所起的作用逐一进行探究，以揭示隐喻在小说文本中的语篇连贯功能。

（一）一个比喻贯穿语篇始终（蜡烛—人性）

小说《洞火》的主题“洞火”本身就是一个隐喻。它的本体是指点燃在黑乎乎的古矿井中那微弱而摇曳的烛火，其喻体不仅象征着逃生的出路和希望之火，也象征着不断变化膨胀的欲望和死亡之火，同时也象征着人的理性、仁爱之火。“蜡烛”一词在文中多次出现并贯穿全文，作者借助概念隐喻，赋予了蜡烛更为深刻的寓意，将蜡烛比作人性，蜡烛的三种状态（图1）实则也是人性的三个方面。这一概念隐喻激活了始源域与目标域之间的对应关系，如表1所示。

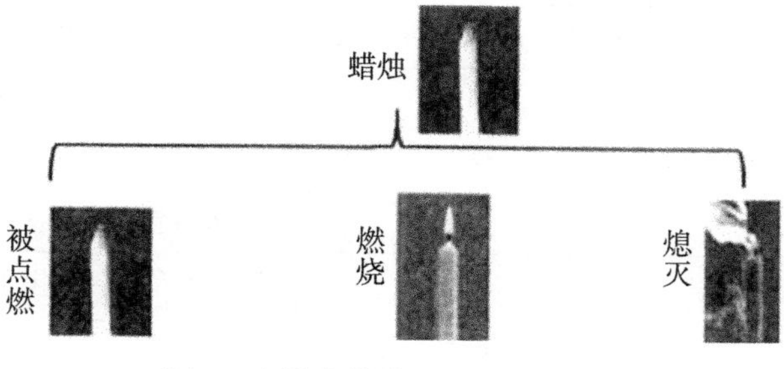

图1　小说中蜡烛呈现的三种状态

表 1 **蜡烛与人性之间的对应关系**

始源域—蜡烛	跨域映射	目标域—人性
被点燃	⟶	黑暗的矿井被照亮，象征着光明和希望
燃烧	⟶	蜡烛的熊熊燃烧，如同不断膨胀的欲望
熄灭	⟶	希望不再，唯有黑暗和面对死亡的恐惧

在漆黑的古矿井中，蜡烛是照明工具，通向光明和希望。如表 1 所示，被点燃的蜡烛瞬间照亮了漆黑的矿井，对于爬行在古矿道中寻求宝藏的“活物”和“头儿”来说无疑是光明和希望，始源域被点燃的蜡烛映射到目标域人性中就是“头儿”最初的情感希望和幻想。熊熊燃烧的蜡烛就如“头儿”不断膨胀的欲望。而在漆黑和密如蛛网的古矿道里，烛火的熄灭无疑意味着恐惧和死亡，也象征着人的希望的破灭、理性的丧失和爱心的泯灭。因为内心没有爱，没有对他人的关怀，“头儿”最终为自己的贪婪、罪恶和自私付出了生命的代价。

该小说是典型的叙事语篇。叙事语篇是在叙事结构的框架内展开的，而语篇的展开与隐喻化的过程并行不悖，相辅相成[14]。作者一开始就设定了一个主题隐喻，即蜡烛是人性的象征，并且围绕蜡烛的三种状态展开故事的情节，如表 2 所示。

表 2

始源域—蜡烛	跨域映射	目标域—人性	文中的体现
蜡烛被点燃—熊熊燃烧	⟶	希望—欲望	“头儿”发现盗取古矿井的一切可能性，萌发了发家致富的欲望（二人寻宝的故事）
蜡烛熊熊燃烧—熄灭	⟶	欲望—死亡	获取“活物”寻宝的方法的欲望诱惑“头儿”一步一步走向死亡（“活物”为果儿报仇的故事）

蜡烛是人性的象征这个隐喻统领全文的发展，故事的情节也是根据蜡烛被点燃——燃烧——熄灭这个过程依次展开的。“头儿”和“活物”寻宝的故事是蜡烛被点燃到熊熊燃烧的过程，即由希望变为欲望的过程。而“活物”为果儿报仇以及“头儿”走向死亡也是蜡烛由盛向衰最后熄灭的过程。

（二）一个中心意象引申出若干相关的次要意象

这就好比树干和树枝的关系。树干是核心比喻或中心意象，而树枝则是引申比喻或次要意象。在小说《洞火》中，蜡烛是中心意象，激活了关于“烛火”“眼睛”“黑乎乎的洞”等次要意象，这些次要意象又与核心隐喻，即蜡烛是人性引出来的三个引申比喻相结合。

1. 烛火—希望

《洞火》中烛光的意象多次出现，与被点燃的蜡烛相一致，烛光也代表着美好和希望。

在小说第一段，烛火是“长蛇”，是“幽蓝的火花”。“这时倘若能停下来，观赏一番身前身后的满洞的烛火，我想那景致一定不错，一定让人想起那童话世界里的圣诞节之夜。”这里把“烛火”比作“美丽的圣诞节之夜”，圣诞节之夜是希望、美好的象征。而古矿井里坑木的脆响“如钟如磬”，这样就形成了有关希望的语义场，如“幽蓝的火花”“圣诞节之夜”“钟磬”等。古矿井是“头儿”的希望，是他发家致富的渠道，而果儿是“活物”心爱的女人，虽然果儿已经成为别人的妻子，但仍旧是他的希望，是他的精神寄托和支柱。

小说围绕希望，展开了一系列准备工作的描写，“有时，夜深人静了，碰巧各家还真的能听见自家屋基下的响声，轰隆隆，像是极远的地方在打雷”。把矿井里的声响比作打雷，地下的构造和真实存在的声响无疑给人无限遐想，激发人们盗取古矿井的欲望的同时也给人以希望，特别是对于一直想发家致富而又无所事事的“头儿”来说。接着由于“活物”深谙古矿井的地下道，这又增添了盗取古矿井孔雀石的可行性，果儿和“活物”当年的情分触发了最后的合作。这一系列的可行性也是希望的累计叠加。

当准备工作就绪，一切都变得实际起来。于是开始了小说的第一个故事“头儿”和“活物”的寻宝传奇。

2. 眼睛—欲望

另一个在小说中多次出现的意象是眼睛。眼睛可以观察一切，从一个人的眼睛也可以看出对方的心理。

> “这回，该不会再耍弄我了吧?”头儿狐疑地问，眼里有一种威逼的光。
>
> “我发现这时候他那双眼睛特别亮，昏暗的烛光下，鹰隼般烁烁闪光，那是一双被欲望燃烧的眼，仿佛要穿透土层，急不可耐地寻找那一块块幽蓝的宝石。”
>
> “你……又在耍弄我?”头儿阴冷的目光望着那活物。先前的那恭谦全然不见了。
>
> “头儿有些焦躁了，暴戾了，眼睛被欲望烧得通红。”
>
> “头儿的眼睛在奕奕闪光。”

这几句话全部是描写“头儿”的眼睛，如“鹰隼”“被欲望烧得通红”“烁烁闪光”等。眼睛在这里被赋予了特殊的含义，并与烛火相结合，而熊熊燃烧的烛火又被喻为“欲望”，于是就有了“被欲望烧红的眼睛”。“头儿”的欲望是希望通过盗取孔雀石发家致富，是想获取“活物”探取宝石的秘密。而“活物”的欲望是情欲，是对果儿的念念不忘。此时熊熊燃烧的烛火是欲望，而赤裸裸的欲望由眼睛直接表达出来，是由希望衍生出来的欲望。

此时，已经尝了数次甜头的“头儿”的欲望进一步滋长，这种欲望是获取更多孔雀石的欲望，是对财富的欲望，更是对获取“活物”探寻孔雀石方法的欲望。而“活物”在果儿死后，失去精神支柱的他唯一的欲望就是为果儿报仇。小说在此也进入第二个故事，即“活物”为果儿报仇的故事。

3. 黑乎乎的洞—死亡

与“希望”相对应的就是“死亡”。在黑黢黢的古矿井里，烛火正常摇曳是希望，但当矿井坍塌，空气不再流动，烛火慢慢熄灭时，此时就是死亡将至和面对死亡的恐惧了。而概念隐喻“蜡烛的熄灭是死亡”也是有一系列形成基础的，即有关“死亡”的语义场，这也是蜡烛的第三层含义。而死亡总是与黑乎乎的洞，黑黢黢的世界，黑乎乎的大口等字眼相结合。

首先是“远古时期沉淀下来的空气层被搅动了，带着沉重的腐霉气味让人窒息”。这里“我们”渺小得就像一个“搅拌器”，而古矿井就像是一个硕大的“容器”。随着“我们”进一步深入，“主坑道变得扑朔迷离，黑乎乎的岔道口一个接着一个，让人分不清哪里是这地下迷宫的主要通道，唯有我背的那个活物，才对这密如蛛网的坑道了如指掌”，此时的古矿井是“迷宫”，是“蛛网”。而到最后“黑乎乎的洞壁好像随时都会压下来；弯弯叉叉的坑道里，无数的洞口好像是张开的黑乎乎的大口；顶壁上的水渗透下来，滴在脖子里透心儿的凉；偶尔还能见到一两节动物的骨头，让人联想到是人身上的哪个部位，我心里有一种钻进历史坟墓的恐怖感”。此时的古矿井是“黑乎乎的大口”，即将吞噬所有的一切，是“历史的坟墓”。“活物还会神经质地大喊起来：‘来了，来了……你们还没听见？轰隆隆？轰隆隆！……白盔白甲，来了，来了……咱们全完了！完了，完了……’”“白盔白甲”就是“死神”。

中心隐喻为“死亡”，“地下迷宫”“蛛网”“黑乎乎的大口”“历史坟墓”和“白盔白甲”等一系列的隐喻都围绕这一主题，并且相互关联构成一个语义场，形成一个语义链。这些喻体都是以该中心展开的，各个喻体之间具有关联性，使每个段落之间相互联系，从而构成了语篇的衔接与连贯。

小说中，各怀鬼胎的“头儿”和“活物”再一次进入矿井，寻求财富。“头儿”执迷于“活物”寻宝的绝招，而“活物”为替果儿报仇不顾自身性命。“活物”探寻宝藏的绝招诱惑着“头儿”一步一步走向死亡，这也是“头儿”的欲望驱使使然。

（三）其他隐喻

在叙事语篇中，隐喻以经验作为基础，而语篇正是以经验的方式展开的。隐喻要借助形象进行经验陈述，在经验的陈述和隐喻形象所激发的图示结构知识的相互作用下，语篇便在整体上取得连贯[15]。以“我”对“活物”的评价为例：

“可我还是只得往前爬，背着那重物往前爬。”

“背上的活物水蛭般地紧贴着我，越来越沉。”

“影影绰绰的光亮里，看得见他的两条光秃秃的腿杆子在身后拖着，倘若是在松软的沙地上，一定能画出两条极均匀的平行线，我想。”

“鬼！他哪用了什么方法，只见他一动不动地坐着，泥塑木雕一般；烟头一闪一闪，他双眼紧闭，凝神静坐，活脱脱的如高僧坐禅或是面壁受罚的佛家弟子。”

“时而闻闻，时而放到烛光下照照，仿佛是古董商在鉴赏一件稀世珍宝。”

“一进到洞里，他就身不由己地抖颤起来，一双手铁爪似的紧紧抠到了我的肉里去。”

在“我”的眼里，添加“活物”是“重物”，是负担，是“水蛭”，不仅是因为他紧紧地压在“我”的背上，更是因为失去双腿的他只能依附于别人而存在；他的腿像“光秃秃的杆子”，说明他外型丑陋，而当他判断孔雀石时则像“泥塑木雕”一样，“面壁受罚的佛家弟子”则说明他的专注；“古董商在鉴赏一件稀世珍宝”则说明了他的专业。正是这份专注和专业给探寻古矿井带来了可行性，即前文提到的希望的叠加。而当面对死亡时，他的手像“铁爪”一般深深地抓到了“我”的肉里，那是面对死亡的恐惧和惊慌。“我”对“活物”的评价也是根据故事的情节慢慢发展的，而其中的隐喻形象也是在经验陈述的框架内进行。“活物”专业的探索方法对“头儿”来说是希望，指引着下文的发展，而“活物”的手之所以变成“铁爪”也是因为死亡将至，符合“希望”到“死亡”的转变。

胡燕怀克服日常语言的局限性，追求小说意象，运用新鲜的隐喻、幻想手法，通过视觉形象（烛火、洞、眼睛等）表达了人物细微复杂的思想感情，在描写外物和表达内心两方面都达到了高度的准确性和真实性，达到了意与象的自然结合、达到了小说的内在人性主题与外在语言形象的相互交融，这使得小说更富有表现力和阐释的力量，也让读者获得极大的审美自由和深度的精神震撼。

四、结语

某些概念隐喻在一部文学作品中反复出现并反映作品的主题，它贯穿于整个文本，体现了文本内的一致性。在进行文学欣赏和批评时，读者要重视对文学语言本身进行分析和欣赏，因为抓住文本中的主要隐喻有助于读者理解文学作品的主旨和关键意义。而主要隐喻由多个反映其主旨的小隐喻组成，隐喻的跳跃和变化对语篇的建构和组织起着重要作用。

在小说《洞火》中，作者设定了一个隐喻，即黑暗的古矿井是人性的象征，以这个隐喻作为整个语篇的模式支配语篇的脉络，并且将这一核心比喻划分为三个不同的层面以代表人性的不同内容，形成三个次要的引申比喻。通过主题隐喻支配其他三个次要隐喻，帮助构建作品主题，形成一个框架并借助一系列相关的隐喻表达式形成系统的词汇衔接网络，使得语篇在这一框架内展开，最终达到语篇内部、语篇底层，即语义上的连贯。小说是具有连贯性的叙事语篇，从小说语篇层面来研究隐喻可以使我们更贴切地理解小说的内涵，为小说语篇分析拓展了一个新的领域；而且深入分析小说文本的隐喻性语言，有助于读者更好地理解文学语言的功能，更准确地领会小说作者的创作意图，也更好地享受文学语言给读者带来的审美认知和情感体验。

◎ 参考文献

[1] Lakoff G, Johnson M. Metaphors We Live By [M]. Chicago: The University of Chicago Press, 1980.

[2] 张玮，张德禄．隐喻性特征与语篇连贯研究 [J]．外语学刊，2008 (1)：99-103.

[3] 魏在江．隐喻的语篇功能——兼论语篇分析与认知语言学的界面研究 [J]．外语教学，2006 (5)：10-15.

[4] 周进珍，等．黄石矿冶文学研究 [M]．武汉：湖北人民出版社，2009.

[5] 陈新瑶．古矿井中的人性之思——评胡燕怀矿冶题材小说《洞火》的叙事意义 [J]．黄石理工学院学报，2009 (2)：6-8.

[6] 魏在江．隐喻与文学语篇的建构 [J]．外语与外语教学，2008 (3)：13-16.

[7] 束定芳．隐喻学研究 [M]．上海：上海外语教育出版社，2001.

[8] 张沛．隐喻的生命 [M]．北京：北京大学出版社，2004.

[9] 廖美珍．英语比喻的语篇粘合作用 [J]．现代外语，1992 (2)：32-35.

[10] 方小青．概念隐喻与卡明斯诗歌语篇连贯的建构 [J]．广西师范大学学报，2010 (4)：25-29.

[11] 张锦峰．英语诗歌中的隐喻与语篇连贯 [J]．忻州师范学院学报，2011 (3)：63-65.

[12] 刘艳春．解读《我有一个梦想》中隐喻的语篇功能 [J]．东北农业大

学学报, 2010 (4): 87-89.
[13] 朱立元. 当代西方文艺理论 [M]. 上海: 华东师范大学出版社, 2005.
[14] 任绍曾. 概念隐喻和语篇连贯 [J]. 外语教学与研究, 2006 (3): 91-100.
[15] 张云红. 从隐喻的视角解读《走出非洲》[J]. 牡丹江大学学报, 2010 (2): 26-29.

第四节　基于概念合成理论的矿冶戏剧认知诗学分析*

——以《钢铁夫人》为例

A CBT-based Cognitive Poetic Analysis of Mining Drama *The Steel Lady*

摘要：从认知诗学的角度，探讨概念合成理论对矿冶文学戏剧《钢铁夫人》在词汇层、语义层以及语篇层意义的建构和理解，揭示话剧理解的认知过程，使读者能够清楚地了解该话剧情节的发展过程以及剧目之间的内在联系网络。验证概念合成理论对话剧理解的解释力，旨在为中国本土的文学作品研究提供新的理论支持，为研究黄石矿冶文学作品提供一种新的方法。

关键词：《钢铁夫人》；矿冶戏剧；概念合成理论；认知诗学

戏剧内涵丰富，艺术手段多样，是一种独特的文学体裁。“剧本”既可以作为文学作品供读者欣赏，也可以作为舞台演出的蓝本与观众见面[1]；它如同小说一样强调情节节奏、人物性格等，但却有独特的语言方式。

侯涛提出，戏剧文体学从描写性研究发展为解释性研究，目前已进入戏剧话语语用和文学认知关系的研究[2]。如：俞东明、左进探究了语用模

* 作者李金妹、吴晓云，原载于《安徽理工大学学报》（社会科学版）第16卷第1期，2014年。

糊、会话策略这两类语用方法对戏剧人物刻画的作用[3]；侯涛、俞东明从语用文体认知的角度分析了《雷雨》人物对话和文学话语的语用建构和文体特征，提出了戏剧文本话语多层分析方法[4]；高剑妩、申丹采用礼貌策略和人物塑造理论对《慈善家》剧本进行了文体分析[5]；高剑妩在修正Brandt等的四空间模式的基础上，以《伽利略传》为例提出戏剧认知诗学分析的一般模式[6]；徐海云运用认知语言学的典型理论、认知模型和文化模型诠释了莎士比亚戏剧的欣赏和批评方法[7]。

由此可见，国内学者大都运用语用学的理论，如礼貌策略、会话分析和合作原则等对剧本进行文学认知分析，但从其他学科角度对剧本进行研究的比较少。本文力求对“认知诗学视域下的矿冶文学的研究”这一课题有所贡献，从认知诗学的角度，探讨概念合成理论对矿冶戏剧《钢铁夫人》在作者构思和读者理解方面的认知机理，从而验证概念合成理论对话剧的解释力，旨在为中国本土的话剧分析提供实际的指导作用，为研究矿冶文学作品提供一种新的方法。

一、话剧《钢铁夫人》简介

大型话剧《钢铁夫人》[8]是湖北剧作家裴有猷的著名作品，也是长江中下游矿冶戏剧的代表作之一。它以改革大潮中的现实为题材，描绘了钢铁工人的生活画面，围绕厂内资金紧缺，原钢铁厂厂长胡涓进行机构调整、人才培训、设备改造等一系列措施展开故事情节，领导与领导之间、领导与工人之间发生的矛盾和冲突将剧情逐步推向高潮。最终经过大家锲而不舍的艰苦努力，排除障碍，钢铁厂在改革大潮中稳步前进。《钢铁夫人》塑造了以原钢铁厂厂长胡涓为代表的大批钢铁工人的形象，反映了今天的矿冶人的精神风貌，展现了改革大潮中黄石矿冶人身上那种特有的无私奉献、乐观向上、刚性的精神风貌，以及理性与感性结合的特质。同时它以现实主义创作手法、生动鲜明的人物形象、典型独特的时代场景、别出心裁的开放式结构和浓厚的富有人情味的地方特色方言，使得我们感受到一幅幅生动的画面，同时也吸引了广大矿冶文学研究学者的注意[9-10]。

二、概念合成理论及其发展应用

概念合成理论（Conceptual Blending Theory）是在心理空间理论基础上发展形成的，是认知语言学的一个重要成果，属于认知语义学范畴[11]。心理空间可建立起一系列概念，如时间、信念等。概念合成理论认为意义的生成和理解是通过非组合性的概念整合积极建构意义的实时动态过程，是人们进行创造性思维和活动时的一种认知过程，它为文学的创造性与新意义的动态建构提供了系统的解释。

Fauconnier 和 Turner 指出，基本的概念整合网络模式是由四个空间构成的，即两个输入空间，一个类属空间和一个合成空间。类属空间反映的是两个输入空间共有的普遍概念结构；合成空间除了包含类属空间中的普遍结构外，还包含两个输入空间选择性投射的特定结构以及合成空间本身通过组合、完善、扩展而建立起的新创空间（emergent structure）。新创空间不存在于原有的输入空间中，这体现了概念整合的创造性。这四个心理空间通过投射彼此连接起来，构成了一个概念整合网络[12-13]。

概念合成理论自问世以来，被广泛地应用于语言、文学、艺术、音乐理论、宗教、计算机科学等领域，并取得丰硕成果。

三、认知诗学模式下概念合成理论对《钢铁夫人》的解读

戏剧文本的研究不但要对戏剧语言进行一般的静态描述，还应通过描述把戏剧语言与内容联系起来，借助全新的语言学理论着重研究话语意义的生成和理解的动态过程[14]。对于读者而言，阅读是发生于作者与读者之间的一种互动活动，作者所创造的语篇并非完整的，需要读者在阅读过程中，利用背景知识和概念整合的认知加工方式加以补充和完善，也就是说读者处于一个重新创造的过程[15]。

将认知语言学的概念合成理论用于探讨剧本解读的认知过程属于认知诗学的研究范畴。概念合成理论，作为一种认知操作模式，为话剧分析提供了比常规分析理论更加理想的推理机制。本文基于概念合成理论，以黄

石矿冶文学戏剧《钢铁夫人》为语料进行认知分析，讨论概念合成在词汇层、语义层以及语篇层的认知建构，揭示话剧理解的认知过程，使读者清楚地了解该话剧情节的发展过程以及剧目之间的内在联系网络。

（一）词汇层面

例 1

杨世杰："来这么三个人就能扭转局面了？"

胡涓："这不是三个人，是一批人。"

孟辉："怎么？还有人？"

胡涓："你忘了那个典故了？燕王濒临灭亡的时候，燕昭王重用了一个郭瑰，不是招来了乐毅、邹衍、剧辛那一批人杰吗？"

例 1 中的典故出自于《史记》。该典故的源认知域与剧本中描述的剧情背景空间具有很大的相似性：一个是陷入窘境的钢铁厂，另一个是濒临灭亡的燕国。读者在理解该句时，典故中描述的地点、角色、事件被纳入输入空间Ⅰ，而话剧描述的厂内情况则被纳入输入空间Ⅱ。两个空间中的事物通过跨空间映射起来，产生一个具有共同联系的类属空间，其内涵便是依靠人的智力，困境可以得到扭转。最后，通过一系列的层创，读者在合成空间中产生新的意义：厂内必须引入新的人才，局面才会得到改变(见图 1)。

例 2

胡涓："这有什么？"

碧茜："好轻松！老杨刚才那个样子你没看出来？他和老代怎么相处？你的女儿胡撞是你和老代生的，她要是知道了，她在两个爸爸之间的距离怎么摆？会给孩子心里种下什么？还有苏云那伙人的流言蜚语你怎么对付？别像尼克松，当了四年总统被水门事件纠缠了三年，

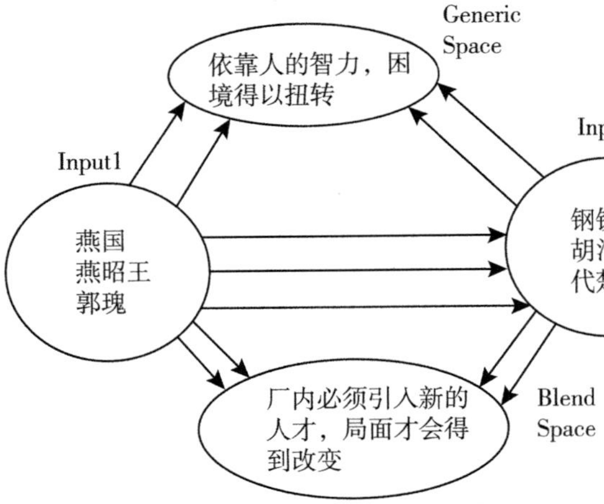

图 1　例 1 的概念合成示意图

落得身败名裂，舆论能杀人哪，即便是无中生有也能逼得人投河上吊的。”

碧茜认为如果胡涓让自己的前任丈夫进入钢铁厂帮忙，那么就会让只顾眼前利益的障碍者——苏云等人制造出绯闻，使得胡涓失去人心。从概念合成理论来看，读者头脑里形成两个输入空间——输入空间Ⅰ，里面有尼克松、水门事件、舆论；输入空间Ⅱ，里面有胡涓、胡涓与前任丈夫的关系、厂内工人的反应。同时，当两个空间内输入的元素彼此映射时，读者的头脑会将输入空间Ⅰ和输入空间Ⅱ中所具有的共同元素放入类属空间，即绯闻会让人走投无路。于是，通过类属空间的加工，读者形成一个合成空间来理解剧目的内涵——流言蜚语的作用非同小可，胡涓不能忽视。

（二）语义层面

例 1

胡涓：“暂时，代楚雄任决策中心办公室主任。他外出，对外是法人的全权代表，我外出，对内行使厂长职权。孟总经济师的辞职，理由不充分，继任原职。”

巩川：“很好！我走了。嗨，你怎么互撞？”

胡撞：“谁叫我妈替我取这么个名字？嘻……”

例中作者巧妙地运用双关的修辞手法，取得幽默的前景化效果。此时的“胡撞”涵盖了两层意义：第一，胡涓与前夫代楚雄所生女儿的名字；第二，表达一种动作方式，“胡”可以理解为“乱”，这样一来，通过读音相似让读者建立起了两个输入空间，虽然两个输入空间的字面表达相同，但却表达了不同的意思，而以字音相同的类属空间通过整合让读者充满联想，有如身临其境的感觉，从而得出这样一个合成空间：胡撞走路时不小心与巩川相碰。这种语音结构的安排，不仅体现了巩川风趣机智的性格特点，也让读者产生愉快的体验。

例 2

胡涓：“东江哥，你别觉得受了什么委屈了，革命对你是公平的！过去革命需要那样，你那样做了，给了你荣誉了嘛，今天需要科学技术文化，要四化，你为什么不化？没有劝你？没有批评没有拉你？像一截系牛桩，摇不动拔不起移不走，还要把周围的人都系住，你，你成了绊脚石了！”

刘东江：“我是绊脚石？好！好！我去市委告你？”

剧本中，作者把固执、停滞不前的刘东江比作坚硬、不易动摇的系牛桩。这种比喻的修辞手法的运用产生了一种生动形象、贴切精准、耐人寻味的文体效果。通过认知加工，读者分别将因循守旧的刘东江和根深蒂固的系牛桩放入输入空间Ⅰ和输入空间Ⅱ，在类属空间中抽象出两个输入空间共有的特性：顽固不化、故步自封、墨守成规。最后通过合成空间的扩展和完善，读者理解了剧本并得出结论：刘东江的保守和古板，在改革中无疑会被淘汰。

例 3

胡涓："你怎么还不结婚?"

代楚雄："说不清楚，也许是失去的东西附着在记忆里太牢固了。"

胡涓："……应该连那篇记忆一起失去，在现实中事情的确储存在记忆里，一跳出记忆就品尝现实中失落的痛苦。何必? 过去，随着光阴消逝了，以每秒三十万公里的光速消逝得无影无踪了……成个家吧。有人给你介绍过吗?"

作者在本句中运用了夸张的修辞手法，表达了人物丰富的想象和强烈的情感，使描写的事件更加生动形象。在这里，读者建构起一个过去的输入空间Ⅰ，胡涓与代楚雄原来是夫妻，但由于种种原因，迫不得已他们离婚了。而在现实的输入空间Ⅱ里，胡涓已经成家，但代楚雄却仍旧一个人，投射到类属空间表现出来的就是时光飞逝，事过境迁，最后在合成空间里得到组合和完善。读者在合成空间得出：胡涓认为代楚雄应当忘记他们以前在一起的生活经历，开始新的生活，早日成家。作者恰当地使用夸张，体现了身为钢铁厂厂长的胡涓也不缺乏应有的柔情和细腻，表达了她对前夫的真诚而恰如其分的建议和亲情如水的关心，真心希望他能过得好的想法。

（三）语篇层面

在整个剧目中，语篇整体的理解成为最重要的部分，语篇是由语句组成的表达多层意思的具有内在逻辑相关性的结构系统[16]。下表是对《钢铁夫人》十个剧目的剧情发展进行的简单概括：

表1　　《钢铁夫人》十个剧目的剧情概括

剧目编号	剧情概括
剧目一	钢铁厂濒临倒闭，胡涓四处借钱，厂内捣乱分子拉轧机卖，胡涓苦心劝导，不计前嫌请前夫代楚雄入厂
剧目二	胡涓想方设法改造旧设备，多方筹借资金
剧目三	苏云百般为改革设置障碍，职工集资被迫停止，厂内陷入窘境
剧目四	捣乱分子无端闹事，代楚雄正式入厂并出谋划策
剧目五	胡涓不畏权势，秉公处事，果断换人
剧目六	胡涓教育工人科学办事，厂内情况扭转
剧目七	厂内举办员工舞会，孟辉借机制造绯闻
剧目八	“相片”风波引起亲人与工人误解
剧目九	胡涓对女儿倾诉苦衷，厂内设备改造再次停止
剧目十	澄清事实，冲破阻挠，在群众的支持下，钢铁厂起死回生

1. 相邻剧目的概念合成

《钢铁夫人》中人物众多、事件较为复杂，头绪纷繁，加之故事所涉及的时间跨度较长，作者采用了开放式结构，剧情按照故事的发生、发展、高潮、结局的自然顺序展开，能够让观众非常清楚地从头至尾原原本本地了解剧情的自然发展过程。这种结构方式能够较为完整地展示人物性格的发展过程，而读者也能够通过剧情的不同发展阶段上的人物动作，比较方便地透视人物的整体面貌及其性格变化。由于戏剧艺术的时空限制性，作者在剧目和剧目之间的组织和安排力求严密、紧凑、最大限度地展示出尽可能丰富的内容。

（1）剧目二与剧目三的概念合成。在概念合成理论下，剧目二与剧目三分别建立起两个输入空间Ⅰ和Ⅱ，即工人争论卖楼以及轧机，苏云挑拨孟辉并对调入人才阳奉阴违。厂内进行集资的输入空间Ⅰ和罗满因卖轧机事件调入废钢库，苏云仍未落实调入代楚雄一事，厂内集资被迫停止，厂内情况陷入窘境的输入空间Ⅱ。两个输入空间通过跨空间映射建立起对应连接形成包含调入人才、职位调动以及厂内集资这三个元素的类属空间。输入空间各元素通过投射进入合成空间，经过组合、完善和扩展形成层创结，即厂内部分职工只顾眼前利益，阻碍厂的前进，资金问题并不是集资就能解决的。此时，通过概念合成，读者感受到胡涓身上的坚强和乐观向上的精神——即使遇到了许多人为或者其他客观因素的干扰，她也没有犹豫和退缩，一如既往迎难而上（见图 2）。

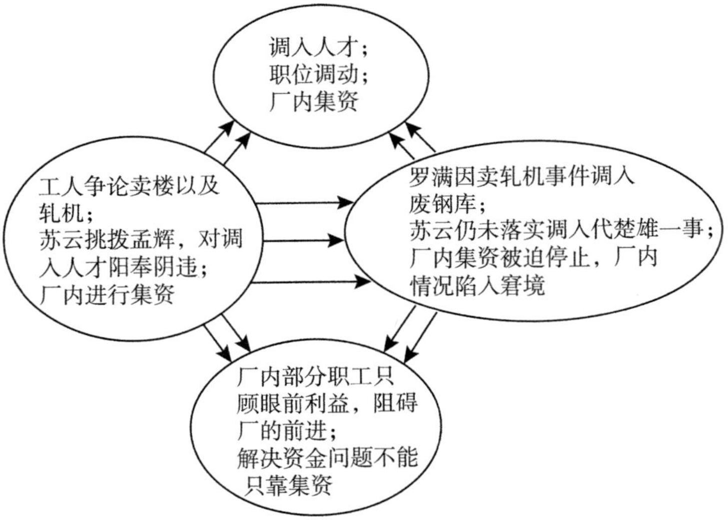

图 2　剧目一与剧目二的概念合成

（2）剧目三与剧目四的概念合成。在理解剧目三和剧目四时，我们的大脑中也存在着剧目三的事件框架Ⅰ和剧目四的事件框架Ⅱ这两个输入空间。输入空间Ⅰ包含罗满因卖轧机事件调入废钢库，苏云仍未落实调入代楚雄一事，厂内集资被迫停止，厂内情况陷入窘境等元素，输入空间Ⅱ包含胡涓请代楚雄来家中做客，罗满进行报复，代楚雄解决厂内资金问题等元素。类属空间提取了两个空间的共同元素：调入人才、资金问题以及职员职位变化。两个空间跨空间映射得到合成空间：引入了优秀人才，厂内看到了生机，钢铁厂的工作有了向好的方向发展的可能。围绕转产的问题，还有机制改革、机构调整、班组成本核算、规范管理、人才培训、设备改造等问题，胡涓根据钢铁厂的实际情况，在周密的调查研究、严格的理论论证和有关专家的指导基础上，进行一系列措施，让读者在理解剧本的过程中能够深刻感受到胡涓尊重科学、坚持真理、按科学规律管理工厂的优秀品质，同时这也是胡涓理性品质的完美体现（见图 3）。

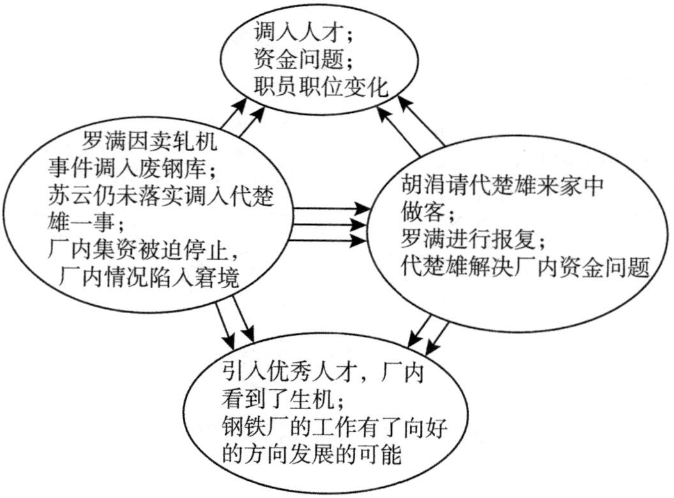

图 3　剧目三与剧目四的概念合成

2. 跨剧目的概念合成

（1）剧目三、剧目五、剧目七的概念合成。在概念合成理论下，剧目三的剧情形成了输入空间 I，它包含了罗满因卖轧机事件被调入废钢库对胡涓产生不满，苏云百般为改革设置障碍，职工集资被迫停止，厂内陷入窘境等元素；剧目五的剧情形成了输入空间 II，它包含了罗满和向荣私吞运费，厂内制度有漏洞，执行不得力等元素。剧目七的剧目形成了输入空间 III，它包含了厂内举办员工舞会，孟辉借机制造绯闻等元素。三个输入空间通过跨空间的映射对应连接得到包含障碍者阻碍改革这一共同元素的类属空间。最后经过认知能动性，得到一个合成空间：厂内障碍者制造的麻烦不断，必须彻底铲除障碍者，合理运用人才，厂内情况才会好转。这也让读者感受到胡涓作为厂长该有的魄力：在人为干扰面前，不畏权势，果断换人，秉公处理无端闹事者。在日常工作中，胡涓为人正直，不弄虚作假，不口是心非，时时闪烁着“钢铁夫人”的自豪感和责任感（见图 4）。

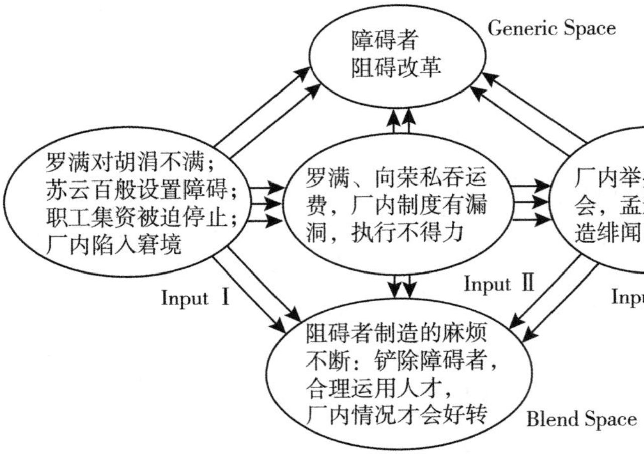

图 4　剧目三、剧目四、剧目七的概念合成

（2）剧目一、剧目四、剧目十的概念合成。实际上，我们可以把剧目一、剧目四、剧目十看作三个不同的输入空间。输入空间 I 是钢铁厂濒临倒闭，胡涓四处借钱，厂内捣乱分子拉轧机卖，胡涓苦心劝导，不计前嫌请前夫入厂。输入空间 II 是胡涓请代楚雄来家中做客，罗满进行报复，代楚雄解决厂内资金问题。输入空间 III 是照片事件真相大白，捣乱分子受到处分，杨世杰与代楚雄及时回厂，厂内设备改造与资金问题得以解决。三个输入空间对接产生了包含厂内资金问题、厂内障碍者以及胡涓得到帮助的类属空间，类属空间将各空间中的元素投射后得到新的合成空间：只有解决厂内资金问题，梳理好厂内人际关系，在众人的努力和支持下，钢铁厂才能起死回生。这三个剧目分别在剧目的前、中、后位置，通过跨空间的概念合成以及剧目结合，胡涓的一言一行都在我们的脑海里留下了深刻印象，一个沉着、刚毅、无畏、坚持真理的改革者的形象也因此产生

（见图 5）。

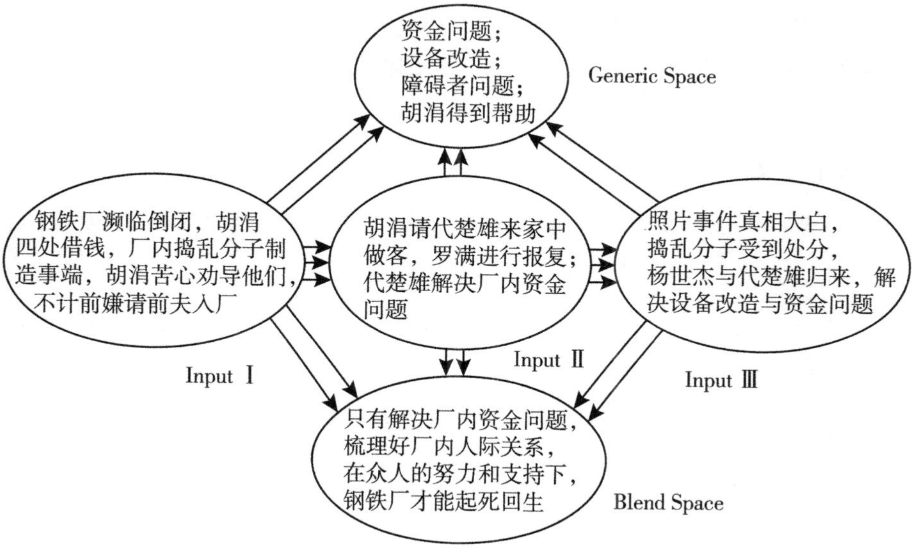

图 5　剧目一、剧目四、剧目十的概念合成

在概念合成理论下，我们可以看到剧目与剧目之间都有一定的联系，并且这些联系通过跨剧目的合成使剧情显得紧凑，深入人心。前面分别例举了相邻空间的概念合成以及跨剧目概念合成的过程，通过理解剧情以及剧情的发展，读者可以清楚地理解该剧本的主题，即主人公胡涓为了把企业搞活，她坚持不放弃，这与剧本题目“钢铁夫人”相呼应，彰显了黄石矿冶人的“刚性”，展现了新时期矿冶人为了钢铁事业艰苦奋斗和前赴后继的精神，进而能够让读者领悟矿冶人积极向上、不屈不挠的精神风貌。

四、结语

话剧作为一种文学创作的手法，将人物的真实情感用语言形式表达出来，因而，对话剧的解读不应该只探究作品本身，同时也可以用来体会人物的情感。用不同的理论来解读话剧可以使得读者更加深入、全面地体会其丰富的艺术价值。概念合成理论作为认知语言学新兴的学科，已经证明对多种语言现象具有独到的解释力。本文正是基于该理论对矿冶戏剧《钢铁夫人》进行全新的解读，通过对剧目写作手法的详细分析，构建了不同的整合网络，最终证明该理论对话剧有很强的阐释力。同时，概念合成理论视角也能帮助我们进一步加深对矿冶文化的理解。

◎ 参考文献

[1] 杨雪燕．试论戏剧在语言文体学中的地位 [J]. 外国语，1989 (1)：67-70.

[2] 侯涛．文学语用学视角下的戏剧话语分析 [J]. 外语教学，2011 (1)：16-19.

[3] 俞东明，左进．语用模糊、会话策略与戏剧人物刻画 [J]. 外语教学与研究，2004 (5)：379-384.

[4] 侯涛，俞东明．戏剧话语：语用建构和文体认知——基于《雷雨》的研究之一 [J]. 哈尔滨工业大学学报（社会科学版），2010 (4)：115-123.

[5] 高剑妩，申丹．礼貌策略、人物塑造理论与戏剧文体学——综合性实例分析及模式修正 [J]. 外语教学与研究，2006 (6)：428-436.

[6] 高剑妩．基于概念复合的戏剧认知诗学分析一般模式 [J]. 外语与外语教学，2009 (9)：7-13.

[7] 徐海云．认知语言学与戏剧欣赏和批评初探 [J]. 安徽农业大学学报（社会科学版），2004 (2)：122-125.

[8] 李社教．黄石矿冶文学作品选 [M]. 武汉：湖北人民出版社，2010.

[9] 周进珍．黄石矿冶文学研究 [M]. 武汉：湖北人民出版社，2009.

[10] 王昭，周进珍．黄石矿冶戏剧的美学价值 [J]. 黄石理工学院学报（人文社会科学版），2011 (2)：6-9.

[11] Fauconnier G M, Turner. The Way We Think：Conceptual Blending and the Minds Hidden Complexities [M]. New York：Basic Books, 2002.

[12] 李福印．认知语言学概论 [M]. 北京：北京大学出版社，2008：174.
[13] 王文斌．概念合成理论研究与应用的回顾和思考 [J]. 外语研究，2004 (1)：6-12.
[14] 俞东明．戏剧文体与戏剧文体学 [J]. 浙江大学学报（社会科学版)，1996 (1)：100-103.
[15] 陈海庆．文学语篇的语用学阐释：互动性及其取效行为 [J]. 外语教学，2009 (1)：30-34.
[16] 王全智．可能世界、心理空间与语篇的意义建构 [J]. 外语教学，2005 (7)：5-8.

第五节　语篇视点与矿冶文学小说《古巷道》的叙事策略*

Discourse Point of View and Narrative Strategies of Mining Novel *Ancient Roadway*

摘要：从认知诗学的理论出发，结合语篇视点，分析矿冶文学的代表作品《古巷道》的叙事与聚焦特征，指出作者选择双层并行叙述框架，运用全知全能零聚焦视点和第三人称内聚焦视点交替叙述的叙事模式，叙述视点和时空视点的转换巧妙自然，小说意识流的写作手法在知觉视点的选择和安排上，传达了主人公起子和作者隐含的心理认知和观念视点。同时，这也验证了认知诗学可以对本土作品进行解读。

关键词：《古巷道》；矿冶文学；视点；认知诗学；本土化

《古巷道》[1]是由著名作家古清生创作的黄石矿冶文学的代表作。它以黄石市大冶铜绿山发掘的我国春秋战国时期的古矿冶遗址为创作背景，以20世纪80年代中后期大冶地区矿山村民大肆盗取国家矿产资源为题材内容。由于其艺术价值和题材的特殊性和代表性，《古巷道》这部小说引起了很多黄石矿冶文学研究学者的关注。如：周进珍介绍了该小说创作的历

---

* 作者李金妹，原载于《河北经贸大学学报》（综合版）第13卷第1期，2013年。

史背景和深刻的主题意义，分析了其写作手法及作品的不足之处；[2]黄燕阐释了“古巷道”与“青铜斧”的象征意义及小说中人物的性格特点，探析了小说中的人性世界。[3]这些学者都是从传统的文学批评角度来分析这部小说的。

李金妹运用“图形—背景理论”探讨了黄石矿冶文学的代表作《古巷道》在语音、词汇、语义和整体语篇结构等层面的文体风格。[4]本文从认知诗学的角度，结合语篇视点理论，分析黄石矿冶小说《古巷道》中的叙事与聚焦特征，认为古清生在创作这部小说的过程中，对叙事视点的处理别具一格，采用双层并行叙述框架，叙述视点和时空视点的转换巧妙自然，同时在知觉视点的选择和安排上，传达了主人公起子和作者隐含的心理认知和观念视点。本文试图运用国外认知诗学理论对中国文学作品进行分析，这不仅可以验证这一全新的解读方法对本土作品的解释力，同时也能为中国文学文本的研究提供一种新的方法。

一、认知诗学视野下的视点

视点（Point of view）是修辞学与文学批评领域的术语。在国外，自20世纪70年代以来，语篇视点在文体学、叙事学、文艺批评、功能语义学等学科中得到深刻的探讨和广泛的运用。它是“制约语篇深层结构（即语义）的一种图式，反映人们看待对象世界的角度和态度，支配着对象的选择与组合，从而影响语篇表层结构（即形式句法）的组织”。它有四种类型：时空视点、观念视点、叙述视点和知觉视点。[5]其中，时空视点是人们观察或呈现对象世界时采用的时空角度和位置，包括时空的起点和移动的顺序；观念视点指作者或人物通过文字体现出来的立场、信仰体系和价值观等；叙述视点指篇章中对陈述内容进行观察和讲述的角度，侧重关注作者和人物参与者之间谁“说”，谁“看”或者“聚焦”。谁“说”涉及对第一、第二或第三人称叙述者的选择。而谁“看”或者“聚焦”，反映了叙述中认知参照点的选择和安排，可以分为无聚焦或零聚焦、内聚焦、外聚焦和多重聚焦。[6]知觉视点关注知觉的对象，有起始和终结两个方面，它事实上是信息的选择与组合。语篇的构建中，语言的起始话题就是知觉的起点，内容就是知觉的终点，也就是新信息。

视点是叙事理论的一个核心概念，而视点的安排和选择是一种认知处理过程，涉及图式、脚本、方案等认知方式的运用；观察角度、方向或立场的差异以及叙述方法的改变都会影响作者或读者对某一个事物的认知体验，从而影响其对文本语言和意义的理解。因此视点的选择和分析对文学文本的解读起着十分重要的作用，[7-8]同时也体现了作为“文学与语言学的新接面”[5]的认知诗学的研究方法。

二、解构小说的叙述策略和语篇视点

（一）叙述视点和聚焦

《古巷道》从宏观上可以分为两部分，采用双层并行叙述框架。第一部分（即外框架）是作者按照人物的行踪交代故事的发展进程，描写了贪婪又聪明的起子在利益的诱惑和驱使下，走进年久失修的古巷道，蜗行在黑暗崎岖的狭道中为了寻找传说中的一把青铜斧，以及在巷道里，起子、九疤子、凤子和豺狗为了争夺青铜斧，相互猜忌厮杀的故事。这一部分作者采用第三人称零聚焦的叙述视点进行观察。第三人称零聚焦是从与故事无关的旁观者立场进行的叙述，其特点是叙述者的全知全能，无视角的限制。叙述者可以同一时间出现在不同的地点，对景物、事件、人物的内心世界和情感活动了如指掌，不动声色地将故事娓娓道来，拉近作者与故事的距离，让读者觉得更真实。如小说一开始作者就为我们描绘了像迷宫一样神秘的古巷道里面阴森恐怖的景象：霉腐浑浊的空气，低矮又不断滴水的巷顶，坑洼不平的窄道，巷壁凹处不下百十条的土蛇，日本人留下的刺刀和盗矿者的尸骨，巷道随时坍塌和涨水的危险等。

第二部分（即内框架）作者避免平面、线性地直观描写，通过对故事情节的处理，设置悬念，以吸引读者。作者采用主人公起子的视角来回忆往事，小说交代了他们进入古巷道的背景、缘由，同时也交代了起子的出身和主要人物起子、九疤子、王经理、凤子和豺狗的相互关系，以及主人公起子的生活背景和个性特征等。这一部分作者采用第三人称内聚焦的视角进行叙述。内聚焦是指叙述者把聚焦者的地位让位于故事中的人物，采用人物的视角对故事情景进行描述。[9]叙述者对事件的理解受限于人物的道德水平和知识能力，所叙述的只是局部情况，这种视角也可以深入人物的内心。

作者运用全知全能零聚焦视点和第三人称内聚焦视点交替叙述的叙事模式，让双层叙述框架并行发展，相辅相成，形成有机整体，使小说情节完整，布局合理。在外框架中，作者即叙述者高于故事层面，从一开始他就已经知道故事的来龙去脉。在内框架中，作者把自己的感知限制在人物起子身上。《古巷道》中故事的外叙述和故事内聚焦的结合丰富了故事的情节，增强了小说的艺术张力，控制了小说叙述的节奏。

（二）时空视点

叙述是在一定的时空进行的。古清生在叙述时间的处理上采用了电影中的蒙太奇手法，呈现出故事的历时性叙述和穿插倒叙。小说结构严谨，布局缜密，随着起子意识的流动，有限的篇幅中自然地插入起子的八段回忆。“意识流”作为一种结构形式，打破常规的因果、逻辑关系，具有跳跃性、逆时性、散乱性和交叉性，是对人心灵隐秘的一种原生状态的如实呈现。[10]

《古巷道》中叙述时间的频繁变化，小说中全知叙述者的叙述和人物起子的意识之间的频繁转换都体现出这部作品具有意识流小说的特点。作者采用全知叙述视点描述人物活动的背景，采用第三人称内聚焦视点表现起子在古巷道中绵绵不断的思绪和飘忽不定的意识：看到九疤子“歹毒贪婪”的眼神，他想到和九疤子、王经理相识的经过；听到古巷道里坍塌的响声，起子心里升起一种不祥的感觉，进而想到他进入古巷道寻找价值连城的古人用来采矿的青铜斧的原因；王经理狡猾恶毒的暗算和挑拨及九疤子凶狠自私的行为让起子产生强烈愤恨，又让他想到童年受人欺压的经历，及他和队长发生过节，为了报复，他放火烧队长家的房子的情景；看到手中燃着的松明子的火光，起子想起用石子打死曾经羞辱过他的赵四家的公鸡；怀抱着被误伤的凤子，他又不自觉地想到最初来到土矿桥受凤子的关照以及和人争夺地盘的情况……古清生巧妙准确地将叙述视点和时空视点进行转换，使与起子有关的过去时空在叙述中自由叠现，让读者从不同的侧面积累一些相互关联的信息，从而了解起子的性格特点，也为故事的高潮的到来做好铺垫。

（三）知觉视点

知觉视点反映了作者在认知过程中信息的选择与组合方式，是观念视点、时空视点和叙述视点的载体。[11]在小说语篇的构建中，故事的起始话题就是知觉的起点，故事内容和所要表达的主题是新信息，也是知觉的终点。古清生在建构语篇时，体现了人们从已知到未知的认知规律。外框架下，小说开篇用全知全能零聚焦的叙述视点描绘了古巷道中的现实场景，描绘了起子和九疤子在年代久远、恐怖阴森的古巷道中寻找青铜斧的场景，这是故事的起始话题，即知觉的起点。随着情节的展开，起子和九疤子在古巷道中历尽艰辛却一无所获。原来青铜斧早已被先进入古巷道中的豺狗和凤子找到，并据为己有。故事的高潮是为了争夺青铜斧，本是表兄弟的九疤子和豺狗互相残杀，起子和凤子一对热恋中的情人相互猜忌和暗算。结尾是，到手的青铜斧不翼而飞，凤子也“没了影踪”，刚刚死去的“九疤子已化为一堆白骨……”最后，起子在万分恐惧下，出现人格分裂、精神失常。一场八级地震将这一切化为乌有，谁也没得到青铜斧，谁也没能走出古巷道。

在内框架中，《古巷道》对于信息焦点的选取是以起子的视角展开的大量断点式叙述。故事中起子的思绪打破一般的时空顺序和逻辑联系，他的思维随意跳跃、凌乱无序，意识胡乱闪接和怪异地流动，有时还带有怪诞离奇的幻想，以至于让人感觉类似于精神病患者的错乱意识。然而把起子意识中的信息碎片重新整理、拼装和分析，我们发现起子的意识流与整个故事情节浑然一体，是小说重要的内容和题材，成为故事发展必不可少的组成部分。在这部小说中，古清生对意识流手法的运用，不仅体现了他独特的创作手法和娴熟的文字驾驭能力，而且也反映了他在认知过程中对于焦点信息的选择与组合方式。更重要的是，叙述者采用第三人称内聚焦，以起子视角进行叙述，不仅将人物复杂的生活经历、思想及情感揭示出来，而且把起子在瞬间产生的自我迷失、惶恐、精神分裂的心理状态如实、真切地呈现出来。而这些是传统的叙述方法所达不到的。

（四）观念视点

“视角蕴含着小说的价值体系和各种态度的集合”。[12] Stevick 说的这个“视角”等同于本文的观念视点。观念视点指作者或人物通过文字体现出来的立场、信仰体系和价值观等。在《古巷道》中作者刻意渲染了一种神秘的、恐怖的氛围。如文中写到：

> 1940 年日本侵略军开来一个探矿队，钻进古巷道就再也没有出来。当时日本人又派了一个中队去找，除了中队长跑出来，其余的也都没了踪影。那个中队长，一出来就疯了，扒了军衣乱喊乱叫，被他的最高指挥官——山田大队长一枪崩了。后来，在月黑风高的晚上，人们路过古巷道的洞口时，仿佛还听到那个中队长的喊叫，骇得这一方人不敢拢近。

又如在古巷道中，九疤子和起子谈论关于鬼的话题；以及豺狗带着假面具，装成鬼恐吓起子和九疤子：

> ……头披长发，尖下巴，两只眼睛极大，闪着阴森的光。……露着一口白森森的尖利的牙……伸展开十个又尖又长的手指，又吐出红红的舌头，边跳边往这头挪动。

还有小说中描写到在黑漆漆的古巷道中一大堆骷髅和人的尸骨，日本人的刺刀，以及青铜斧神秘的消失等。

小说的结尾还体现了佛家文化对人物的影响。”这些描写增强了小说悬疑、灵异、恐怖的神秘色彩，体现了故事中人物强烈的、根深蒂固的神灵意识，也增强了小说的审美价值，深化了作品的主题：人类精神世界广袤复杂，变化多端，以及人性的脆弱。

同时小说采用全知全能的叙述视角可以任意透视人物的内心世界，自由地进出叙事本身，也因此享有对人物进行评论的极大自由。《古巷道》中全知叙述者经常会中断叙述，时不时发表评论，进行道德评价，褒贬是非。如在古巷道中，九疤子提出“人为财死”的人生观，并夸口说：“老子这辈子为财杀过人，为财……起子，你放心，大江大海都闯过，绝对在这翻不了船。”叙述者在此中断叙述评论道：“翻不了船？谁能断定呢？世间事本说不清。”以此表明作者对九疤子流露出一种不赞同、斥责、鄙视的态度。小说的结尾，起子费尽心机得到的青铜斧却不翼而飞，叙述者又做出评论道：“起子，你本应该老老实实呆在母亲身边，种三亩田……吃份安稳饭，在那么些年的屈辱中，最渴望的难道不是一份安稳？”这里的评价表明了叙述者的态度及道德评价观点，劝诫世人。正是全知全能零聚焦的叙述方式凸显叙述者的权威、主导地位，发出居高临下的评论，以权威的口吻建立道德标准，引导读者实现价值认同。

另外，叙述者采用第三人称内聚焦的视角对起子进行聚焦，频繁地进入他的内心世界，拉近他与读者的距离，引起读者对他的思考。作品中，作者肯定了起子顽强向上、从不向命运低头的抗争精神，但同时又批判他被利益驱使的“盗矿”和“盗宝”的疯狂行为，劝诫世人在改变自己生活和命运的过程中，要保持清醒和理性，不要在欲望中迷失了自我。

三、结论

视点的选择和安排是叙述策略的体现，不仅表现出作者的创作技巧，而且也蕴含了作者的态度和价值观；同时也影响读者对于作品的理解与评价。读者在解读文学作品时，要仔细分析作者或叙述者的视点和叙事策略。本文从认知诗学的角度，结合语篇视点，分析了黄石矿冶小说《古巷道》中的叙事与聚焦特征，不仅验证了这一全新的解读方法对本土作品的解释力，同时也为中国文学文本的研究提供了一种新的方法。

◎ 参考文献

[1] 古清生．古巷道［J］．小说月报，1992，(5)：95.

[2] 周进珍．黄石矿冶文学研究［M］．武汉：湖北人民出版社，2009.

[3] 黄燕．道德评判与生命关怀——探析《古巷道》中的人性世界［J］．黄石理工学院学报（人文社会科学版），2009，(3)：1-3.

[4] 李金姝．论《古巷道》的文体风格——基于图形—背景理论的视角［J］．长沙理工大学学报，2013，(1)：129-132.

[5] 熊沐清．论语篇视点［J］．外语教学与研究，2001，(1)：21-28.

[6] 熊荣敏．聚焦理论的认知参照点阐释［J］．外国语文，2011，(3)：85-88.

[7] Stock Well，P Cognitve. Poetics：An Introduction［M］. London and New York：Routledge，2002.

[8] 李金姝．语篇视点和认知诗学在英语诗歌解读中的运用［J］．河北北方学院学报，2012，(4)：33-36.

[9] 赵秀凤．语篇视点的语言表达——以“言语场景”为基础的认知构建模式［J］．山东外语教学，2006，(1)：22-25.

[10] 魏石当．“生活流”与“意识流”——对新时期小说文体特征的研究［J］．河南社会科学，2001，(4)：153-156.

[11] 彭正银．知觉视点在翻译作用的转换与等值效果［J］．外国语文，2010，(2)：105-110.

[12] Stevick P. The Theory and the Novel［M］. NewYork：The Free Press，1967：86.

第六节　论《古巷道》的文体风格

——基于图形—背景理论的视角*

Stylistic Features of Mining Novel *Ancient Roadway* in the Perspective of Figure-ground Theory

摘要：运用认知诗学中的图形—背景理论探讨黄石矿冶文学的代表作《古巷道》在语音、词汇、语义，以及整体语篇结构等层面的文体风格，分析文中前景化的拟声词、隐喻和叙事特征产生的突出的文体效果及其对小说主题的推动作用。验证认知诗学这一解读方法对本土作品的解释力和适用性，为研究矿冶文学作品提供一种新的方法。

关键词：《古巷道》；矿冶文学；图形—背景；认知诗学；本土化

《古巷道》是当代知名作家古清生创作的一部中篇小说。这是一部反映20世纪80年代湖北大冶矿区村民与矿区利益冲突矛盾的小说，小说具有浓郁的地域和行业特色，本文试图以图形—背景理论对其进行文体和语言分析。作为国外认知诗学研究范畴的图形—背景理论很少被运用于汉语文本，尤其是矿冶文学的文本文体分析。运用“图形—背景理论”探讨《古巷道》的文体风格，分析文中前景化的拟声词、隐喻和叙事特征，挖

---

* 作者李金妹、李社教，原载于《长沙理工大学学报》（社会科学版）第28卷第1期，2013年。

掘其内在的认知理据，以更深刻地阐释该作品的主题意义，旨在验证认知诗学这一解读方法对本土作品的解释力和适用性，在一定程度上填补该研究领域的空白，同时也为研究黄石矿冶文学作品提供一种新思路。

一、图形—背景理论与语言文学研究图形

背景理论起源于心理学以突显原则为基础的认知观，由 Rubin 首先提出。图形—背景分离理论指的是通常人们不能同时感知到图形和背景，在某个场景中，有些部分是注意的焦点，成为图形，而其他的部分被忽视而成为背景。[1]图形和背景不但可以分离，在特定的条件下图形和背景也可以被选择和相互转换。图形的选择取决于观察者的视角、识解方式、兴趣爱好、知识经验、认知需求等，同时还取决于作者创作的动机和情绪、采用的语用修辞和文体风格等。[2]图形—背景分离和转换不仅反映在日常生活感知的体验上，也反映在语言结构上和文学作品中。图形—背景理论是语言组织信息的一个基本认知原则。Talmy 首先将图形—背景理论应用于语言研究，并列举了语言中的图形和背景的定义特征和联想特征。[3]作为有效的研究工具，它在解释句法多样性、介词的运用、时间状语的确定、倒装句、断裂句、被动结构等语言现象有巨大的优越性和可靠性。[4]

认知诗学是一门运用认知科学研究文学的学科，关注文本的解读，以及故事的讲述对读者产生的情感、移情及审美效果。图形—背景理论体现了人们通过选择不同的视角、聚焦某部分加以详细观察和论述，以及忽略其他部分加以轻描谈写来解释场景的一种认知能力。因此，图形和背景是反映凸显、感知前景化的主要心理运作机制，是前景化的认知基础。[5]本文将结合图形—背景理论，从语音、词汇、语义和整体语篇结构等层面来分析矿冶题材小说《古巷道》的文体风格。

二、《古巷道》图形—背景分析

Stockwell 认为文学语篇中的某些方面比其他一些方面更重要或更突出。[7]突出是一个心理概念，突出的程度和类型为读者识别文体风格提供

一个主观认知基础。[7] 有些常规语言经过反复使用而产生一种量的突出，形成认知概念或感知中突出的部分，以吸引读者的注意力，从而在读者大脑产生一种由图形和背景的对比和分离所带来的特殊文体效应，这在《古巷道》中表现得很明显。

（一）语音层面的图形与背景

拟声词是借助语音手段对自然界的各种声音进行模拟。《古巷道》中出现的各种拟声词有 45 处，作者叙述起子和九疤子在古巷道寻找青铜斧的故事的同时，准确形象地运用了拟声词来表现人物的生活、情感、心理以及事物的特征，唤起读者的听觉想象，产生对事物的丰富联想。从摹拟的对象看，《古巷道》中的拟声词大致分为三类。

一是拟人声。文中作者借用拟声词来展现各色人物的言行举止，音容笑貌，以进一步揭示其丰富的内心活动，给读者留下深刻的印象。如：

（1）“嘿嘿，嘿嘿……” 王经理意味深长地笑。

（2）“危险？你怕危险？哈……哈……哈！” 王经理仰头大笑……

（3）……那家伙本能地一颤，九疤子得意地嘿嘿一笑。

（4）起子就吃吃地笑。

（5）凤子笑嘻嘻地松了手……

作者描写人的笑声时，十分注意声音与人物心情、性格的协调。不同的笑声让读者联想到不同人物的性格特点及内心想法。如王经理阴险狡猾、险恶贪婪的本性在意味深长的笑声中显露无遗；九疤子的“嘿嘿一笑”暴露了他的阴险与凶残；起子和凤子这对恋人在一起发出的笑声，表现了他们俩快乐善良的生活气息。

此外，作者还运用拟声词来描摹没有声音的动态，唤起读者对事物动态的联想，借助读者对声音的感觉来创造一种无声胜有声的意境，使语句产生生动、形象的效果，增强句子的表现力。

（1）起子头嗡的一响，腿肚子一软，便坐在了水里。

（2）凤子点点头，禁不住眼泪刷刷地淌。

(3) 起子心里咯噔一下。

二是拟水声。环境描写烘托了人物心理、故事情节和意境氛围。文中出现的三次描写古巷道中不同地段水的声音，把古巷道中黑暗崎岖、阴森恐怖、随时都可能坍塌的危险处境真实形象地展现在读者面前，传达了一种紧张惊险的气氛。如：

(1) 他一晃一晃地往前钻，两脚趟得积水哗哗地响。

(2) 巷道里的水渗得更厉害了，滴答滴答地响成一片。

(3) 起子喘着气……隆隆的大水冲击的声音撞击耳膜。

三是拟物声。小说中对物声的摹拟，比比皆是。细细体会，发现这些精心选用的拟声词都是符合特定场景的"音响词"。古清生在《古巷道》中恰如其分地运用大量的拟声词增强了情景的语言立体感，让读者如闻其声，如见其人，如临其境，强化了语言的审美功能。如：

(1)"当当!"响起两下敲门声，吓得起子一惊……

(2) 火苗一直往上涌……噼噼啪啪烧得干透的房梁发出令人愉悦地爆响。

(3) 松明子烧得沸腾的松节油带着火尾子噗噗地滴在潮湿的地上。

(4) 哐当一声，刺刀从九疤子的手上滑落到地上。

(5) ……那鸡顿时仰翻在地，扑翅伸爪，扑腾扑腾地光荣牺牲了。

(6) 啪嚓！九疤子的胳膊断为两截……

认知诗学的理论认为，概念是通过体验，特别是通过感知和肌肉运动而得到的。人们在经验和行为中形成了概念和范畴，同时形成语义。现实生活中，人们凭借自己的生活经验和语言意识，不仅十分熟悉许多事物的声音，而且对于发声的动作或状态也很熟悉，所以在读到拟声词的时候，既能感受到声音，也会自然地联想到发声的动作或状态，并依照传统的习惯来理解拟声词的抽象意义。[8]作者对拟声词的巧妙运用增强了作品的写景、状物、叙事等方面的艺术感染力，产生出引人入胜的文体效果，唤起了读者对于声音的体验。

(二) 词汇、语义层面的图形与背景

这部小说所使用的语义修辞手法也独具特色。小说描写的是 20 世纪 80 年代末 90 年代初期发生在黄石大冶地区古老的矿山土地上的故事和人物的命运。矿山附近的农民纷纷涌入矿山，他们“昼伏夜出”，秘密地偷矿、抢矿，私自盗取国家的矿产资源，起子，九疤子、豺狗和秤砣就是他们中的一员，而矿山的警察也是那个时期的产物。文中真实、野蛮而又原始的气息极具浓郁的地域色彩，非常具有表现力，反映了当时黄石大冶地区的风土人情。小说使用的大多是普通常用的词语，而文中人物的语言有不少是方言口语、粗话和黑话，这些语言都与人物的性格、身份相符合。

认知语言学认为，明喻和暗喻涉及语义的跨域、概念的映射，应归属于隐喻。《古巷道》运用多种修辞手段，如隐喻、夸张、象征等，其中，隐喻是一大亮点，别具一格，有 30 余处，以人们日常生活中的具体的动物形象为喻体的比喻就有 14 处。如：

(1) 循着光望去，巷壁和巷顶犬牙交错，一些地方渗着水……

(2) 王经理面带微笑，点了支烟，便在沙发上坐下，翘起腿悠悠地晃着，那双鳝鱼眼睛久久地盯着起子……

(3) 王经理仰头大笑，笑得像猫头鹰叫似的……

(4) 起子举着火把，火烈烈地燃着像一只栖落枝头的火蝴蝶，不住地振颤翅膀。

(5) 起子扔了烟蒂，绕过一块龟背似的大石头……

(6) 石头砸下去，那家伙杀猪样地叫了一声，触电似的颤抖着……

以村民非常熟悉的事物做喻体的句子有 10 余处，如：

(1) 不下百十条的土蛇相互绞在一起，像一大团乱草绳子。

(2) 母亲如遭雷击，木桩般立着，脸像纸一样白，眼睛里满是哀怨怯懦的光。

(3) 那一次，他把队长家的厦屋烧了。火苗一直往上涌，跳到正房顶上，像冲锋的士兵占领下山头，疯狂地在屋顶上跳跃、欢呼，噼噼啪啪烧

得干透的房梁令人愉悦地爆响。

（4）九疤子的胳膊断为两截，那前面一截像折了的高粱秆样倒垂下来。

认知语言学认为隐喻源于日常人类共有的经验。“隐喻的生成依靠经验知识，通过把不同的认知领域相互联系起来，引导读者展开对比和推理，将某一个领域的知识、经验映射到另一个领域。”[9]作者运用大量日常生活中人们熟悉的经验结构（“鳝鱼”“猫头鹰”“蝴蝶”“乌龟”“猪”“草绳”“高粱秆”等）来表现另外一些事物的属性特点。根据范畴化理论，这些词都属于基本范畴，具有构词能力高、词义丰富、界限模糊、使用频率高等特点。因此，丰富的隐喻在小说中的使用增加了作品的丰富性和立体感，增加了小说的新颖性，也显示了作者的原创力、想象力和对生活敏锐的观察力。另外，作者使用处于社会下层的普通人常使用的语言形式，短句居多，语言简洁明了，多用隐喻，精练贴切，反映了文中人物的农民身份、性格、社会地位、所受教育程度和居住区域等。

如果我们把常规语言作为背景或陪衬，那么采用这些修辞手段的语言因为数量和性质的突出而形成图形，让读者产生一种强烈视觉化效果，对已经熟悉的事情产生一种新奇感、陌生感，从而延长关注的时间，由此产生的文体效果不言而喻。

（三）语篇结构层面的图形与背景

认知诗学认为，文学作品的阅读是一种不断根据图形与背景的切换来改变注意力，并能由注意力的变化而重新形成图形和背景的动态过程。在整个语篇中，文本的语言特征和文体特色可以使读者的注意力集中在某一点上。随着文体特色的不断变化，图形和背景不断形成和改变，从而产生令人震撼、引人注目的形象和效应，读者的注意力也随之发生变化。文学的语篇特征、主题意义及联想意义正是在这一动态的过程中产生的。[10]

《古巷道》从宏观上采用双层并行的叙述框架。外框架，即小说叙事手法上的背景部分，是作者按照人物的行踪交代故事的发展进程，描写了起子走进古巷道寻找传说中的一把青铜斧，以及在巷道里，起子、九疤子、凤子和豺狗为了争夺青铜斧，相互猜忌厮杀的故事。内框架，即图形部分，作者采用意识流的手法，以主人公起子的视角来追溯往事。通过起子的回忆，作者交代了他们进入古巷道的背景、缘由，同时交代了起子的出身和主要人物起子、九疤子、王经理、凤子和豺狗的相互关系，以及主人公起子的生活背景和个性特征等。

作者在文中自然地插入起子的八段回忆，让读者的注意力时而随着起子的视角和回忆回到过去，时而回到古巷道的现实场景中。这种叙事方式反映了作者在认知过程中对于焦点信息的选择与组合方式，也让读者在图形和背景不断形成和改变的过程中，不自觉地跟进故事的发展过程，了解人物复杂的生活经历、思想及情感，体验起子在瞬间产生的恐慌和精神分裂的心理状态。这种突出的叙事方法展现了丰富的人物形象，揭示了作品深刻的主题意义，即人在金钱和利益的驱使下，人性发生扭曲和异化的过程，最终取得引人入胜的文体效果，让读者产生强烈的阅读兴趣。

三、结论

本文分析了古清生的矿冶文学小说《古巷道》在不同语言层面上，由图形—背景的对比和分离带来的突出的文体效果。图形—背景理论在该小说中的现实化研究表明：该理论对汉语文本的阐释也是有力的理论工具，是研究文体风格的一个崭新而重要的方法，对于文学作品的解读具有特别的美学价值，是认知诗学“本土化”研究的有力尝试。

◎ 参考文献

[1] 李金姝．从认知诗学的角度解读英语诗歌［J］．内蒙古农业大学学报，2012（4）．

[2] 米卫文．从认知诗学的角度看海明威《一个干净、明亮的地方》的主题［J］．外国语文，2010（5）．

[3] Talmy L. Towards a Cognitive Semantics（Vol. 1）［M］. Cambridge,

Mass: The MIT Press, 2000.

[4] 李疆彤. 论图形—背景理论在认知语言学领域运用的优势及不足 [J]. 宜宾学院学报, 2008 (2).

[5] 李金姝. 认知诗学视角下前景化与图形/背景的关系 [J]. 黄冈师范学院学报, 2012 (5).

[6] Stockwell P. Cognitve Poetics: An Introduction [M]. London New York: Routledge, 2002.

[7] 吴显友. 他山之石: 从陌生化到前景化 [J]. 河南师范大学学报, 2004 (1): 142-146.

[8] 李树红. 试论汉语拟声词的语言审美功能 [J]. 学术交流, 2009 (8): 141-143.

[9] 尹丕安. 模因论与隐喻的认知理据 [J]. 西安外国语学院学报, 2005 (2).

[10] 杨颖. 基于图形背景理论的《哈利·波特》认知解读 [J]. 安徽理工大学学报, 2009 (1).

第七节　图式理论和意象图式与矿冶小说《古巷道》的语篇理解*

Schema Theory and Image Schema in Discourse Comprehension of Mining Novel *Ancient Roadway*

摘要：从认知诗学的角度，运用图式理论和意象图式探讨矿冶文学的代表作《古巷道》在语篇理解上的功用，旨在为中国本土的文学作品研究提供新的理论支持，为研究黄石矿冶文学作品提供一种新的方法。运用文学语篇构思图式和意象图式来分析小说，可以探索作者生成语篇的认知过程，了解小说情节的整合组接方式，分析读者理解语篇的认知过程，帮助读者理解语篇意义、体验作品所蕴含的情感。

关键词：《古巷道》；矿冶文学；图式理论；意象图式；认知诗学

图式理论和意象图式分别是心理学和认知语言学中最重要的概念之一，也被认知诗学作为主要的“理论特征”来讨论。经历了 200 多年的发展历史，图式理论因具有强大的概括性和解释力，已被广泛应用于翻译、语篇理解以及阅读、写作、听力技能的培养等领域[1]。意象图式理论的研究在国外英语文献中已有较大规模，但是该话题在近十年才引起国内学界

---

* 作者李金妹，原载于《重庆交通大学学报》（社会科学版）第 13 卷第 3 期，2013 年。

的关注。而且西方的学者已经将意象图式运用于文学作品的分析和诗歌的研究[2]。国内有少量学者把意象图式与中国古典诗词相结合进行研究，如吴欣欣[3]、杨俊峰[4]、李东[5]等。而把意象图式运用于文学作品，特别是中国本土小说的研究比较罕见。

中篇小说《古巷道》是黄石矿冶文学的代表作，近年来引起大批学者的关注和研究。笔者已从认知诗学的角度分析了它的文体风格和叙事策略[6-7]。基于前期研究，本文继续从认知诗学的角度探讨图式理论和意象图式对中国本土作品《古巷道》的阐释空间，从根本上把握作者的文学语篇构思图式和小说情节的整合组接方式，分析读者语篇理解的认知过程，帮助读者理解语篇意义和体验作品蕴含的情感，进一步验证认知诗学这一全新的解读方法对本土作品的解释力和适用性。

一、图式理论与语篇理解

康德认为图式是连接感知和概念的纽带，是建立概念与物体之间联系的手段，是建立意象、创造意义的必要程序，是个体共有的想象结构[8]。Rumelhart 阐述了图式与语篇理解的关系，认为图式就是“以等级层次形式储存于长期记忆中的一组相互作用的知识结构”，或者是“构成认知能力的建筑砌块”[9]。他认为人们头脑中已有的图式会影响其对新信息的理解。

Filmore 在语篇理解中提出三种图式：语篇图式、风格图式、内容图式。Carel 和 Eisterhold 将图式分为形式图式、内容图式。Bower 和 Girilo 在语篇结构研究中，把图式分为故事图式和说明文图式[10]。田延明等把图式分为语言图式、语体图式、文化图式和百科知识图式，并结合语料的分析总结了语篇理解的动态图式认知模式[11]。

认知诗学运用心理学的脚本和图式概念，不仅从作者角度剖析作品产生的原因和背景，也同样探讨读者是如何理解文本的。Stockwell 把用于文学领域的图式理论称为文学图式，认为它是一种“建构性的、组织文学阅读的更高水平的概念结构”，具有增长性、调节性和重构性等特点[12]。

可见，图式理论对语篇理解具有指导意义。

二、意象图式与语篇理解

Stockwell 认为，意象图式就是“空间（以及从隐喻意义上说的时间）的方位表达”[13]。它来自人们的体验经验，是语言和思维的重要组成部分，赋予人类认知世界的能力，在理解过程中具有预测和推理作用，对理解经验非常重要，也是隐喻的认知基础[14]。

Evans 和 Green 列举的意象图式的特性和功能对古典诗歌中的意象翻译有现实意义[4]，对以小说为代表的文学语篇的理解也有较强的阐释力。具体说来：（1）意象图式具有前概念性。它与感官经验相联系，是形成概念体系的基础概念。因此意象图式能够通过隐喻等方式向抽象域映射始源域的特性和功能。这样，意象图式在帮助读者分析和视觉化小说中呈现的空间描写的同时，还能帮助读者理解语篇中象征和比喻意义的成因。（2）意象图式具有体验性。它来自与外界的互动和对外界的观察，这与作者创作小说的过程是一致的，这也是意象图式可以用来分析小说语篇的构思图式的原因之一。（3）意象图式具有抽象性和简单性，可以当作可操作性的工具来分析作者和读者头脑中复杂的想象。（4）意象图式具有多模态性，是多种感官经验的抽象模式，因此，对于文学作品中的听觉、视觉、味觉、嗅觉、触觉等意象都有解释力。（5）意象图式具有转换性，可以从一种意象图式变成另一种意象图式，由此产生意义的引申，可以帮助读者理解作品中深刻的文化意义和主题意义。（6）意象图式具有密集性，即相互关联的意象图式可以以群或者网络的方式出现，可以帮助读者分析小说情节的整合组接方式。

Turner 认为人们思考问题的方式是图式性质的，头脑中的意象图式是故事、寓言及其他文学作品的基础[15]。意象图式沿着一定的路径向前运动，途经的各点与故事发展的各个阶段相对应。因此，意象图式和图式理论完全可以用来对以小说为代表的文学作品进行分析和研究。

三、图式理论和意象图式对矿冶小说《古巷道》语篇理解的功用

（一）语篇构思图式与《古巷道》的解读

《古巷道》以黄石市大冶铜绿山发掘的我国春秋战国时期的古矿冶遗址为创作背景，以 20 世纪 80 年代中后期大冶地区矿山村民大肆盗取国家矿产资源为题材内容的中篇小说。人们在阅读小说时，总是将它作为一个故事来读，寻找其开端、发展、高潮和结局，琢磨其间的因果关系，区分人物和情节的主次，归纳作品的中心思想和深刻含义。这是“小说”体裁在人们头脑中的一般图式。Bower 和 Girilo 认为作者通常根据四个步骤去构建故事，读者根据这一图式理解传统小说的故事模式。(见图 1)

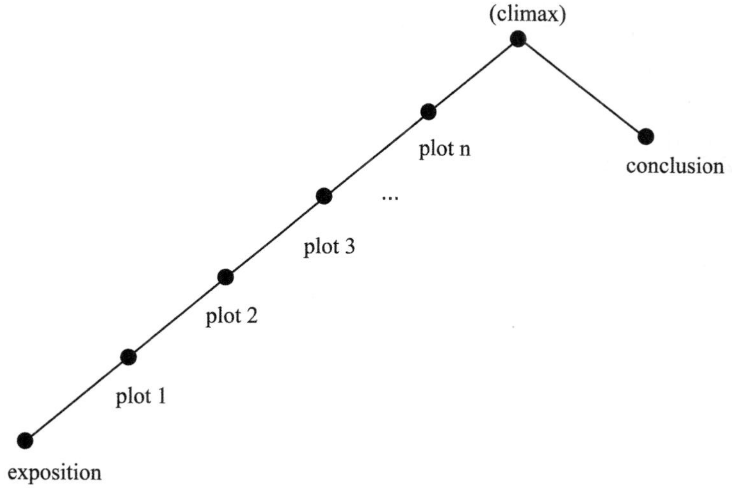

图 1 传统小说的故事模式

在该模式中，exposition 交代故事发生的时间、地点、人物等。读者根据这一模式去了解故事的相关信息。故事中出现的一个个情节（plots）使故事得到发展（development），逐步达到高潮（climax），高潮后，故事

结尾（conclusion）。图式在语篇理解中除了有预期、搜索、选择和提取相关信息的作用之外，它还有以下功能：（1）根据图式的总体框架和图式成分之间的联系，推测未知信息，补充“缺省值”；（2）把新信息整合到已有的图式框架中，构建内在心理表征，更新旧知识，形成新的理解。因此，读者根据小说的一般图式，结合《古巷道》跌宕起伏的情节安排和巧妙的语篇构思，会在头脑里连续不断地组织记忆并更新已有的图式。（见图 2）

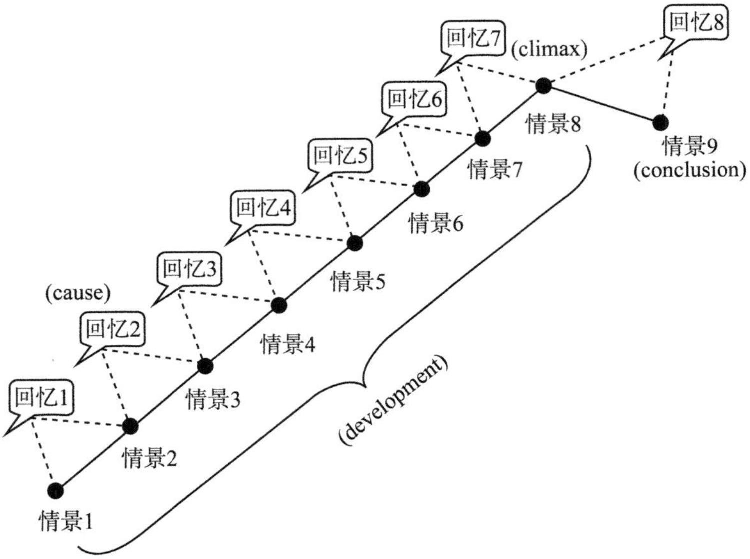

图 2　《古巷道》故事图式

从作者的小说构思图式可以看出，这篇小说通过两条线来叙述故事，一条是主线，即明线，用顺序按照人物的行踪交代故事的发展进程，即图式中的黑色粗实线（情景 1~9）。概括地说，情景 1 即故事的开端，作者以起子的一句“回照啊！”为开场白，交代了故事的地点和人物，把读者一下子拉入古巷道中。随着故事的发展（情景 2~7），起子和九疤子在像迷宫一样神秘、阴森恐怖的古巷道中历尽艰辛，寻找青铜斧。情景 8 是故事的高潮，原来青铜斧早已被先进入古巷道的豺狗和凤子找到，并据为己有。豺狗和九疤子展开厮杀，起子也身受重伤，混乱之中，起子伺机得到梦寐以求的青铜斧，并认出被他误伤的恋人凤子。情景 9 是故事的结尾，凤子偷走了青铜斧，就在此时，本地发生 8 级地震，转眼一切化为乌有，唯独古巷道纹丝不动。

另一条是辅线，即暗线，通过主人公起子的回忆追溯往事。在故事线性发展的过程中，主人公起子的思维随意跳跃、零零散散，整个寻宝的过程中自然地插入起子的八段回忆，交代故事发生的背景、缘由，主人公起子的生活背景、成长经历和个性特征，以及起子、九疤子、王经理、豺狗、凤子、秤砣等人物的相互关系等。这两条线并行发展，相辅相成，构成了有机的整体。在阅读小说时，读者的注意力时而随着起子的视角和回忆回到过去，时而回到古巷道的现实中，让人觉得小说的结构严谨、布局巧妙。

分析得出，本小说并不像传统的故事图式那样开头就交代故事的起因，而是在故事的发展中通过人物的回忆（即回忆 2）慢慢道来。中、长篇小说一般以繁多的故事情节和错综复杂的人物关系为特点，运用构思图式对小说主要内容进行呈现，可以帮助读者构建并重现作者当时创作这部小说的思路，理清丰富的故事情节的整合组接方式和复杂的人物关系，加深对整个语篇内容的认知和理解，并最终感受作者意识流叙述手法的运用而产生的引人入胜的文体效果和审美感。

（二）意象图式与《古巷道》的解读

意象图式源自人体对空间关系的感知，是对空间关系抽象的认知结构。为检验意象图式在解读中国本土文学作品的语篇理解中的实用性，现从意象图式来分析矿冶文学《古巷道》中的隐喻和象征意义、人物的价值观、主题意义、情节组合等。

1. 容器图式

容器图式结构具备里、外和边界三个要素，人们将身体作为容器和容器里的东西，通过身体得到体验。小说中的“古巷道”是古人在采矿、开矿的过程中开凿的小小的通道，是人们采矿冶炼的场所。它是我国古代劳动人民开发、利用自然资源的有力见证，也是古代大冶人民顽强意志力的见证[14]。“古巷道”也是本故事发生的地点，起子、九疤子、豺狗、凤子等人为了抢夺价值连城的青铜斧，在它狭小的身躯里演绎了一场触目惊心的搏斗和厮杀。文中还提到许多人进入古巷道寻找传说中的宝藏，但是最终都命丧古巷道，其中包括 20 世纪 30 年代入侵黄石大冶的日本人，只在巷道里留下“露出银白的光泽”的刺刀，谁也没有真正地走出古巷道。由此看来，古巷道本身就是一个容器，里面承载着丰富的历史故事、各色人物及青铜斧、孔雀石、铁矿等宝藏。“古巷道”和“青铜斧”也因此具有了隐喻和象征意义：“古巷道”象征着历史；“青铜斧”象征着财富，指向人们的精神世界，通过人们对它的疯狂追逐，为我们揭开在新的历史条件下人被金钱和物欲异化的历程，展现了人性丑陋的一面。

2. 上下图式

根据人类对空间的体验和感受以及对社会生活经验的归纳，上下图式可以用来分析情感的状态和社会等级结构。小说中主人公的名字运用了谐音的手法，“起子”具有奋发向上、逐步出人头地的意思。他通过自己的努力改善生活水平，提高自己的社会地位：从最初为了改变凄凉贫穷的生活，不安于在农村种田而跑去烧窑，之后又跑去偷矿，偷矿时不满被欺负和被掠夺，逐步当上收矿老板，“出落成一条汉子了”；从最初处于社会底层，从小就被人欺负，被人骂成“汉奸崽子”，钻同伴的裤裆，长大后受队长的欺压、赵四的羞辱，到后来在抢矿时对付经济警察的过程中表现出过人的智慧和胆量，“逐步在土桥矿站住脚跟”，受到众多盗矿人的拥戴，并拥有了一定的社会地位。我们抛开道德的评判，从个人的生存状态和发展过程来看，起子身上具有人性的顽强和不屈的精神，他的一生也是不断向上、不断拼搏努力的过程。因此，上下图式用于对小说人物的分析，不仅反映了作者对以起子为代表的个体盗矿者的社会和道德审判，也深刻揭示并肯定了人性中决不屈服的抗争精神。

3. 始源—路径—目的图式

路径图式来自人类在走路时有起点、路径和目的地的经验，其结构成分包括起点、路径、方向和目的地等要素。例如：图 2 的暗线讲述了人物的发展历程，起子从乡村走出，到外地烧窑，再走进矿山，进而又走进古巷道，最终再也没有出来。始源—路径—目的图式真实地描绘了起子的人生轨迹，交代了起子的生活背景、成长经历以及最终悲惨的结局，为读者了解人物性格提供了必要的内容和情节。

主人公起子白手起家，历尽艰辛，不断追求财富，在改变生活和命运的过程中丧失理性，误入歧途，最终一无所有，导致了自我的迷失与毁灭。故事新颖独特的构思、精细巧妙的悬念、小说情节安排跌宕起伏、出乎意料的结尾，读来令人欲罢不能。

4. 力图式

力图式是一种包含施力者、受力者、迫力运动、受力结果四个成分及其相互关系的经验结构。在语篇理解中，可以看作情节中的矛盾冲突。冲突分为内部冲突和外部冲突两种。前者指人和自己内心的冲突，后者包括个体的人和社会之间的冲突、人和环境的冲突以及人和人之间的冲突。

小说中，起子的童年是屈辱和贫穷的。年幼的起子因为家庭出身不好常常被人欺负，他人频繁的打骂和羞辱摧残着起子的心灵，扭曲了他的人格。这是人和社会之间的冲突。随着年龄的增长，起子压抑扭曲的性格中倔强和顽强的一面开始凸现。母亲因为贫穷和饥饿，“卷起袖子和裤脚”偷了公社几粒粮食，被队长发现并羞辱，母亲晕倒在地。起子为了报复，烧了队长家的房子。后来因为打牌时受到邻村赵四的羞辱，起子打死了他家的公鸡。这是起子和他人之间的冲突。后来，起子为了改变生活和命运走出乡村，去烧窑、偷矿，他身上表现出来的顽强不屈的抗争精神是人和环境之间冲突的体现。正是这些冲突和抗争带来的结果让起子明白，人只能靠自己的努力和反抗去改变自己的命运。在描写起子反抗不公正的命运的过程中，在为读者揭示起子奋斗的外部原因时，文章中也交织着对历史的评判和对人性的思考[16]。

四、结语

运用文学语篇构思图式和意象图式来分析小说，可以探索作者生成语篇的认知过程，了解小说情节的整合组接方式，分析读者理解语篇的认知过程，帮助读者理解语篇意义、体验作品所蕴含的情感。同时，图式理论和意象图式作为认知诗学的重要理论之一，把人的感知和想象结合起来。本研究从认知诗学的角度，把图式理论和意象图式用于黄石矿冶文学小说的理解分析上，为中国本土文学作品的研究提供了新的理论支持。

◎ 参考文献

[1] 韦汉，章柏成．图式理论和中国外语教学研究的回顾与前瞻 [J]．西安外国语学院学报，2004 (3)：63-66.

[2] 李福印．意象图式理论 [J]．四川外语学院学报，2007 (1)：80-85.

[3] 吴欣欣．意象图式理论视角下毛泽东诗词英译的意象传递研究 [D]．沈阳：辽宁师范大学，2009.

[4] 杨俊峰．从古典诗歌中的意象翻译看意象图式理论的阐释空间 [J]．外语教学与研究，2011 (4)：66-70.

[5] 李东，平坦．从意象图式解析中国唐代诗歌的英译策略 [J]．辽宁工业大学学报，2011 (6)：51-53.

[6] 李金妹．论《古巷道》的文体风格——基于图景理论的视角 [J]．长沙理工大学学报，2013 (1)：129-132.

[7] 李金妹．语篇视点与矿冶文学小说《古巷道》的叙事策略 [J]．河北经贸大学学报，2013 (1)：46-49.

[8] 王寅．认知语言学 [M]．上海：上海外语教育出版社，2007.

[9] Rumelhart O E. Schemeta: The Building Blocks of Cognition [C] // Spiro R J, Bruce B C, Brewer W F. Theroterical Issues in Reading Comprehension. Hillsadle NJ: Lawrence Erlbaum Associates, 1980.

[10] 高翼．图式理论在文学语篇解读中的功用 [J]. 贵州民族学院学报：哲学社会科学版，2009 (3)：177-180.

[11] 田延明，王淑杰．图式理论框架下的语篇理解模式研究 [J]. 西安外国语学院学报，2006 (4)：16-20.

[12] 熊沐清．语言学与文学研究的新接面——两本认知诗学著作述评 [J]. 外语教学与研究，2008 (4)：299-305.

[13] Stockwell P. Cognitve Poetics：An Introduction [M]. London & New York：Routledge，2002.

[14] 刘丽华，李明君．意象图式理论研究的进展与前沿 [J]. 哈尔滨工业大学学报，2008 (4)：110-117.

[15] Turner M. The Literary Mind [M]. Oxford：Oxford University Press，1996.

[16] 黄燕．道德评判与生命关怀——探析《古巷道》中的人性世界 [J]. 黄石理工学院学报（人文社会科学版），2009 (3)：1-3.

附录1　矿冶文化中英文术语
Terminology of Mining and Metallurgical Culture (Chinese and English)

次生富集带 secondary enrichment zone

搭接式支护 lap joint supporting

地下采场 underground stope

地下开采 underground mining

垛盘结构 buttress plate structure

富矿带 rich ore belt

共生关系 symbiotic relationship

挂杆支护 suspended rod support

挂网支护 suspended net support

接触带 contact zone

阶梯式斜井 stepped inclined shaft

井巷 shaft and tunnel

矿床 deposit

矿脉 vein

矿泥 sludge

矿石 ore

矿石矿物 ore mineral

矿体 ore body

矿冶文化 mining and metallurgical culture

炼炉 smelting furnace

炼渣 slag

露天铁矿 open pit iron mine

露头矿 exposed mine

炉缸 furnace vat

炉基 furnace base

炉身 furnace body

脉石矿物 gangue mineral

盲井 blind shaft

配矿 ore blending

喷浆支护 gunite support

棚式支护 shed supporting

平巷 level tunnel

青铜时代 Bronze Age

青铜文化 bronze culture

上向式开采 upward mining

深部勘探 deep exploration

竖井 vertical shaft

榫卯式支护 tenon mortise supporting

铁器时代 Iron Age

下向式开采 downward mining

斜巷 inclined tunnel

岩层 rock strata

岩芯 core

氧化带 oxidation zone

氧化富集带 oxidation enrichment zone

遗物 relic

遗址 site

硬岩复垦基地 hard rock reclamation base

原生带 original zone

造渣 slag forming

掌子面 tunnel face

整粒 granulation

重砂分析法 heavy minerals analysis

附录 2　矿冶文化器物和遗址图片及中英文介绍

Pictures and Descriptions of Artifacts and Sites of Mining and Metallurgical Culture (Chinese and English)

1. 陶鬲（pottery li-pot）

陶鬲（lì），中国古代陶制炊器，新石器时代晚期出现，中国商周时期继续流行。其形状多为侈（chǐ）口、圆腹、三个袋状足，有的颈部有双耳。

Pottery li-pot is an ancient Chinese ceramic cooker which appeared in the late Neolithic period. It continued to be popular in China till the Shang and Zhou Dynasties. It has wide flared mouth, round belly, and three bag-shaped feet. Some have ears on the neck.

图片来源：https：//baike. so. com/doc/6304463-6517989. html

2. 陶甗（pottery yan-steamer）

陶甗（yǎn）为古代陶制炊器，相当于现在的蒸锅。上部是无底甑（zèng），放食物，下部是鬲（lì），放水，中部置箅（bì），箅上有用来通蒸汽的洞孔，可以蒸食物。

Pottery yan-steamer is an ancient ceramic cooker, equivalent to the current steamer. The upper part is a bottomless steamer where food is placed. The lower part is a li which is filled with water. The middle part is a grate in which there are holes for steam to steam food.

图片来源：https：//baike. so. com/doc/568881-602200. html

3. 铜锛（bronze adze）

铜锛（bēn），青铜器，砍削木料用的工具，古代常称为斤。体呈单斜面或双斜面，銎（qióng）形和装柄方式与镢（jué）相同。青铜锛始见于商代，春秋战国时数量增多。有不少流传到后世。

Bronze adze is a tool for cutting wood which was often called jin in ancient times. The body is single-slope or double-slope. The hole on it for installing a handle and its handle are the same as jue. Bronze adze began to appear in the Shang Dynasty, and the number increased during the Spring and Autumn Period and the Warring States Period. Many have been passed on to later generations.

图片来源：https：//baike. so. com/doc/674566-714058. html

4. 铜镢（bronze hoe）

铜镢（jué），青铜器，破土起土用的农具，古书里也称为鐯（zhuō）。青铜镢体长而大，单斜面或双斜面刃，顶端有长方銎，銎中安方木，方木上装柄，柄与镢体成直角。最早见于商代，春秋战国时较多。有的铜镢上部，装饰有花纹。

Bronze hoe is a farm tool used to break up soil which is also called zhuo in ancient books. The body of bronze hoe is long and large, with single-beveled or double-beveled blades. On its top there is a rectangular hole in which a piece of square wood is installed. A handle is installed on the wood. The handle and the hoe body are at right angles. It was first seen in the Shang Dynasty. Many appeared during the Spring and Autumn period and the Warring States Period. Some copper hoes are decorated with patterns at the upper part.

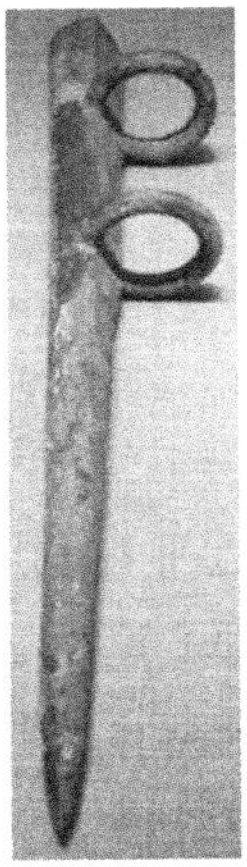

图片来源：https：//sucai. redocn. com/yishuwenhua_6795751. html

5. 陶瓮（pottery pot）

陶瓮（wèng），古代陶制储藏器或水器。原始社会时也有用作葬具的。器形较高大，口和底较小。

Pottery pot is an ancient storage or water vessel. It was also used as a burial tool in primitive society. Its shape is tall and large with a small mouth and bottom.

图片来源：https：//image. so. com

6. 陶豆 (pottery bean)

陶豆为古代陶制食器，形似高足盘，或有盖，用于盛食物，出现于新石器时代晚期，流行于新石器时代至汉代，盛于商周，距今有6000多年。

Pottery bean is an ancient ceramic food utensil, shaped like a high-footed plate. Sometimes it was covered with a lid which was used to hold food. It appeared in the late Neolithic Age, and was popular from the Neolithic Age to the Han Dynasty which has been prevailing in the Shang and Zhou Dynasties more than 6000 years ago.

图片来源：https：//www.360kuai.com/pc/9099498ad853c47b7？cota = 4&kuai_so = 1&tj_url=so_rec&sign=360_57c3bbd1&refer_scene=so_1

7. 铁戟 (iron halberd)

戟（jǐ）是一种古代长兵器，青铜制，将矛、戈合成一体，既能直刺，又能横击。出现于商、周，盛行于战国、汉晋各代。铁戟是比青铜戟更为实用的一种兵器。

Iron halberd is an ancient long weapon made of bronze. It combines spear and ge into one, which can pierce directly and strike horizontally.

It appeared in the Shang and Zhou Dynasties, and prevailed in the Warring States Period and Han and Jin Dynasties. The iron halberd is a more practical weapon than the bronze one.

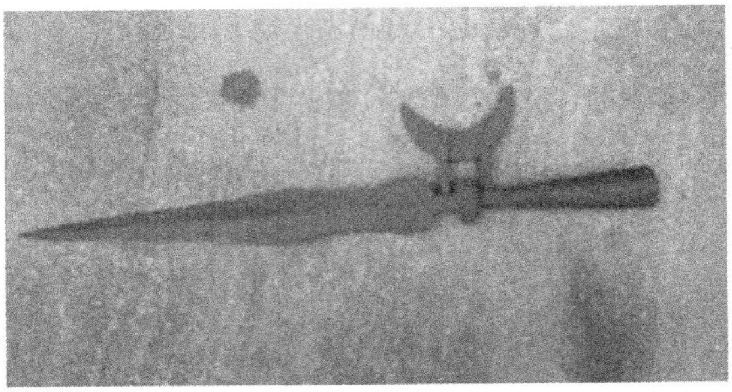

图片来源：https：//image. so. com

8. 大冶铁矿东露天采场旧址（Site of the East Open Mining Pit of Daye Iron Mine）

大冶铁矿东露天采场位于湖北省黄石市铁山区。整个采场东西长 2400 米，南北宽 900 米，上下落差 444 米，坑口面积达 108 万平方米。最早开采于三国时期。大冶铁矿露天采场是中国第一座采用机械化开采的大型露天矿山，代表着当时生产力的先进水平，是世界第一高陡边坡和亚洲最大的人工露天采坑。

The East Open Mining Pit of Daye Iron Mine is located in Tieshan District, Huangshi City, Hubei Province. The entire stope is 2,400 meters long from east to west, 900 meters wide from north to south, and has a height difference of 444 meters. The area of the pit entrance is 1. 08 million square meters. It was first mined during the Three Kingdoms Period. It is China's first large-scale open mining pit which adopts mechanized mining, representing the advanced level of productivity at that time. It is the highest steep side slope in the world and the largest artificial open mining pit in Asia.

图片来源：https：//image. so. com

9. 汉冶萍煤铁厂矿旧址（Site of Han-Ye-Ping Coal and Iron Factory and Mine Co. , Ltd.）

汉冶萍煤铁厂矿旧址位于湖北省黄石市西塞山区、黄石港区，近现代（1890—1948年）代表性厂矿建筑。1890年（光绪十六年），为修建芦汉铁路，湖广总督张之洞创建汉阳铁厂。1908年，在汉阳铁厂、大冶铁矿、萍乡煤矿的基础上，成立了汉冶萍煤铁厂矿有限公司（简称汉冶萍公司），它集勘探、冶炼、销售于一身，是中国历史上第一家用新式机械设备进行大规模生产的、规模最大的钢铁煤联合企业，有中国“钢铁工业的摇篮”之称。

Han-Ye-Ping Coal and Iron Factory and Mine Co. , Ltd. is located in Xisaishan District and Huangshigang District of Huangshi City, Hubei Province. It is a representative modern (1890—1948) factory building. In 1890 (16th year of Guangxu), in order to build the Luhan Railway, Zhang Zhidong, Governor of Huguang, established Hanyang Iron Plant. In 1908,

Han-Ye-Ping Coal and Iron Factory and Mine Co. , Ltd. (referred to as Han-Ye-Ping Co. , Ltd.) was established on the basis of Hanyang Iron Plant, Daye Iron Mine and Pingxiang Coal Mine, which combines exploration with smelting and sales. It is the first steel and coal joint venture in China's history adopting new machinery and equipment for large-scale production. It is called China's "cradle of the steel industry".

图片来源：https：//image. so. com

参考文献

Bibliography

[1] Bigelow Allison Margaret. Mining Language: Racial Thinking, Indigenous Knowledge, and Colonial Metallurgy in the Early Modern Iberian World [M]. North Carolina: University of North Carolina Press, 2020.

[2] Habashi F. Cultural Heritage in Geosciences, Mining, and Metallurgy [J]. Journal of Cultural Heritage, 2003 (4): 377-378.

[3] Liu Manzhong. On Constructing a Virtual Museum of Mining and Metallurgy Culture in Huangshi, China [C] //Lam, Meen & Prior (Eds). Proceedings of the 2010 IEEE International Conference on Information, Communication and Engineering. New York: AMSE Press, 2010.

[4] Long Pamela O. The Openness of Knowledge: An Ideal and Its Context in 16th-Century Writings on Mining and Metallurgy [J]. Technology and Culture, 1991, 32 (2): 318-355.

[5] Ou Xie, Tu Yuansheng. Discussion on the Integration of Road Landscape Design and Urban Mining and metallurgical culture in Huangshi City [J]. Applied Mechanics and Materials, 2013, 357-360.

[6] Rae John B. The Herbert Hoover Collection of Mining and Metallurgy [J]. Technology and Culture, 1980, 21 (4): 614-616.

[7] 蔡明伦．东楚文化视野下的黄石矿冶文化 [J]. 湖北师范学院学报

(哲学社会科学版), 2012, 32 (6): 88-90.
[8] 曹明伦. 谈翻译中的文化移植和信息补偿——兼答“自学之友”栏目读者的相关问题 [J]. 中国翻译, 2012, 33 (4): 119-121.
[9] 曹庆波. 论矿冶文化与黄石城市现代化 [J]. 黄石理工学院学报 (人文社会科学版), 2010, 27 (2): 1-3, 7.
[10] 曹宇. 黄石矿冶文化景观研究 [D]. 武汉: 华中科技大学, 2019.
[11] 曹芸. 博物馆矿冶类文本的翻译原则——以黄石博物馆为例 [J]. 开封教育学院学报, 2014, 34 (2): 22-23.
[12] 曹芸. 矿冶类外宣文本的翻译研究——以文化操纵派为视角 [J]. 郑州航空工业管理学院学报 (社会科学版), 2015, 34 (5): 142-144.
[13] 陈欢. 城市文化资本与城市文化形象建构——以黄石市为例 [J]. 湖北师范学院学报 (哲学社会科学版), 2012, 32 (3): 68-71.
[14] 陈继林, 等. 黄石——矿冶文明之都 [M]. 武汉: 湖北人民出版社, 2009.
[15] 陈继林, 钟丽萍. 太阳石的文明——黄石煤炭百年历程 [M]. 武汉: 湖北人民出版社, 2009.
[16] 陈军. 我市矿冶文化资源的特点与开发 [N]. 黄石日报, 2010-07-14.
[17] 陈维维. 矿冶古都黄石对外旅游宣传资料英译现状调查及对策研究 [J]. 华章, 2014 (15): 98-99.
[18] 陈新瑶. 钢与火的缠绵——武钢工人文学创作研究 [M]. 北京: 冶金工业出版社, 2014.
[19] 程里, 程国强. 矿冶文化的建设路径 [N]. 黄石日报, 2010-07-21.
[20] 程鑫, 李芙蓉, 王其丽, 等. 对接·融合·互动: 矿冶文化与黄石城市发展研究——基于“矿冶文化”新闻报道 (2005—2017 年) [J]. 湖北理工学院学报 (人文社会科学版), 2018, 35 (5): 10-13, 34.

[21] 程幼金，周永胜．矿冶文化研究文集（1）［M］．武汉：长江出版社，2011.

[22] 丁珊，谢晨．以矿冶文化为指标的黄石城市形象的解构与重塑［J］．太原城市职业技术学院学报，2019（5）：18-19.

[23] 方红，等．春秋百年——大冶铁矿企业文化启示录［M］．武汉：湖北人民出版社，2012.

[24] 方晓梅，邵春美．公知性矿冶外宣文本英译质量研究［J］．湖北师范学院学报（哲学社会科学版），2014，34（4）：16-19.

[25] 高磊．大冶铁矿文化产业发展的实践与思考［J］．钢铁文化，2013（5）：26-28.

[26] 郭淑英．黄石矿冶文化外宣翻译问题探析——以“铜绿山古铜矿遗址”为例［J］．湖北理工学院学报（人文社会科学版），2016，33（3）：10-15.

[27] 郭远东．黄石矿冶文化源远流长［N］．黄石日报，2010-05-27.

[28] 郭远东．矿冶文化研究文集（2）［M］．北京：中国文史出版社，2013.

[29] 郭远东．以矿冶文化精神为动力 推动资源枯竭型城市转型发展［N］．黄石日报，2012-09-19.

[30] 郭远东．刍论矿冶文化［N］．黄石日报，2010-08-20.

[31] 胡一娟，李金妹．篇章修辞学视角下《红煤》的文本解读［J］．现代企业教育，2014（14）：380-381.

[32] 胡永炎．黄石矿冶文化溯源［N］．黄石日报，2010-06-16.

[33] 黄友义．坚持“外宣三贴近”原则，处理好外宣翻译中的难点问题［J］．中国翻译，2004（6）：29-30.

[34] 姜逸云，邵春美．矿冶类文本的信息类型及翻译［J］．海外英语，2012（16）：142-143.

[35] 柯梦琪，李国英．黄石特色文化融入中小学校园文化路径探究［J］．湖北师范学院学报（哲学社会科学版），2016，36（4）：123-125.

[36] 李金妹．图式理论和意象图式与矿冶小说《古巷道》的语篇理解［J］．重庆交通大学学报（社会科学版），2013，13（3）：125-128.
[37] 李金妹．语篇视点与矿冶文学小说《古巷道》的叙事策略［J］．河北经贸大学学报（综合版），2013，13（1）：46-49.
[38] 李金妹，李社教．论《古巷道》的文体风格——基于图形—背景理论的视角［J］．长沙理工大学学报（社会科学版），2013，28（1）：129-132.
[39] 李金妹，吕青青．矿冶小说《洞火》中的隐喻与语篇连贯的建构［J］．电子科技大学学报（社科版），2014，16（1）：71-75.
[40] 李金妹，吴晓云．基于概念合成理论的矿冶戏剧认知诗学分析——以《钢铁夫人》为例［J］．安徽理工大学学报（社会科学版），2014，16（1）：74-79.
[41] 李蕾蕾．逆工业化与工业遗产旅游开发：德国鲁尔区的实践过程与开发模式［J］．世界地理研究，2002（3）：57-65.
[42] 李儒科．黄石矿冶文化形成的特殊环境及其特色［J］．中国文化研究，2012（4）：179-182.
[43] 李睿．矿冶文化外宣翻译探析：生态翻译学视角［J］．湖南科技学院学报，2020，41（2）：122-125.
[44] 李社教．黄石矿冶文化的历史地位及现实反思［J］．黄石理工学院学报（人文社会科学版），2011，28（1）：1-3.
[45] 李社教．黄石矿冶文学作品选［M］．武汉：湖北人民出版社，2010.
[46] 李社教．矿冶文化研究文集（3）［M］．武汉：湖北人民出版社，2015.
[47] 李社教，周进珍．在历史的踪迹中追寻黄石发展的文化底蕴——论研究黄石矿冶文学的意义［J］．黄石理工学院学报（人文社会科学版），2008，25（6）：1-7.
[48] 黎晓艳．矿冶文化孕育黄石旅游之花［N］．黄石日报，2010-05-21.
[49] 廖作鸿．国内有色金属企业文化研究综述及对赣州矿业文化建设的

启示 [J]. 江西理工大学学报，2013，34 (2)：10-12.
[50] 刘海峰，陈虹利，白国柱. 南京矿冶文化遗产研究与保护模式探索 [J]. 阅江学刊，2018，10 (6)：122-132，136.
[51] 刘金林. 黄石工业遗产开发与利用对策研究 [J]. 湖北理工学院学报 (人文社会科学版)，2016，33 (2)：7-10.
[52] 刘金林，王军. 中国工业遗产旅游的百年实践与探索研究——以黄石汉冶萍铁路工业遗产旅游为例 [J]. 中国旅游评论，2016 (4)：111-120.
[53] 刘满中. 数字技术在黄石矿冶文化遗产保护中的运用 [J]. 湖北理工学院学报 (人文社会科学版)，2016，33 (3)：5-9.
[54] 刘梦恒，吴堪. 产业转型背景下黄石市发展矿冶文化的 SWOT 分析 [J]. 中国市场，2012 (15)：112-114.
[55] 刘茵. "十二五"旅游业打矿冶文化牌 [N]. 黄石日报，2010-12-22.
[56] 刘媛媛. 将黄石矿冶文化推向海外 [N]. 黄石日报，2010-07-22.
[57] 刘志强. 弘扬矿冶文化塑造城市"灵魂" [N]. 黄石日报，2010-02-03.
[58] 梅定祥. 弘扬矿冶文化塑造城市精神 [N]. 黄石日报，2010-06-02.
[59] 倪京，邵春美. 西方现代修辞学视角下矿冶文化的外宣翻译 [J]. 海外英语，2014 (23)：155-157.
[60] 邵春美. 矿冶类文本的多元化特点及翻译原则 [J]. 黄石理工学院学报 (人文社会科学版)，2011，28 (1)：63-67.
[61] 石璋铭，项锐. 矿冶文化内涵的探寻 [J]. 黄石理工学院学报 (人文社会科学版)，2008，25 (1)：78-82.
[62] 舒韶雄，张红英. 黄石矿冶文化旅游开发研究 (一) [J]. 黄石理工学院学报 (人文社会科学版)，2011a，28 (3)：5-8，18.
[63] 舒韶雄，张红英. 黄石矿冶文化旅游开发研究 (二) [J]. 黄石理工学院学报 (人文社会科学版)，2011b，28 (4)：1-4，8.

[64] 孙少山，孙发友. 黄石矿冶文化市场定位与开发 [J]. 湖北理工学院学报（人文社会科学版），2012，29（6）：13-15.

[65] 孙淑云. 中国古代矿冶文化的传承和发展 [J]. 黄石理工学院学报（人文社会科学版），2010，27（6）：1-5.

[66] 太阳. 矿冶文化研究综述（一）[J]. 黄石理工学院学报（人文社会科学版），2011，28（6）：1-2.

[67] 谭元敏，李社教. 黄石矿冶文化建设调查研究 [J]. 湖北理工学院学报（人文社会科学版），2016，33（2）：1-6.

[68] 谭元敏，李社教. 黄石矿冶文化研究述评 [J]. 湖北理工学院学报（人文社会科学版），2014，31（4）：10-15.

[69] 汤强松，胡雅年. 黄石矿冶工业遗产的内涵和价值 [J]. 中国文化遗产，2016（3）：45-51.

[70] 王琼杰. 弘扬矿冶文明 推动矿城转型 [N]. 中国矿业报，2016-08-31（007）.

[71] 王勇刚. 基于黄石市建设鄂东特大城市——黄石矿冶文化城市景观形象的构建研究 [J]. 湖北师范学院学报（哲学社会科学版），2014，34（6）：54-56.

[72] 王载册. 重塑矿冶文化品牌 助推城市战略转型——论黄石矿冶文化在城市转型过程中的作用和路径 [J]. 社科纵横，2013，28（5）：43-46.

[73] 王载册. 论黄石矿冶文化与城市品牌的塑造 [J]. 黄石理工学院学报（人文社会科学版），2009，26（4）：1-3.

[74] 王志超. 矿冶文化与工业文明——黄石矿冶文化的价值定位研究 [J]. 黄石理工学院学报（人文社会科学版），2010，27（4）：1-4，9.

[75] 吴建刚，胡雅年. 黄石矿冶工业遗产保护与利用探索 [N]. 中国文物报，2014-02-21（008）.

[76] 夏恩德，石璋铭. 矿冶文化的内涵与表现形式探析 [J]. 黄石理工

学院学报（人文社会科学版），2012，29（3）：1-4.
［77］夏剑锋，殷丽红．黄石矿冶文化在荆楚文化旅游中的地位［N］．黄石日报，2010-03-03.
［78］肖步云．黄石“三位一体”的矿冶文化建设模式研究［J］．湖北师范学院学报（哲学社会科学版），2011，31（4）：88-91.
［79］肖步云．基于信息技术的黄石矿冶文化宣传平台建设［J］．求知导刊，2016（4）：35.
［80］徐明强．外宣翻译的苦恼［J］．中国翻译，2014，35（3）：11-12.
［81］严凌．我市矿冶文化研究成果初显［N］．黄石日报，2010-01-21.
［82］杨丹丹．黄石城市旅游视觉形象的设计与策划——矿冶文化节为例［J］．旅游纵览（下半月），2016（10）：102.
［83］尹春霞．“矿冶文化研究”特色栏目建设十年回眸［J］．湖北理工学院学报（人文社会科学版），2018，35（1）：10-15.
［84］余立国．黄石矿冶文化的精神内涵及其现实启迪［J］．黄石理工学院学报（人文社会科学版），2010，27（5）：1-4.
［85］张大鹏．资源枯竭型城市旅游资源活化与形象重塑——以湖北省黄石市为例［J］．中南财经政法大学学报，2015（6）：61-66.
［86］张大鹏，涂精华，刑禹鹤．资源枯竭型城市旅游形象定位研究——以黄石市为例［J］．湖北理工学院学报（人文社会科学版），2019，36（2）：76-81.
［87］张美芳，陈曦．巧传信息 适应读者——以故宫博物院网站材料翻译为例［J］．中国翻译，2013，34（4）：99-103.
［88］张祥胜．弘扬矿冶精神发掘矿冶文化［N］．黄石日报，2010-05-05.
［89］张亚微．黄石市城市形象传播策略分析［D］．南宁：广西大学，2018.
［90］张远望．城市建设应重视矿冶文化元素［N］．黄石日报，2012-05-09.
［91］张云宽．铜绿山遗址与中国矿冶文化［N］．湖北日报，2012-02-07.

[92] 赵青．黄石打造历史文化名城的 CIS 战略研究 [J]. 湖北理工学院学报（人文社会科学版），2018，35（2）：39-42.

[93] 赵小红，陈维维，李雅颖．矿冶小说中隐喻的语篇功能研究——以《窗外的灯光》为例 [J]. 湖北理工学院学报（人文社会科学版），2015，32（1）：70-72，82.

[94] 赵艺博．从考古学角度初探大冶古代矿冶文化 [J]. 文化产业，2019（9）：15-17.

[95] 郑馨念，邵春美．语域理论视角下矿冶文化的翻译策略探析 [J]. 湖北理工学院学报（人文社会科学版），2014，31（2）：82-86.

[96] 周进珍，等．黄石矿冶文学研究 [M]. 武汉：湖北人民出版社，2009，3.

[97] 周熠．黄石矿冶文化资源在当地小学美术校本课程中的开发和利用——以黄石中山小学为例 [D]. 黄石：湖北师范大学，2017.

[98] 朱移德．基于矿冶文化的黄石旅游业发展研究 [J]. 当代经济，2015（19）：68-72.

后　记
Afterword

本书缘于2013年湖北理工学院优秀青年科技创新团队资助计划项目“跨文化视域下的矿冶文化传译”（项目编号：13xtr05），作者作为该团队负责人，自立项以来，积极组织团队成员按照研究计划有序开展工作，主动与黄石市各矿冶文化场馆联系，完成矿冶文化外宣资料的收集与整理。组织团队成员前往大冶市铜绿山古铜矿遗址、黄石国家矿山公园、大冶铁矿博物馆和黄石博物馆进行实地调研，体验矿冶文化，从感性上认识矿冶文化。同时组织团队成员阅读矿冶文化文献，开展学习与讨论，从理论上夯实基础。经反复沟通和周密安排，将团队成员分成四个小组，分别由陈维维老师、王盛老师、邵秀荣老师和刘文飞老师担任组长，参与人员有方晓梅老师、郭淑英老师、曹芸老师、张嵋琳老师、李雅颖老师、刘俊老师、丁怡君老师、胡凯老师、陈铭老师、李晓云老师、张俊老师、李蓓老师、宋来根老师、张岚老师以及作者本人。前后一共有19人实际参与了该项翻译工作，经过一年多的共同努力，完成了三轮翻译。但是作者统稿发现，无论是中文原文还是英文译文都不尽人意。在咨询相关专业人士的基础上，作者对原文进行了较大修改，同时对译文也进行了全面修改与完善。在前期翻译实践与文献积累的基础上，赵小红、方晓梅、郭淑英、李金妹、邵春美、曹芸、陈维维等团队成员从翻译学和语言学角度对矿冶文化和矿冶文学进行了研究，主要研究成果亦收入本书。

经过这样一项工作的历练，作者深刻体会到了翻译之不易，学术之艰难。全书统稿后，作者在近四年时间里进行了六次大规模的修改与校对，参考了大量文献资料。在这个过程中，方晓梅老师和郭淑英老师给予了无私的帮助和指导，作者在此致以诚挚的谢意。同时感谢参与该项翻译与研究工作的所有老师。还要感谢大冶市铜绿山古铜矿遗址、黄石国家矿山公园、大冶铁矿博物馆和黄石博物馆等黄石市主要矿冶文化场馆的管理人员和工作人员，是他们提供了实地参观的便利，并毫无保留地提供了第一手的解说词。没有他们的支持、帮助与鼓励，完成本书基本上是一件不可能的事情。

矿冶文化是黄石的地方特色文化，希望更多学者从事这方面的研究，更希望地方政府和相关机构支持这种研究。

由于作者自身水平、精力和时间的限制，书中难免有错谬之处，敬请各位读者加以指正。凡有错漏，皆由作者本人负责。